IMAGES OF POWER AND THE POWER OF IMAGES

Space and Place

Bodily, geographic, and architectural sites are embedded with cultural knowledge and social value. The Anthropology of Space and Place series provides ethnographically rich analyses of the cultural organization and meanings of these sites of space, architecture, landscape, and places of the body. Contributions to this series will examine the symbolic meanings of space and place, the cultural and historical processes involved in their construction and contestation, and how they are in dialogue with wider political, religious, social, and economic ideas, values, and institutions.

Volume 1
Berlin, Alexanderplatz: Transforming Place in a Unified Germany
Gisa Weszkalnys

Volume 2
Cultural Diversity in Russian Cities: The Urban Landscape in the post-Soviet Era
Edited by Cordula Gdaniec

Volume 3
Settling for Less: The Planned Resettlement of Israel's Negev Bedouin
Steven C. Dinero

Volume 4
Contested Mediterranean Spaces: Ethnographic Essays in Honour of Charles Tilly
Edited by Maria Kousis, Tom Selwyn, and David Clark

Volume 5
Ernst L. Freud, Architect, and the Case of the Modern Bourgeois Home
Volker M. Welter

Volume 6
Extreme Heritage Management: The Practices and Policies of Densely Populated Islands
Edited by Godfrey Baldacchino

Volume 7
Images of Power and the Power of Images
Edited by Judith Kapferer

IMAGES OF POWER AND THE POWER OF IMAGES

Edited by

Judith Kapferer

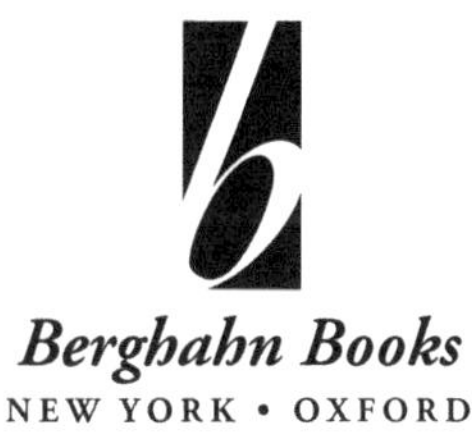

Berghahn Books
NEW YORK · OXFORD

First published in 2012 by

Berghahn Books

www.berghahnbooks.com

© 2012 Berghahn Books

Originally published as a special issue of *Social Analysis*, volume 54, issue 2.

Library of Congress Cataloging-in-Publication Data

Images of power and the power of images / edited by Judith Kapferer.
        p. cm. — (Space and place ; v. 7)
    Includes bibliographical references and index.
    ISBN 978-0-85745-514-7 (pbk. : alk. paper); ISBN 978-0-85745-515-4 (ebook)
        1. Art and society. 2. Visual communication. I. Kapferer, Judith.

    N72.S6I517 2012
    701'.03—dc23

                                                              2012004988

British Library Cataloguing in Publication Data

A catalogue record for this book is available from the British Library.

Printed on acid-free paper

❧ CONTENTS ❦

❧ ILLUSTRATIONS ❧

Images of Power and the Power of Images

JUDITH KAPFERER

Symbols of power in diverse areas of public life surround us, from insignificant street signs and little-known corners to grand monuments and great buildings. Concrete expressions of abstract conceptions—churches (religion), seats of government (Parliament), railway stations (transport policy), shopping malls (commerce), and newsvendors (mass media), for instance—are regularly translated from these solidities into ideas, for the most part unthinkingly. Images of the control and ownership of public space in everyday matters have great significance in the conduct of human affairs—social, political, and cultural—and they dominate our generally accepted beliefs in the order of things. As we move through and around our work and leisure places, memorials, and construction sites, we rarely pause to contemplate the symbolic meanings of these spaces. Instead, we take the fact of their actual forms for granted, allowing for a glossing over of their symbolism. This is the force of the 'social imaginary' (see Taylor 2004), a phenomenon that will be explored in this volume as part of an ongoing examination of the relation between the arts and the state (see Kapferer 2008).

The Aestheticization of Power and Everyday Life

The social imaginary is integral to understandings of the conception, formulation, and design—the imagining—of worlds that range from the most commonplace to the most exotic. I am primarily concerned here with power and its aestheticization with specific relation to the everyday circumstances of life for which such an aesthetics is intended to have both effect and affect. I am thinking of various forms of representation and technical construction, since these both embody and refract dimensions of the socio-political orders in which they achieve expression. In many respects, these phenomena are active in constituting both the way that they are perceived and the kinds of conception that are enlivened in their presence. They do not declare what they are and how they are

References for this section are located on page 8.

to be interpreted; rather, their potency gains force by drawing perceivers into a dynamic that is not apart from them but rather involves those who engage with them in a mutually participatory act.

Ambrogio Lorenzetti's fresco series on the allegory and effects of good and bad government, painted in 1338–1339 in Siena's Palazzo Pubblico (see Meoni 2005), provides a text for a moral lesson that is highly pertinent to an exploration of images of power. The paintings impart a lesson that, in its teaching, is not totally unfamiliar to contemporary audiences, although it advances its burden of instruction in a more straightforward way than similar lessons of today. Indeed, it might be argued that postmodernist arts actually follow an amoral script, privileging as they do ideas of innumerable, equally plausible interpretations—as many meanings as there are personal perceptions. The fourteenth-century audience that viewed the frescoes, on the other hand, saw the inhabited social world as a given, that is, as unchanging and non-analyzable.

Lorenzetti's work comprises three paintings. The *Allegory of Good Government* and the *Allegory of Bad Government* flank the *Effects of Good Government* (or the *Well-Governed City*). The notion of the 'well-governed city' brought together images of civic rectitude, peace, and prosperity with an unapologetic didactic intent. The relation between the state and its aesthetic was firmly coupled with the idea of the thoroughly legitimate power of authority within the city-state, and, in this respect, the frescoes served as an object lesson to the populace. The artwork is a depiction of power that does not conceive of any message other than itself—a phenomenon that is now unfamiliar. However, this contrast provides contemporary viewers with a wealth of perspectives from which to interrogate the present and future of virtual and actual constructions and deconstructions of everyday life.

I want to focus here on a kind of art that is different from the straightforwardly instructional monumental art that dominates the perceptions of its audience while not including viewers within it. The polysemic nature of postmodern imagery and meaning is at odds with the unambiguity of the aesthetic messages of didactic intent that lie at the heart of the art of earlier eras. As a one-way process, the art, architecture, and literature of the late medieval and early Renaissance periods, for example, are forcefully contradicted by postmodern emphases on individual exegesis and the negotiation of perception. And while individualism is seen by many as a defining characteristic of the Enlightenment and subsequent periods, contemporary understandings of individualism and individuality are open to many other interpretations with regard to the intentions and the practices of art workers. These analyses allow for the circulation of more free-floating ideas that may indeed be internally contradictory, a situation that is celebrated for its multi-directionality of art, technics, craft, and design. But at the same time, the likelihood of cooperative meaning negotiation—the possibility of taking the role of the other—is diminished, both in the arts and in workaday social interaction.

Facets of state power that I will address encompass, firstly, the use of the townscape as a focal point symbolizing society and the state; secondly, the usage of secular and sacred motifs to signify fundamental conceptions of faith, sociality, and cultural difference; and, thirdly, the role of communicative action such as exhibitions and publications in interpreting commonplace human activities. While this might appear to be a rather idiosyncratic selection of subjects (of the thousands available), they serve to demonstrate some of the ideas of the aesthetics of state power that will be explored here and in subsequent chapters of this book. The central question is how social institutions—formal education, religion, the family, for example—are/could be/should be imagined, planned, organized, and actualized. The imagining of other worlds, physical or fantastical, is fundamental to an understanding of that otherness of humanity that informs and inspires the invention, discovery, and aesthetic recognition of itself.

I concentrate on the relation of material phenomena to the symbolic representation that is brought to bear on a range of mundane events at various sites. The relations between real and unreal, concrete and abstract, image and substance are entwined in these representations of a social imaginary that simultaneously expresses and signifies the prosaic and the poetic of customary practice, wrapped up in the familiarity of banal existence.

It might be useful in this context to locate specific social geographical and metaphorical spaces in concrete places and events to give some shape to analyses of state activity and effects in both the arts and elsewhere. To illustrate: the imaginaries and the imagery of equal and unequal social relations are a universal theme. Spaces of power are entangled with spaces of resistance in situations of resignation, unease, or outright hostility, not only in state-people relations, but also in and among factions and conflicting perceptions of otherness. Similarly, social subordination and dominance are marked in significant spaces, where the ownership and control of certain zones within wider areas of the city, the polity, and the economy are contested or conceded. The conjunction of material place and imagined space produces many of the most potent images of social formations and their realities.

The Interrelationship between the State and the Arts

In exploring the expression and materialization of state (and market) power, as well as the ability of ordinary citizens to influence or direct everyday lives in contemporary social formations, the potential of symbols and images to refashion taken-for-granted political, social, economic, and cultural life is central. While such beliefs may offer only a semblance of personal participation through the aura (or the illusion) of democratic sharing, their efficacy nonetheless depends on how well or ill the ideological apparatuses of the state handle the instruments of dominance and persuasion at their disposal. These methods have become more complicated with the spread of popular education, but the habit of skepticism and disagreement has survived, if not exactly flourished.

I emphasize the interrelationship between the arts and the state, whereby the arts, however indirectly, are seen as the product and inspiration of state processes. Such processes constitute art as opening up a distance from the situations it represents, allowing for the critique and judgment of artworks from myriad perspectives—from the personal and subjective to the ostensibly objective and impersonal. At the same time, artworks themselves may provide a platform for understanding, publicizing, or querying state practices.

The state and the arts are frequently at odds with each other's evaluations and priorities, as notorious clashes between the authority of art and the authority of the state attest. Selecting from a long list of examples, I adduce the furious reception of Diaghilev and Stravinsky's *The Rite of Spring* (1913), Eliot's *The Waste Land* (1922), Ginsberg's *Howl* (1956), Lawrence's *Lady Chatterley's Lover* (first published in Florence in 1928 but not until 1960 in Britain), and the 1997 *Sensation* exhibition of the works of Young British Artists.

Everyday Images and Social Orders

The focus of the chapters presented here is on the connections between those often unremarked images that ground our understandings (and misunderstandings) of the social orders of the city and the state. Our concern is with a range of works that is wide open to a multitude of perceptions centering on the relation between artworkers and the meanings that they and their perceivers attach to their creations. This is an idea that has only comparatively recently engaged the attention of artists and designers, who have generally dismissed the end-users' views of their works. The intention of the artist has often been denied, claiming indifference to the views of lay people and leaving the perceivers to make of the artwork whatever they will. This anti-representational trend—not so much arrogant as perfunctory—has been a part of both modern and postmodern conceptions of artwork. The lionizing and self-regard of architects and their attitudes toward their clients have frequently been observed (see, e.g., luminaries such as Norman Foster, Rem Koolhaas, and Richard Rogers). Furthermore, the aura of the creator extends to the concrete work and, crucially to the owners and proprietors of the buildings themselves. Such an attitude spills over to other modish creators, including chefs, hair dressers, or interior decorators, generically known as 'celebrities'. Nonetheless, an increasing number of arts practitioners are concerned with holding their own creations up for discussion, explanation, and debate (see Jencks and Kropf 2006). The relation of the actor to the audience (see Bensman and Lilienfeld 1991) becomes important to the whole process of sharing ideas, rather than loftily pronouncing upon them.

An analysis of the connections among the quotidian images that ground our cognizance of the interrelationships between the social order and its realities is important for understanding the uses to which these symbols, emblems, and brand names may be put in advancing disparate ends. While canny users of information technology and further education have become more self-consciously aware of the attitudes and the social construction (and deconstruction) of everyday life (see Berger and Luckman 1966; Schutz 1970), much potential knowledge and its deployment remain opaque or dissimulated, with no ready-made guides to meaning. It is these latter significations that we concentrate on in this volume. From a wide variety of angles, the authors examine issues that are in general taken for granted by the subjects, whose experiences and their relationships to other aspects of daily existence are the topics of our investigations. These experiences are the stuff of commonplace events and social interactions that are important to people caught up in the midst of their own life-worlds, however much they might be unaware of or disinclined to probe the causes and consequences of their actions. The authors seek to analyze and understand the ideas and attitudes of those engaged in these (often unwitting) partnerships.

Lorenzetti's frescoes preach a sermon to a people always on the brink of misfortune and rebellion. The iconography is grounded in the dialectical structure of the allegory on good and bad government. The idea of the three panels of the painting portrays a clear political—even ideological—intent in what seems to be a very modern interpretation of a time-honored topic: the relationship between the state and the people. But here it is the taken-for-grantedness of Lorenzetti's work that is its meaning.

Social Structures and State Practices

Social structures that have materialized through the use of metaphor and artistic license have the effect of persistently obscuring state practices while claiming their informational content and legitimating their power. Picasso's *Guernica*, Goya's *The Disasters of War* series, and Hogarth's *A Rake's Progress* are 'personified' to make an unmistakable point: an ill-governed people will be visited by war, misery, and death. The moral lesson to be drawn is one that concentrates on the positive aspects of the effects of a well-governed people, who are conscious of the benefits that they receive from the state—in the building of roads, the construction of housing, or, less directly, in the contemplation of religious icons, landscapes, or townscapes.

Thus, in the chapters that follow we can discern, for instance, religious observances and icons now including members of the congregation, who are active in the orchestration of worshipful events and circumstances. While this might once have been considered a recognizably Christian idea, the present approach to such images indicates a shift toward a different relationship between signifier and signified. The use of the vernacular rather than the heightened language of the Mass is one sign of this change, as is the dismantling of the arm's-length distance previously maintained between the priest and his flock, well illustrated by the practice of breaking bread in a circle of believers without the benefit of an interlocutor. This is a process whereby devotees have fashioned a new relationship with the object of their piety. It is not only Christians who exhibit such changing stances: in a post-positivist world, all kinds of spiritual and religious practices—Buddhist, Hindu, Muslim, and others—and their depiction are opened up to the scrutiny of a postmodern, globalized consciousness (see Vadakkiniyil and Verdi in this volume).

Similarly, the eye of the beholder now assumes a more central position in attending to the work of art as a knowing observer. The act of contemplating a wall, a bridge, a street, or a public building enfolds observers in the meanings of such structures (see Handelman and Harvey in this volume). These structures also implicate onlookers in their reception, thereby shaping their very reactions to the place. The state remains a central actor in these public works of art and architecture, but the people themselves become actors in their own drama, while more tightly binding people and state together—in some cases wittingly, in other cases not.

The creation and utilization of public works to teach or imply an alternative reading of state practices and state effects offer other instances of the shifting relationship between builder and beholder of images of significance in everyday life. In one case, such effects involve readjusting the state versus people relation—as road creators versus road users (see Harvey in this volume)—in the construction of a road in an out-of-the-way location. The two groups do not see eye to eye on the merits of the government transport program, with engineers finding their creation damaged by the road users and the local people seeing the road as having unintended and even alarming consequences for their livelihood. In much the same way, the designers of public housing units have rarely attended to the dwellers who must live in these often intimidatingly impersonal structures that have been thoughtlessly sited without considering contexts or surroundings (see Glendinning in this volume).

In contrast with the motif of creation, the shock of death is chillingly concretized in many exhibitions and memorials relating to war, military occupation, and torture. One such is the exhibition 'Body Worlds'. Devised and curated by German anatomist Gunther von Hagens, this display has perplexed and/or sickened viewers in diverse sites since it began touring in 1996. The 'plastinated' bodies of the dead hold up to public scrutiny the remembered or half-remembered experience of wartime destruction and subsequent efforts to educate and re-educate contemporary generations about post-denazification in Germany and farther afield (see Linke in this volume). Once again, the juxtaposition of artist and perceiver, mediated by the execution, content, and context of the work, realizes a new association between them—one in which the viewer is an active participant.

The apposition of creator and perceiver (including sellers, buyers, and onlookers) is further complicated by the presence of third parties: professional critics and reviewers (see chapter 1). At art fairs (as with other trade fairs), most creators and designers of artworks have an ambivalent relationship with those who assess their offerings for 'public' approbation and/or sale. Many will profess to be unaware of or uninterested in the critiques of viewers, while others (Andy Warhol, Damien Hirst) claim to be nakedly interested in profit making. However, an art fair focuses on a smaller, closed circle of cognoscenti, and while the didactic appraisals of professional critics and reviewers have implications for the long-term success of the artists concerned, it is the wider public of educated lay persons whose estimation is sought after more often than in earlier eras (see, e.g., Birnbaum and Graw 2008).

Within temples, shrines, and other spiritual centers, the attitude of the perceiver of the work is of a different order. In a Zen garden, initially mediated by

Zen masters (see Weiss in this volume), observers become more than onlookers. The garden envelops them, and they become one with it, ingesting its structure and its philosophical meanings. The distance between creator and participant is negated within the object itself: its we-they relation almost disappears. As with many of the other topics explored in these chapters, autodidacticism comes into the foreground of the work, whether consciously or unconsciously experienced by the perceivers of these messages.

Such realities, as I have suggested, may be a village road in Peru, a Zen garden in Japan, the built environment in Jerusalem, and public housing in the United Kingdom. All have as their centerpiece townscapes or landscapes that express the relation between the people and the state, and they all embrace a spectrum of ideas that utilize abstract qualities and figures of the imagination to analyze state power as it affects the lives of those taking part in their construction and being acted upon by it. Some of these concepts are of ancient lineage, for example, the striving for peace and tranquility, security, and national or local prestige. Some are seen as being directly related to the welfare of citizens and conceptions of the modern. Here the figure of a suffering Christ and the contemporary embodiment of the god Muttappan (see Verdi and Vadakkiniyil in this volume) are iconic with the reverence, compassion, and faith that bespeak a direct relationship with beliefs in the power of intercession and supplication to bring succor to the devout. At the same time, they display a present-day understanding of older truths, with the result that worshippers now pursue more personal ends than previously.

Of perhaps more contemporary application, images of the communicative action of media and exhibition express more ambivalent understandings of the links between the market and the state in the service of the people: a German exhibition evokes images of death, and a London art fair calls up greed and envy. These analyses of intercultural friction examine racism, capitalist transactions, memory, and imaginaries of collective guilt as they are depicted in newspapers, magazines, and occasional installations of street theater in Europe, North America, and other outposts of empire.

The Social Imaginary at Work

The spaces and places that supply the contexts with which we deal here are generally rather more opaque than representational artworks, such as paintings or sculptures. This conclusion is based not only on the habit of the interpretation of such works (common perhaps to all expressive uses of imagery and imagination) but also on the obfuscation involving less obvious subjects, such as state (or market) practices that are realized in tall buildings and suburban housing estates, wide boulevards and country roads. The semiotics of such phenomena structures the raw material of social imaginaries of power and subordination, consent and dissent, conflict and persuasion. Icons and exhibitions are interpellated in terms of their discursive properties and their ability to concretize abstract formulations of, for example, hegemonic elites at an art fair or state-sanctioned and state-promoted installations, such as Zen gardens, walls in Jerusalem or the US Southwest, or Holocaust museums in Israel and elsewhere.

Symbolic manifestations of legitimated power—achieved through media such as artworks, architecture, town planning, landscaping, and dramatic performances—are easy enough to find. But their importance lies in unraveling the shifting relations between image and reality. Those relations constantly discover novel interpretations of fundamental beliefs and values that are thought to characterize the well-governed nation-state. Or, conversely, they lay bare a narrative of deception and propaganda, exposing the perils of the ill-governed state. The power of images is such that they may be bent to multiple forms and purposes, to the construction and expression of the social imaginaries of modernity. It is this capacity that separates the imagery of the pre-modern world from that of the modern and characterizes the diversity of images available to the practice of the arts and humanities today. The construction and deconstruction of images and mythologies of power is thereby vital in the analysis of the ever-changing social assemblages of postmodern global formations, the discovery and invention of new ways of recasting new realities. This is the social imaginary at work.

Acknowledgments

The Norwegian Research Council has made the production of this volume possible. Through it, both the Social Anthropology Institute of the University of Bergen's 'Challenging the State' project and its tireless and inspirational convener Bruce Kapferer have supported us unswervingly. My heartfelt thanks go to them, to the participants in the program, and to the members of the 2008 seminar who contributed to our discussions, of which this publication is the result. Thanks are also due to the editorial staff at Berghahn and especially to Shawn Kendrick, master copy editor.

References

Bensman, Joseph, and Robert Lilienfeld. 1991. *Craft and Consciousness: Occupational Technique and the Development of World Images.* 2nd ed. New York: De Gruyter.
Berger, Peter, and Thomas Luckman. 1966. *The Social Construction of Reality.* New York: Anchor.
Birnbaum, Daniel, and Isabelle Graw, eds. 2008. *Canvases and Careers Today: Criticism and Its Markets.* Berlin: Sternberg.
Jencks, Charles, and Karl Kropf, eds. 2006. *Theories and Manifestoes of Contemporary Architecture.* 2nd ed. New York: Wiley.
Kapferer, Judith, ed. 2007. *The Arts and the State.* New York: Berghahn Books.
Meoni, Maria Luisa. 2005. *Utopia and Reality in Ambrogio Lorenzetti's Good Government.* Florence: Edizioni IFI.
Schutz, Alfred. 1970. *On Phenomenology and Social Relations.* Ed. Helmut R. Wagner. Chicago, IL: University of Chicago.
Taylor, Charles. 2004. *Modern Social Imaginaries.* Durham, NC: Duke University Press.

❧ Chapter 1 ☙

Twilight of the Enlightenment

*The Art Fair, the Culture Industry,
and the 'Creative Class'*

JUDITH KAPFERER

In Western Europe and North America today, the reconfiguring of the ideologies and institutions of state apparatuses has significant consequences for the arts of postmodern society in the dispensing of social, political, and cultural power and influence. Taking the social situation of the art market at the Frieze Art Fair in London from 2006–2009 as the grounds of my analysis, I propose to investigate here some of the ways by which late modernity has reworked the values of national and post-national thinking in the direction of taken-for-granted meanings of class and status. Class, in the traditional sense of relation to the means of production, and status, as social esteem identified by lifestyle, are everywhere in the process of being breached and overcome by the efforts of individuals to secure and maintain positions of prestige and a favorable relation to the socio-economic practices of the post-industrial world.

Privatization and globalization are the twin pillars upon which current evaluations of social power and influence rest. In the arts, as elsewhere, the legitimation

Notes for this chapter are located on page 25.

of private wealth and corporate profit is essential to the legitimation of state power (Habermas 1980); indeed, the one supports the other. The fiscal policies of the state mirror the financial decisions of the major transnational business institutions, and this is nowhere more clearly demonstrated than by the state of the arts and their relations with commerce and industry.

This chapter essays a critique of the 'creative industries' (Caves 2000), 'creative economy' (Howkins 2002), and 'Creative Class' (Florida 2002) as examples of the shifting assessments of those cultural productions that cater to a culture-consuming society while belittling a culture-debating one (Habermas 1989). My purpose is to tease out some of the strands of contention in relation to the advent of the 'creative industries' as a postmodern financial and transnational phenomenon. The analysis I propose turns on an assumption that the core Enlightenment traditions of criticality, rationality, radical doubt, skepticism, and argumentation have been steadily eroded throughout the twentieth and into the twenty-first centuries (and indeed earlier), being replaced by an intense concentration on material profit and an easy acceptance of unequal economic power, at least in the Western capitalist nations. These outcomes, supported by state politics and policies, are grounded in beliefs about the naturalness of social inequalities as individual difference, rather than on a structural understanding of social formations. Central to this stance is the separation of the public sphere from the private domain, a separation that finds the former shrinking while the latter expands triumphantly.

That public sphere consists of two modes: the first is composed of the physical and concrete places and spaces of public encounter and interaction, and the second is the non-material world of the dissemination of knowledge and ideas beyond physical boundaries. I contend that the rise of the culture-consuming society of contemporary social formations and the waning of the culture-debating society of the eighteenth and early nineteenth centuries have consequences for the collective culture of those democratic, civil, and civic manifestations of public spirit thought to have been at the core of twentieth- and now twenty-first-century understandings of public rectitude and probity. The spaces of public encounter, I suggest, are iconic with the spaces of discussion and debate that, from time to time, flourish in the interstices of financial and commercial institutions and personal budgetary concerns. Examples include university and college seminars and tutorials; public lectures and talks in art galleries, museums, and civic auditoriums; and popular demonstrations of a political nature in places such as Trafalgar Square and Hyde Park in London (see Kapferer 2008).

Such is the Frieze Art Fair, where what Habermas (1989) calls the 'culture-debating public' (of students, connoisseurs, artists, and critics) comes face to face with the culture-consuming society of Horkheimer and Adorno's ([1944] 1972) despised culture industry—the buyers and sellers of cultural products. Frieze, like all other fairs of its type (e.g., Basel, Miami Beach, Berlin, Cologne, Turin, Venice), cuts to the heart of the relations between art, economics, and aesthetics. Here I am using the term 'culture' in its restricted usage as an expression of works of the liberal arts—art, music, literature, etc. This distinction is important because of the way in which culture is central to the four fields of cultural consumption explored in this chapter: (1) the culture industry; (2) cultural studies; (3) the creative industries; and (4) the 'Creative Class', the producers and consumers of creativity. Clearly, there are labyrinthine connections between and among these fields (only some of which I pursue here), and they all revolve around the central conception of the art market and the art fair as commercial sites.

I explore the idea of an increasingly influential fraction of the ruling class that supports the production and consumption of—and competition for—artwork of all kinds in the pursuit of financial profit and enhanced social status. At the same time, the culture-debating role of art workers has consistently diminished in favor of stock market quotations and journalists' opinions. In this connection, I investigate the social relations of cultural production and consumption by reference to art fairs and the role of the state in fostering the arts in cooperation with the corporate interests of the art market.

Fascination with the arts, culture, and the creative industries has grown apace since Horkheimer and Adorno first used the term 'culture industry' in 1944 to designate the world of the mass media and the burgeoning communications industries of the immediate post–World War II period in North America and northern Europe. From the 1950s onward, the purveyors of persuasion strategies, opinion polling, and market research filled the airwaves and other means of mass communication with new methods of promoting the policies and practices of governments, businesses, and industries. Fueled by the inventors and designers of electronic and technologically advanced devices, especially in television and film, artists of all kinds were quick to exploit opportunities for the expression of new art forms in video, graffiti, 'happenings', performances, and installations, whether temporary or permanent. The expansion and popularization of these novel or rejuvenated artistic techniques, along with the rash of mixed-media messages that accompanied them, produced an explosion of fresh approaches to painting, sculpture, craft, architecture, urban planning, music, speech, literature, performance, and kinetic experimentation. Today, the changing topography of the art world can be read in the events taking place at art fairs, biennials, and exhibitions all over the world.

After World War II, the victorious nation-states of 'the West'—striving to convince people that, despite commodity shortages and a million private griefs, the war had been worth it—were at pains to improve their image as freedom-loving, optimistic, employment-dispensing benefactors in manufacturing and industry. Their largesse was extended to the erstwhile Axis enemy, the Federal Republic of Germany, in the form of the Marshall Plan (sponsored by the United States) as a means of restarting the Western European economy and shoring up the fragile borders between Eastern and Western Europe. The Great Depression was forgotten, and consumerism spread rapidly. Offe's (1984) work on the contradictions of the welfare state—inherent in the drive to maintain payments to the unemployed, for example—could be seen as a direct result of the need of the state, as expressed by public authorities, to maintain consumption levels.

The period of the Cold War entrenched the manipulation of public opinion in ways both subtle and blatant (Marchand 1989; Mattelart 1979), a practice continuing today in, for example, the policy of 'embedded journalism', in which news reporters are attached to front-line combatants in theaters of war. The expansion of the advertising industry and the increasing number of film and, later, television productions (both commercial and state-subsidized) that extolled the ideology of 'choice' attested to the power of the mass media and the economic benefit of cultures of control. The censure of the role of propagandists and specialized agents of persuasion was at the heart of the Frankfurt School's critique of the culture industry, in which its members laid out their fears for the fate of democracy in a world controlled by those same experts, referred to these days as 'spin doctors'.[1] The use of those techniques was exposed by, among others, Herbert Marcuse ([1964] 2002: xxxix) as "the paralysis of criticism" in a "society without opposition" and also characterized as "repressive tolerance" (Marcuse 1969: 95; see also Herman and Chomsky 1998). Yet this critique is now submerged in a welter of self-congratulatory practices that throw together artists, writers, architects, critics, and commentators—all the stars of the arts firmament—whose purpose is the production and dissemination of innovative or merely fashionable cultural action.

Central to the development of the modern culture industry has been the rise of an academic territory known as cultural studies, a perversion of Horkheimer and Adorno's original definition of the culture industry, although now thought to be cognate with it. The vicissitudes of university politics and economics in the post-Thatcher era in the United Kingdom and the British Commonwealth were grounded in a belief in economic rationalism and a celebration of superficiality and immediate gratification. Cultural studies allowed for a rationalization of those intellectual pursuits considered to be impractical and/or merely recreational (e.g., faculties of arts and departments of literature, languages, history, philosophy, and social science). These departments were often cheap to run (only books and teachers were required) and popular with students, but the interests of what was called 'the real world' were bent on the erasure of all studies not believed to have a straightforward application to economic, commercial, and industrial fields—that did not attend to the *training*, as opposed to the *education*, of the rising generation. The solution was to constitute cultural studies as a refuge for some few scholars of the old disciplines and to undertake a massive revamping of former academic divisions to encompass studies of, for example, communications, media, journalism, advertising, and so forth, thereby ushering in practical training regimens by the back door.

The pursuit of cultural ignorance has been an offshoot of the free trade in university studies and other areas of 'higher' education and has been much lauded by the cultural and creative industries, which have indeed, along with government policies and directives, been instrumental in their creation. An expanded field of activity, of practical training and studies relevant to employment opportunities in a post-industrial world, means that a range of new qualifications and regulations has been established in educational institutions at all levels. These moves have the effect of controlling and managing the aspirations of young people in matters of career choice and suitable routes to specific career goals. The direction and disciplinarity of the world of workers is further constrained by means of quality controls and performance reviews on the job, smacking of school tests, report cards, and the instigation of standardized ratings of success.

The post-industrial field of the jobs market and its relevant qualifications produce an enormous selection of burgeoning occupational opportunities in the newly designated creative industries. These include not only creative workers in what might reasonably have been thought of as creative activities, such as the arts, technics, and design, as well as isolated inventors and scientists. One economist, Richard Florida (2002: ix) also includes, for example, members of business corporations who could be thought of as inventing new methods of production and distribution of valued goods. "[I]f you use your creativity as a key factor in your work in business, education, health care, law or some other profession, you are a member" of what Florida calls the 'Creative Class'—which in the United States alone totals 38 million, more than 30 percent of the workforce (ibid.). The creative industries, according to another economist, Richard E. Caves (2000: 1), include "goods and services that we broadly associate with cultural, artistic, or simply entertainment value. They include book and magazine publishing, the visual arts (painting, sculpture), the performing arts (theatre, opera, concerts, dance), sound recordings, cinema and TV films." Howkins (2002: 123) lists advertising, architecture, art, crafts, design, fashion, film, music, performing arts, publishing, R&D, software, television and radio, toys and games, and video games. Florida (2002: 46) cites *Business Week* as introducing the "concept of a 'Creative Economy'"—a notion to which he and others make constant reference.

An enormous number of enterprises have sprung up, climbing on the creativity bandwagon since the late 1990s. They include, for example, businesses such as Creative and Cultural Skills, whose mission is "to turn creative and cultural talents into productive skills and jobs" under the aegis of Britain's National Skills Academy's Creative and Cultural sector. The company offers a Cultural Leadership Programme and Creative Apprenticeships.[2] A favorite term in relation to management is 'passion'—a passion for 'enterprise' or, in the case of Deutsche Bank's advertising, for 'performance'. Business schools highlight their courses on corporate entrepreneurship, creativity, and motivation, while many have an underpinning of psychology. The emphasis placed on leadership, team and individual entrepreneurship, employment opportunities, and so forth points to the purpose of these initiatives as sectors of a business-dominated focus on production and profit. On 18 November 2008, Global Entrepreneurship Week was opened with fanfare, lauding the ways in which "young entrepreneurs will be the key to kickstarting the economy."[3] The nexus between creativity and economics is indeed a tightly knit one.

A Culture-Debating Society

Like Adorno (1991), Jürgen Habermas (1989) laments the rise of a culture industry that operates in direct opposition to the kind of 'rational-critical debate' deemed necessary to sustain a social and cultural milieu for judging important political, social, and cultural events and disputes. A culture-debating society is predicated on the existence of a reading public engaged in critical discussion of books and literature and participating in the wider world of the arts in general. It requires a common understanding of the rules of engagement embodied in the assumptions of similarly educated and what many 'creative economists' celebrate today as 'culturally capitalized' people—the literate world of the eighteenth century.

Habermas (1989: 158) refers to a perceived decline in rational-critical debate since that era and attributes this to the steady atrophying of the separation between domestic and public life, a retraction of the 'bourgeois public sphere' that he sees as characteristic of the time. The destruction of the relation between the private realm and the public sphere, he argues, has spelled the waning of public critical debate, which has degenerated into "acts of individuated reception" of the offerings of the mass media (ibid.: 161). He attributes the decline in public debate to (among other changes) a change in the design of streets and buildings where encounters among like-minded people might have taken place—coffee houses and cafes, for instance. The salons and reception rooms of an earlier time have given way to inward-facing private (living) rooms centered on the immediate family, now cut off from a connection with the wider world of politics, economics, and cultural production (ibid.: 46). By the same token, writers such as Jane ('Eyes on the Street') Jacobs (1993: 45) and William Whyte (1988) have made the point that the design of streetscapes and landscapes, in seeking privacy, affects the relations between one household and the next, militating against public social engagement in any particular neighborhood. So where is the debate among rational and enlightened citizens to be found?

In reference to cultural tastes, it can be noted that everyday sociality tends to be undemanding in nature. Rational-critical debate is actively eschewed in an effort to maintain cordial relations with neighbors and friends while engaging in activities like playing golf or visiting pubs (see Oldenburg 1989; Putnam 2000) or taking part in community events such as block parties. The habit of informed critique is becoming rarer, excused by an assumption of private opinion and personal preference as the central purpose of any conversation or communication. Such an outcome also affects television and radio talk shows, which often invite their audiences to vote on some issue or other without commentary. Internet communication is of the same type, with no face-to-face activity to enable the argument or critical point to go forward. 'Little' magazines—belles-lettres, academic journals, sheets of political discussion—reach small audiences and still do not encourage face-to-face communication in the public arena.

As I hope to show, an art fair would appear to be an eminently suitable venue for an exploration of the relations between producers and consumers of cultural artifacts and for an exchange of views between them, however mediated by others (reviewers, critics, journalists, etc.). In this instance, the journals of today that are at the forefront of critique are not necessarily confined to a narrow conception of art. Rather, they include a wide range of critical, mostly left-leaning publications, such as *New Left Review* (founded in 1960), *Artforum* (1962),

Radical Philosophy (1972), *October* (1976), *Art Monthly* (1976), and *Frieze* (2003), as well as *Art Review* online, where art and culture news is updated every 60 minutes. At both the Frieze Art Fair and Art Basel, such magazines and journals are displayed and sold in stalls, and they can also be found in specialist bookshops, such as Koenig Books at the Serpentine Gallery and the Institute of Contemporary Art Bookshop in London, for instance.

What is remarkable about the Frieze Art Fair is the often self-deprecatory tone of the artists and commentators on the subject of the fair itself. The earnest tone of advertising in *Frieze* magazine and its frequently playful or quizzical editorial content are mirrored by the writers, critics, and reviewers, who highlight the double-edged nature of art fairs. Although commercially oriented, these events are seriously involved in promoting the arts as being good-in-themselves.

One keynote speaker at the Frieze Art Fair 2007, Dave Hickey, a professor of English at the University of Nevada Las Vegas and a cultural critic, had this to say about the collapse of the art market after the 1990s:[4]

> The public funding disappeared. The power of museums receded. Kunsthalles were closing like little violets across the country. At the same time you have the business world which benefits from a condition of borderline hyperliquidity. And I needn't tell you that hyperliquidity is good for the art world because if you really want to piss away some money, the art world is a good place to do it. You add to this the income from hedge funds, private equity, all of these financial instruments … Not having history doesn't disable ennui. The art world works on ennui. I am bored with giant cibachrome photographs of three Germans standing behind a mailbox. It doesn't mean it's bad, it just means I'm fucking bored with it … When I walk through Frieze I say is 99% of this bullshit? Yes. Is 1% of it interesting? Yes. As exciting as this is, just imagine how exciting the collapse [of the art market] will be. Thousands of Icari plunging to the sea. Eventually all the windows where we sell our soul, will be closed.

I quote these passages at some length because the language vividly captures the mood of the fair. There is an unmistakable touch of *épater la bourgeoisie*—the imprint of the *enfant terrible*, the idiom of the art school. As Baudrillard (2005: 27) put it, art is "mediocrity squared. It claims to be null—'I am null! I am null!'—*and it truly is null.*"[5]

At numerous art fairs, an important place is given to what are called, for instance, Frieze Talks,[6] or Art Basel's more wide-ranging Art Lobby ("a dense program of talks, panels, book signings and other presentations—often informal—by figures active in the international art world") and Conversations (where "distinguished collectors, museum directors, biennial curators, gallery owners, publishers, artists and other art world leaders present their current and upcoming projects and report on their experiences, providing both an insider's view and an opportunity for dynamic dialogue").[7] At Frieze Talks, discussants and the wider audience have engaged in topics ranging from "Criticizing the Critics" and "New Performativity" through "Theory and Practice: Art Education Today" and "Cultural Cartography: Does Art Travel?" to "About Time" and "In Memory of the Image." Participants have included foundation and gallery directors, curators, artists, art school teachers, designers, newspaper and cultural critics, academics, architects, and so forth.

The talks I have listed have a critical edge, albeit a fairly muted one. But I would argue that these occasions, sporadic and not widely publicized, evoke just the kind of content and ambience that constitutes the contemporary public sphere. Many of the speakers' deliberations continued well after the publicized end-of-meeting time. With notable exceptions, the presenters were generally not very broadly educated intellectuals, but in their specialist fields they have a highly knowledgeable grasp of the theory and practice of current debates and issues in the art world. It is debatable whether these infrequent meetings and 'dialogues', many among people who are virtually strangers, can do very much to keep back the rising tide of culture industry practitioners ('cultural commentators' and 'creativity theorists') clamoring for a niche in the 'Creative Class'. If the site and activities characteristic of the public sphere are not regularly activated, the milieu may well collapse, leaving only isolated encounters to maintain a vestigial culture-debating society. As Baudrillard (2005: 75) says, "With writing it is possible to critique from the inside to do a truly *critical* critique. But it is out of the question in a world like the art world, because of the complicity of reciprocal praise."

One headline in *The Art Newspaper* baldly lauded the prime purpose of the event—"Frieze at Five: The Art Scene Transformed. Strong Sales Keep the Original Event at the Centre of the Circus"—and associated auction houses realized remarkable individual sales of, for example, £2.93 million, while at Frieze itself a work by Luc Tuymans sold for $500,000.[8] In 2008, despite a perceptible belt-tightening tone, Lindsay Pollock and Georgina Adam of *The Art Newspaper* opined that the market at Frieze was "Down but Not Out: Sales Fall Significantly but It Could Have Been a Whole Lot Worse",[9] while Melanie Gerlis, Viv Lawes, and Bruce Millar reported a "Strong Start: Fresh Art and Keen Prices Make Zoo [a parallel event] a Hit." They also noted an observation of Zoo's director, Soraya Rodriguez: "The financial markets have changed so quickly, it's a reminder of how virtual money is."[10]

A Culture-Consuming Society

While the role of critics and commentators is to criticize and comment, it is also their job to publicize and delineate the space of the arts and their fairs. Publicity and promotion are what drives the fair and the collectors, gallerists, and curators whom it assembles. The fair is their playground, the site of trendsetters and trend-spotters who are the subject of the gossip columnists and weekly magazines. As at Formula 1 auto racing events, celebrated artists are foregrounded, as are rock stars, fashion models and designers, cinema actors and directors, star architects ('starchitects'), famous authors, well-known journalists, and editors of 'quality' newspapers and glossy magazines, a fraction of 'the new class'.

Louisa Buck (2007) describes the habitat of some of them, the Colony Room (so named in the 1940s, later the Colony Room Club), a private drinking club on Dean Street in Soho that is frequented by 'hard-drinking', well-known artists and their partners. The Groucho Club, situated nearby, is also a favored haunt of people in the world of the media, such as journalists, writers, producers, and successful artists.

On 5 October 2008, however, the weekly BBC television program *Newsnight* featured the imminent demise of the Colony Room Club, where patrons were mourning the loss of this particular artists' hangout, characterized by the BBC announcer as a "salon of salaciousness" and "legendary rudeness." Patrons, the presenter said, have included Dylan Thomas, Francis Bacon, and George Melly. Some items that decorated the club, such as the works of other newer British artists like Damien Hirst and Michael Andrews, would, it was announced, be auctioned off at the end of the club's lease. One of the long-time artist-members, Maggi Hambling, proudly spoke of the Colony Room Club as housing "a history of art in one room." The presenter of the television segment depicted the club as "an oasis of sleaze" and "a heady mixture of great art and great sleaziness." The club, which has also attracted "bibulous journalists ... as well as [admiringly] a rich, maverick pageant" of actors, musicians, politicians, underworld types, and singers, was described as a spot "where everyone is treated with equal contempt." *Les enfants terribles* again. In contrast, 'Lunchtime O'Booze', a columnist for the satirical current affairs magazine *Private Eye*, portrayed the Colony Room Club as "a drinking den frequented by low-life piss-artists for the past 60 years."[11]

These are the very denizens of what one insider calls the 'private view' (the 'quite important' people) at Frieze, who meet at gallery openings and premieres, awards ceremonies, and often annual sporting events like Wimbledon and Ascot—an exclusive and self-contained coterie of buyers, sellers, and entrepreneurs. The customary abode of these luminaries is, as in other cities (e.g. Paris at the turn of the nineteenth century), something of a movable feast, but one that for much of its existence was usually recognized as an element of the lifestyle of Bohemian or other 'creative' people. In Paris, in the early part of the twentieth century, the usually impoverished artists' quarters were generally shifting from Montmartre and Montparnasse to the Latin Quarter and the Left Bank (see Hewitt 1996), wherever living and studio space was cheaper. One thinks of the old Greenwich Village or Monterey in the United States, the Art Nouveau center of Darmstadt, and Berlin's old Jewish quarter as currently thriving cultural centers. In London, the avant-garde of the art world has shifted from Chelsea to Fitzrovia near the West End and to Hoxton or Bethnal Green in the East End. Almost inevitably, such venues become gentrified as art workers of all kinds (e.g. Picasso, Kees van Dongen) become more comfortably situated and wealthier. The self-styled or journalistically inscribed avant-garde notables eventually subscribe to the celebrity lifestyle, and newer exponents of fresh genres and more contemporary schools take their place in new quarters.

The innovative, unconventional, or unorthodox style and rule-breaking behavior of the avant-garde grounds one of Richard Florida's (2002) 'Creativity Indices'—his 'Bohemian Index'. These Bohemians are, of course, members of the arts world—painters, sculptors, musicians, novelists, and essayists, as well as architects, designers, and often craftspeople. But far beyond these rather unsurprising occupations, this 'class' includes academics, business managers, 'knowledge workers', research-and-development workers, health professionals, and those in high-tech fields. They are said to hold at least a bachelor's degree (fields unspecified), are conscious of their 'work-life balance' in day-to-day activities, and appreciate that their lifestyle affords a relaxed and informal workplace. They are also recipients of very decent incomes and live in the suburbs or small cities, which provide an amiable milieu of like-minded, similarly educated people and consciously cater to their recreational needs. Many in this class appear to be relatively young and unencumbered by children or dependent relatives. They are resolutely individualist, but not 'driven',[12] and are characterized by 'Technology, Talent and Tolerance'. Florida (ibid.) says they are the drivers of the kinds of innovation and creativity that feed the 'Creative Economy' and form the 'Creative Class'.

During the question and answer session after one of the talks by millionaires at the Frieze Art Fair 2007, one 'questioner' seized the opportunity to promote her new book. At both scheduled meetings, the speakers were quietly mobbed by young artists endeavoring to have the collectors look at their works in videos and photographs, asking for interviews, offering to send their curricula vitae, and so on. These interludes illuminate the naked competition that fuels art students' efforts to become recognized and embark on a career. But while the aspirants hope for a soda-fountain-style 'discovery' of their talent, collectors and patrons, both corporate and individual, are actually quite immune to, even unaware of, their ambition.

However, a new career path in the art world has grown up over the last 30-odd years: the world of subalterns of the cultural arm of the ruling class. This field encompasses a host of workers and entrepreneurs whose activities are centrally in the arts, or quite reliant on them, as employees and proprietors of small arts-related businesses. What has become more and more important for all of these people is the possession of appropriate qualifications, which can serve to winnow out some of the enormous numbers of job seekers looking for arts-centered occupations in the creative industries.

Professionalization follows in the footsteps of these entrepreneurial awakenings. Whereas once an apprenticeship or on-the-job learning was the accepted route to secure employment, nowadays the neophyte, apart from being immersed in the theory and practice of a particular art or craft, is required to take on workshops and training courses that result in specialist diplomas and degrees—for instance, in curating or arts administration or event management. Partly because of changes in education policy, but more because of the outcomes of global business trends and financial insecurities, professional qualifications now frame training courses in the arts and crafts of the so-called creative industries. These courses represent, for most, the first step on the road to a career—even if the notion of vocation, especially in the arts, has become so outdated as to seem faintly pompous.

Buck (2007: 204) recounts the careers of those whom she designates 'the operators'—those who have, for example, attained successful businesses in arts publicity or what one firm calls "cultural communications consultancy." Other opportunities exist in arts consultancy in the field of matching products to suitable sponsors, in the transport and removal of delicate and heavily insured artifacts such as musical instruments and artwork, and in 'assembling' artwork as part of a retail store's exhibition space, a version of window dressing (see also Becker 1982). Buck (2007: 211) relates that in "the early 1970s Habitat perked up the British aesthetic consciousness by commissioning special prints from [well-known artists], and in the 1990s it resurrected this practice with a series of limited edition prints … Yet this time the household store went one step further by inaugurating an adventurous rolling programme of contemporary art exhibitions in shops across the country." This program has resulted in the establishment of Habitat art awards for students and an annual art show. The retailer is "giving something back" (Kapferer 2008: 75) to the arts community, not from generosity but as a *quid quo pro* mercantile transaction.

The division of labor in the arts has become evermore detailed as members of the creative industries compete for jobs and bankable reputations. In the *MediaGuardian* (8 October 2007), five positions were advertised at the Hospital Club (which sponsored the 'quite important' persons venue at Frieze, serving drinks, coffee, food). The introduction to the advertisement reads as follows: "The Hospital Club is unique because it's the only club designed specifically for *creative entrepreneurs* [emphasis added]—the people who make things and the people that help make those things happen. The Covent Garden Club is the place for members to meet, work, get things done or simply enjoy themselves. So we offer them everything they need to do so—bars, lounges, a members' restaurant, cinema and a gallery alongside state of the art music and television production facilities. We are now looking to add to our growing Communications team." The vacancies were for a marketing manager, a public relations manager, a Web site editor, a club membership manager, and, intriguingly, a philanthropic manager who would "work with the Head of Communications to build and communicate a rolling Philanthropic programme that will nurture and grow creative talent … You will also develop and implement a proactive sponsorship and fundraising strategy."

Workers in the creative industries, as in the culture industry before them, make an important contribution to the continuing hegemony of the capitalist ruling class. It is their efforts that support the 'repressive tolerance' that blankets film and television productions and constitutes the arts as underpinning the advertising and news broadcasts, putting forward the opinions of reporters, interpreters, and scientists embedded within ruling regimes. Meanwhile, apart from some isolated whistle-blowers and descendants of muck-raking journalists, the ironic tones of critical commentators and dissenting voices are almost invariably drowned out by the 'good news' messages of the state and the self-congratulation of the creative industries themselves.

The Arts and the Market

One of the many faces of the culture industry is presented at trade fairs, particularly at art fairs. Despite the concerns of many in the world of the arts today, the agonizing about selling out to commercialism remains a thorny issue. While it may be that painters and poets of the 1920s, playwrights of the 1930s, and musicians of the 1960s had a sharper edge to their critique, many artists today, as presented at and by the Frieze Art Fair, are still greatly concerned to address the same issues, if in more knowing and perhaps ironic ways. Self-parody and sly humor are on frequent display in galleries and exhibitions, particularly of student work. The staple topic of art schools concerning the relation between theory and practice finds multiple expressions at symposia, colloquia, and lectures everywhere. Frieze is no exception. Frieze Talks demonstrate the concern of artists to be considered intellectuals in a postmodern context that focuses on theory at least as much as practice, using the language of narrative, post-colonialism, site specificity, deconstructionism, and virtuality. This is of course not to suggest that artists, architects, writers, and musicians have not always theorized about their work (see, e.g., Jencks and Kropf 2006). What is different now is the self-consciousness of the theorist and the ways in which practice has been inflected by the centrality of the professional art school, its competitiveness and self-promotion. The process of professionalism in the arts is reflected in an increasingly finely drawn division of labor encompassing all of the actors in the drama of the art fair.

One of the better-known art critics in Britain is Germaine Greer, although her critical pieces have little of the flavor of a culture debate. Her apologia for the artist Damien Hirst, who caused a stir when in September 2008 he sold much of his oeuvre at auction with Sotheby's (bypassing his usual dealers), is determinedly contemporary in tone and focuses on the 'old fart' attitudes of Robert Hughes, a critic who had disparaged Hirst's work. After declaring, "I have known Hughes and liked him all my adult life," Greer (2008) takes Hughes to task for his out-of-date understanding of current artistic preoccupations. She chastises him for not being able to "understand a good deal of art," stating that he doesn't "get Basquiat or Baselitz, for example." Greer (ibid.) states:

> Hirst is quite frank about what he doesn't do. He doesn't paint his triumphantly vacuous [!?] spot paintings—the best spot paintings by Damien Hirst are those painted by Rachel Howard. His undeniable genius consists in getting people to buy them. Damien Hirst is a brand, because *the art form of the 21st century is marketing* [emphasis added]. To develop so strong a brand on so conspicuously threadbare a rationale is hugely creative—revolutionary even … The prices his work fetches are verifications of his main point; they are not the point. No one knows better than Hirst that consumers of his work are incapable of getting that point … Bob dear, the Sotheby's auction was the work.

A little less delphically, Hal Foster (2008), in an article entitled "The Medium Is the Market" in the *London Review of Books*, cites Andy Warhol's dictum "Business art is the step that comes after Art" from *The Philosophy of Andy Warhol*. Warhol (1975: 92) claimed that "making money is art" and that "being good in business is the most fascinating kind of art." In a similar vein, Gabriel Orozco's images of banknotes with circular holes cut in them (Serpentine

Gallery, 2004) are a sardonic reference to making money from art and a comment on consumerism. Meanwhile, Hirst's Sotheby's venture fetched him a total of £111.5 million.

The Frieze Art Fair, like all others of its type, cuts to the heart of the relations between art, economics, and aesthetics. Citing an unknown source, Christine Mehring (2008: 325) observes that the Art Dealers Association of America was founded in 1962 "not to create a fair but more generally to 'improve the stature and status of the fine arts business and … to assist its members and others with tax, customs, and related problems.'" Behold the culture-consuming society at its most brazenly unapologetic. The culture industry, cultural studies, the creative industries, and the 'Creative Class'—all are imbricated in the edifice of art and money with the collusion of the state, which constitutes a distinctive fraction of a culture-consuming society. As publics, this culture-consuming society of the art world may include performers, players, and the artists themselves, as well as foundations and grant-giving bodies, supporters and users, critics, curators, dealers, gallery and theatre owners and managers. Also included are fee-paying visitors, audiences, fan clubs, Friends of the X Museum, etc. As individual producers, consumers, or both, all are bound up in the economic nexus of the arts, on display at such places as the Frieze Art Fair. Competition feeds the event, as it does even more egregiously at major auctions.

Such competition has long been a driving force in newly formed nations, as reflected in their desire to establish and maintain expositions, a national art gallery, a museum, and 'flagship' theatre companies and opera houses (Freeland 2001; Karp, Kreamer, and Lavine 1992; Zukin 1995; see also Kuspit 2007; Rydell 1993; Smith 2005). The founding of such institutions signals the national image of a civilized society. In Europe, the institution of the European Cultural Capital (launched in 1985 as the European Cities of Culture and renamed in 1999) is increasingly important as a means to augment a city's trade, especially in tourism, but also as a conference venue and site for business meetings and transactions (see Begg 2002; Kapferer 2003; Lever 2002). Preparations for the annual event (of which the Edinburgh Festival, established in 1947, is probably the template) often include prettifying the city's center and scheduling cultural activities, such as concerts, theatre productions, and street festivals. Cities vie for a place in the roster of venues in order to put themselves 'on the map'. This competition for a place in the cultural sun is thought to be a boost to a city's reputation as a place to do business, an advertisement for its cultured lifestyle,[13] and an occasion for the municipal authorities to pacify the public.

In discussing the "symbolic economy" of contemporary cities, Zukin (1995) claims that what is bought and sold is increasingly focused on a special kind of use value: works of art, for example, that represent the status or prestige of the owner. The owners' tastes are measured by particular kinds of possessions, especially their style. In big cities, where land or real estate is one of the most valued commodities, possession of land and property represents status. Memberships, trusteeships, directorships, the patronage of prestigious bodies such as galleries and museums—all are all strongly valued signs of high cultural standing.

But the symbolic economy or what might be called a cultural fraction of the ruling class is by no means coterminous with Florida's 'Creative Class'. For one thing, Florida's term, alliterative as it is, does not chime with the notion of class in any useful way. Much as he might wish to redraw the statistics he uses to designate 'membership' of that class, he comes up against the intractable fact of class as a relationship, not a collection of people conscious of their position as acknowledged 'creative' leaders, however broadly that leadership might spread. He is writing about occupational status, a favorite quantitative method of 'measuring' social strata in terms of income and its source. Moreover, the symbolic economy and the cultural fraction of the dominant class are bound up with the city's major concerns for its own economy, both symbolic and actual. Here, the creative economy is nothing more than the accountancy of people who make a living by allying themselves with the operatives of the old culture industry, however much they may think of themselves as avant-garde bellwethers. Artists of all kinds, at all times, and in all places are to be distinguished by their individual attributes and characteristics, even when they occasionally form small groups with common goals. They are not a class.

Benefits to the ruling class from the display of wealth and the company of their peers have long been a benchmark for measuring social status, especially in the United States. Thorstein Veblen ([1899] 1970), for example, was particularly concerned to document and analyze, in his *Theory of the Leisure Class*, the pecuniary emulation and conspicuous consumption of the North American robber barons and the displays of their massive wealth. He adduced grand houses, chauffeured limousines, foreign cruises, jewelry, lavish parties, fashionable attire, and so on as status symbols.[14] There is no doubt these individuals collectively constituted a class—a ruling class, whose income derived from ownership of the means of production. The conspicuous consumption of those who owned and used their properties, possessions, employees, and assets to acquire wealth, combined with status competition, set these individuals apart as the ruling class in American society—and has done so ever since.

Conclusion: The Twilight of the Enlightenment

The cultural fraction of this dominant class is an ideological subset of it: cultural capital allows it a special place in the halls of the rulers. Its ownership and promotion of important or voguish artwork designate it as an apparatus of ideological power. Still the objects of patronage, cultural producers whose works have been bought and/or sold by individuals, foundations, and banks (and, in the case of Picasso, Ofili, and Hirst, themselves) have parlayed their products into places of prestige within the dominant class. Their works have graced aristocratic palaces and corporate business establishments, and they move within the same social circles as the owners and controllers of the social formation now globalized.

This state of affairs points to the conclusion that the culture-debating society of the Enlightenment project is now almost entirely defunct. Critique, analysis, discussion, and argument, once the lifeblood of the bourgeois public sphere, have been overwhelmed by the culture-consuming society of corporate directors, bureaucrats, plutocrats, oligarchs, and celebrities. The Enlightenment reverence for scientific discovery and invention, the delight in the expansion of knowledge, and the spread of a habit of rational debate and civil argument have all but disappeared. The public sphere is now thought of as spectacle or pageantry, scandal or titillation. The site of a fractured milieu of ignorant negativity and trite opinion, it is located in awards ceremonies and public buildings, or in the marquees of annual events like Frieze, with its specially commissioned architects. The Frieze Art Fair stands out as a landmark event, as a symbol of the power of the market that extends far beyond the arts.

Now a rampantly culture-consuming society with little regard for the values of the Enlightenment is being rapidly superseded by superficial understanding and indifference to a world beyond the personal and the familiar. Sneering disagreement in radio or television talk shows and displays of histrionic fury increasingly substitute for serious discussion of important social issues. The individual replaces the collective; subjectivity overwhelms objectivity. In the meantime, a small clique of characters famous for being famous, along with a cast of shadowy supporting players, more powerful but less well-known, tread the boards on the stage of the culture-consuming society.

The end of critique and public knowledge is a feature of a society wherein knowledge and education are devalued, and chicanery, fraud, and sharp practice are widespread and admired in high places. At the same time, ideas about luck and happenstance play a major part in popular conceptions of random fortune and individual fate. Coincidence and superstition are thereby compounded by 'new age' mysticism and ignorance. Prejudice and injustice are the outriders of racism and ethnocentrism, while moralism replaces informed reasoning.

Here I want to introduce, tentatively, the idea of a (re-)enchantment of the world. In place of the post-Renaissance conception of the Enlightenment and Weber's 'disenchantment of the world', the post-Enlightenment project heralds a new dawn of fear and ignorance among people who have been suborned by the blandishments of the good life as depicted by a ruling class and a corporatized culture industry. Believing that worldly success is available to all those who work hard and engage in fair competition on a 'level playing field', if only they have a little luck and a modicum of ability, the petite bourgeoisie and the working class see the cultural fraction of the dominant class as examples of the reward for honest endeavor. Thus, the 'society of control' (Deleuze 1995) defuses criticism and actively supports ruling class hegemony. Advertising, as Raymond Williams (1980) maintained, is truly 'a magic system'—one that imposes and maintains the social order of the state through the operations of the culture industry and the creative economy. Capitalist economies/states show no sign of being brought low by this transformation of the culture industry, which has entrenched the notion of private profit as the highest good and the idea of consumerism, in material or cultural goods, as the ambition of entire social formations. The fading of the Enlightenment project, accompanied by the demise of a culture-debating society, heralds a new period of exploitation and appropriation of culture in the service of both the state and global capital.

The power of the culture industry to legitimate and dominate the myths and realities of corporate profit and state sovereignty is testimony to the ascendancy of business and entrepreneurial skills masquerading as innovation. Creativity is regularly misaligned with productivity, imaginative creation with material production, while the emphasis placed on trained teamwork and managerial leadership further devalues the talents and inspirations of artists. Narrowing the focus of general education in order to augment practical skills and amass useful information depreciates the role of the arts and humanities in the civilizing process. While what we call creativity today reflects the belief that it can be trained, hired out, bought and sold, or enhanced by teamwork in order to turn a profit for corporations, creative work can still be distinguished from the smooth interpersonal skills that constitute good management and entrepreneurial expertise in that it has an essential spirit comprising talent, imagination, and dedication.

The widening gap between the private domain and the public sphere means that private, individual opinions are not grounded in any serious discussion with others. The public sphere is limited to the commentators of the culture industry for the dissemination of knowledge or information, which never focuses on any topic, important or trivial, for more than a fleeting moment. The ideas themselves, once adopted, are rarely subjected to any thoughtful consideration of the common good. The Enlightenment project, bereft of the inclination or ability to be the object of rational critique, is thereby further diminished.

The art fair, the creative industries, and a culture-consuming society combine to delineate the social and cultural functions of art today. But the concepts of creativity, entrepreneurialism, and corporate expertise that they define constitute a travesty of the role of the fine arts and the humanities in the civilizing process of our time. Hitching the wagon of creativity, creative industries, and the 'Creative Class' to the star of corporate expansion and private profit proclaims the extinguishment of the Enlightenment project and its public sphere, to the advantage of private capital and to the detriment of the public culture.

Acknowledgments

Bruce Kapferer has been a rock of support in the production of this chapter. Amid a thousand calls on his time, he has been unstinting in his back-stiffening efforts on my behalf. As always, I thank him for his courage, help, and strength, his gimlet anthropological eye, and his compassionate heart.

Judith Kapferer was Professor of Sociology at the University of Bergen in Norway (2000–2010). She has taught and/or conducted research in Australia, Norway, the United Kingdom, the United States, Sri Lanka, and Zambia on the sociology of the arts and urban sociology. Her ongoing research interests are in egalitarianism, individualism, and public, corporate, and private support for the arts. Her current fieldwork focuses on regional or non-metropolitan arts in Australia, Norway, and the United Kingdom. Her most recent publication is *The State and the Arts: Articulating Power and Subversion* (2008).

Notes

1. The use of 'culture' as a pejorative term was also, if in a more radical vein, used by the Situationists and others in their analyses of the art of the spectacle.
2. See http://www.ccskills.org.uk/.
3. "Peter Mandelson: Young Entrepreneurs Will Be the Key to Kickstarting the Economy," *Independent*, 18 November 2008, http://www.independent.co.uk/opinion/commentators/peter-mandelson-young-entrepreneurs-will-be-the-key-to-kickstarting-the-economy-1023127.html. See also http://www.gew.org.uk/
4. "Dave Hickey's Keynote Lecture at Frieze," *The Art Newspaper*, 13–14 October 2007, 4, http://www.theartnewspaper.com/fairs/frieze/2007/4.pdf.
5. In his introduction, Sylvère Lotringer (2005: 13) substitutes "bad" for "null" in this segment of quoted text.
6. See http://www.friezefoundation.org/talks/.
7. See http://www.artbasel.com/go/id/ss/).
8. See http://www.theartnewspaper.com/fairs/frieze/2007/4.pdf.
9. See http://www.theartnewspaper.com/article.asp?id = 16328.
10. See http://www.theartnewspaper.com/fairs/frieze/2008/3.pdf.
11. See *Private Eye* 1219 (2008): 5.
12. This is in contrast to the perception and characterization of the 'organization man' of yesteryear (see Whyte 1956, 1988).
13. Cf. Florida's (2002: 260) reference to "vibrant street life, readily available outdoor recreation and a cutting-edge music scene" as part of a city's ability "to attract talented people and high-tech industries."
14. F. Scott Fitzgerald's *The Great Gatsby* provides the usual example of this lifestyle.

References

Adorno, Theodor. 1991. *The Culture Industry: Selected Essays on Mass Culture*. London: Routledge.

Baudrillard, Jean. 2005. *The Conspiracy of Art: Manifestos, Interviews, Essays.* Ed. Sylvère Lotringer. Trans. Ames Hodges. New York: Semiotext(e).

Becker, Howard S. 1982. *Art Worlds*. Berkeley: University of California Press.

Begg, Iain, ed. 2002. *Urban Competitiveness: Policies for Dynamic Cities*. Bristol, UK: Policy Press.

Buck, Louisa. 2007. *Moving Targets 2: A User's Guide to British Art Now*. Rev. ed. London: Tate Publishing.

Caves, Richard E. 2000. *Creative Industries: Contracts between Art and Commerce*. Cambridge, MA: Harvard University Press.
Deleuze, Gilles. 1995. "Postscript on Control Societies." Pp. 177–182 in *Negotiations 1972–1990*, trans. Martin Joughin. New York: Columbia University Press.
Florida, Richard. 2002. *The Rise of the Creative Class: And How It's Transforming Work, Leisure, Community and Everyday Life*. New York: Basic Books.
______. 2007. *The Flight of the Creative Class: The New Global Competition for Talent*. New York: HarperCollins.
Foster, Hal. 2008. "The Medium Is the Market." *London Review of Books* 30, no. 19: 23–24.
Freeland, Cynthia. 2001. *Art Theory: A Very Short Introduction*. Oxford: Oxford University Press.
Greer, Germaine. 2008. 'Germaine Greer: Note to Robert Hughes." http://www.guardian.co.uk/artanddesign/2008/sep/22/1/print.
Habermas, Jürgen. 1980. *Legitimation Crisis*. Trans. Thomas McCarthy. London: Heinemann.
______. 1989. *The Structural Transformation of the Public Sphere: An Inquiry into a Category of Bourgeois Society*. Trans. Thomas Burger and Frederick Lawrence. Cambridge: Polity Press.
Herman, Edward S., and Noam Chomsky. 1998. *Manufacturing Consent: The Political Economy of the Mass Media*. New York: Pantheon Books.
Hewitt, Nicholas. 1996. "Shifting Cultural Centres in Twentieth Century Paris." Pp. 30–45 in *Parisian Fields*, ed. Michael Sheringham. Oxford: Reaktion Books.
Horkheimer, Max, and Theodor Adorno. [1944] 1972. *Dialectic of Enlightenment*. Trans. John Cumming. New York: Continuum.
Howkins, John. 2002. *The Creative Economy: How People Make Money from Ideas*. London: Penguin Books.
Jacobs, Jane. 1993. *The Death and Life of Great American Cities*. New York: Modern Library.
Jencks, Charles, and Karl Kropf, eds. 2006. *Theories and Manifestoes of Contemporary Architecture*. 2nd ed. Chichester: Wiley-Academy.
Kapferer, Judith L. 2003. "Culture and Commerce: European Culture Cities and Civic Distinction." Pp. 31–42 in *Cultures and Settlement*, ed. Malcolm Miles and Nicola Kirkham. Bristol, UK: Intellect Books.
______. 2008. "Urban Design and State Power: City Spaces and the Public Sphere." Pp. 70–87 in *The State and the Arts: Articulating Power and Subversion*, ed. Judith Kapferer. New York: Berghahn Books.
Karp, Ivan, Christine Mullen Kreamer, and Steven D. Lavine, eds. 1992. *Museums and Communities: The Politics of Public Culture*. Washington, DC: Smithsonian Institution Press.
Kuspit, Donald. 2007. "Art Values or Money Values?" http://www.artnet.com/magazineus/features/kuspit/kuspit3-6-07.asp.
Lever, William F. 2002. "The Knowledge Base and the Competitive City." Pp. 11–31 in Begg 2002.
Lotringer, Sylvère. 2005. "Introduction: The Piracy of Art." Pp. 1–21 in Baudrillard 2005.
Marchand, Roland. 1998. *Creating the Corporate Soul: The Rise of Public Relations and Corporate Imagery in American Big Business*. Berkeley: University of California Press.
Marcuse, Herbert. [1964] 2002. *One-Dimensional Man*. London: Routledge.
______. 1969. "Repressive Tolerance." Pp. 95–137 in *A Critique of Pure Tolerance*, Robert Paul Wolff, Barrington Moore, Jr., and Herbert Marcuse. Boston: Beacon Press.
Mattelart, Armand. 1979. *Multinational Corporations and the Control of Culture*. Sussex. UK: Harvester Press.
Mehring, Christine. 2008. "Emerging Market: Christine Mehring on the Birth of the Contemporary Art Fair." *Artforum* 46, no. 8: 322–329, 390.
Offe, Claus. 1984. *Contradictions of the Welfare State*. Ed. John Keane. London: Hutchinson.
Oldenburg, Ray. 1989. *The Great Good Place*. New York: Marlowe.
Putnam, Robert D. 2000. *Bowling Alone: The Collapse and Revival of American Community*. New York: Simon & Schuster.

Rydell, Robert W. 1993. *World of Fairs: The Century-of-Progress Expositions.* Chicago, IL: University of Chicago Press.

Smith, Roberta. 2005. "Artists' Personal Visions Reveal a Nation to Itself." *New York Times,* 28 December. http://www.nytimes.com/2005/12/28/arts/television/28smit.html.

Veblen, Thorstein. [1899] 1970. *The Theory of the Leisure Class.* London: Allen and Unwin.

Warhol, Andy. 1975. *The Philosophy of Andy Warhol (From A to B and Back Again).* New York: Harcourt.

Whyte, William H. 1956. *The Organization Man.* New York: Simon & Schuster.

______. 1988. *City: Rediscovering the Center.* New York: Doubleday.

Williams, Raymond. 1980. "Advertising: The Magic System." Pp. 170–195 in *Problems in Materialism and Culture.* London: Verso.

Zukin, Sharon. 1995. *The Cultures of Cities.* Malden, MA: Blackwell.

❖ Chapter 2 ❖

Cementing Relations

*The Materiality of Roads and Public Spaces
in Provincial Peru*

PENELOPE HARVEY

When I began to consider the aesthetics of state power, it was the pervasive presence of concrete that caught my attention. Concrete is one of the key materials used for the demarcation and ordering of public space in contemporary Peru. It is, after all, a material that binds together elements that otherwise refuse or fail to cohere. Over the past 25 years, I have watched the use of this material spread from more established urban centers to transform rural towns into peri-urban spaces. Where adobe structures and compacted mud roadways prevailed in the mid-1980s, you now find concrete public buildings, concrete pathways, asphalted concrete roads, and town squares adorned with concrete 'artworks', such as sculptures, fountains, and benches (fig. 2.1).

This chapter sets out to analyze the appeal of concrete—the values that attach to the material and to the forms that are built from it. Embraced and rejected with equal passion in different times and places, concrete is a substance

Notes for this chapter begin on page 44.

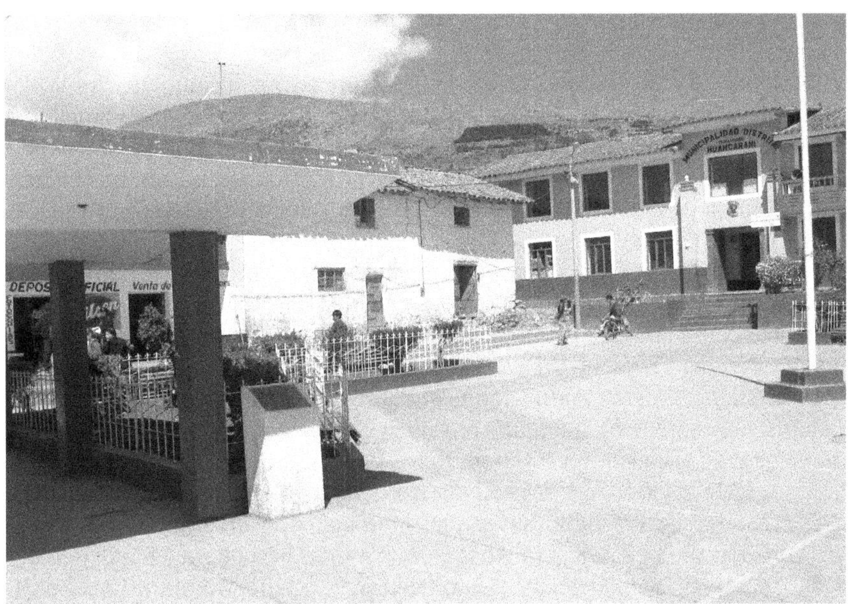

FIGURE 2.1 A new concrete municipal building and paved town square

that has a charged presence in the history of the modern built environment. It is the material that delivered the ambitious public housing projects and public buildings of the post–World War II construction boom, and it was integral to the communications infrastructures—the roads, bridges, and airstrips—that formed the backbone of the twentieth-century modern economy (Gandy 2002). For many, its association with high modernism (whether capitalist or socialist) links it to oppressive, dehumanizing architectures of standardization. Its use in the construction of cheap mass housing connotes poverty and poor living conditions. Yet concrete has always also been a material with which architects and engineers have experimented to produce iconic buildings, public landmarks, and luxury residences (Cohen and Moeller 2006; Jones 2006; Wagenaar and Dings 2005). Concrete has been deployed in large-scale public architecture with the intention of deliberately disrupting a bourgeois aesthetic of discrimination through an appeal to mass production and standard form. But it is also a material that has excited artists and experimental architects and engineers, whose reputations and careers depend on these very notions of creative distinction. In the world of contemporary design, concrete excites because it can be molded to any form and because the openness of this material to non-standard aggregates allows for experimentation and innovative results.

In this chapter, I am primarily concerned with the ways in which concrete is implicated in the transformation of public space in provincial Peru. I am also particularly interested in the potency attributed to concrete, its transformative capacities and its seductive force. Concrete is closely associated with modern industry and contemporary state power, for while 'liquid stone' (Cohen and Moeller 2006) can take any shape initially, this is crucially only a transitional and temporary characteristic. Concrete is useful because it combines this initial flexibility with a powerful fixing capacity, which has led to its ubiquitous and dominant deployment in unruly settings and all kinds of environmental conditions. Its associations with standardized forms that transcend the specificities of local conditions have given the material great value for the regulatory spaces of the modern state.

It is now some 15 years since the Sunday market was moved into its own designated area in the small town of Ocongate in southern Peru, where I have conducted ethnographic research on and off since 1983. The new market very quickly became a regulated space, in contrast to the previous haphazard appearance of stalls, wares, traders, and customers that transformed the otherwise rather sleepy square on a Sunday morning. The new area was concreted over, drainage was installed, a central section was covered, stalls were designated, licenses were issued, and inspections were made. The school buildings have also expanded significantly during the same period, from a handful of adobe structures in the mid-1980s to what is now a large secondary and elementary school complex. Similar changes can be seen in relation to the medical post, the police station, the telephone exchange, and, most dramatically perhaps, the town hall itself. Once a single multi-purpose room with a long wooden balcony that connected the local business of state to the general square, the town hall is now a large concrete building with functionally differentiated rooms: an auditorium, a storeroom, and a whole suite of offices occupied by the various officials who work for local government, including the mayor, the general manager, secretaries, agronomists, engineers, and educationalists.

The appearance of concrete in Ocongate is directly related to changes in the local state that were brought about by decentralization processes associated with the neo-liberal policies of devolved government, which have greatly increased the fiscal resources of local municipalities. New concrete structures continue to appear throughout provincial Peru. Indeed, as I traveled round the Ayacucho region of Peru in 2006, an area that had been the epicenter of the war between the state and the Maoist guerrilla group the Shining Path, in which tens of thousands of people died during the 1980s, I was amazed to find small highland towns displaying ever more elaborate municipal structures in what could only be described as an explosive and competitive demonstration of municipal concrete grandeur. Decentralization processes also respond to decades of popular demand for greater political autonomy and to the desire on the part of municipal governments to develop a range of technical expertise in, for example, agronomy, tourism, and ecology, which allows them to compete for funds from both national and international sources.[1] The devolution of fiscal power to local government has thus produced a more highly differentiated and functional approach to state business.

These new civic buildings thus index changing modes of governance and a radical move away from established regimes of control within Peru's rural political economy. The post-colonial Peruvian state, established in 1824, ceded much political power to the hacienda owners. After the agrarian reform of the late 1960s, local government passed into the hands of new local elites—educated professionals and traders whose capacity to represent the majority was articulated in direct relation to practices of racialized class difference. Today, however, the municipalities are most likely to be controlled by young men whose parents would have been looked down on and excluded by earlier regimes. These new politicians have not 'taken power' in any straightforward way. Elite power is now more specifically focused on capital interests, which seek to exploit resources that are not under the control of the local state. Mineral deposits are at the eye of the storm in these changing configurations of power. Over 90 percent of Peruvian subsoils (owned by the national state) are already granted in concessions to mining companies. The situation is volatile because the municipalities do have a certain amount of political power that they exert, orchestrating protests as they seek to 'defend' their territories and traditional land use in appeals to international environmental and human rights campaigns. It is in this scenario that concrete now appears, carrying with it a highly ambiguous and complex promise.

The control of public offices by a new sector of the population is an important shift that has ramifications yet to be played out on the national and international scene. But the ubiquity of concrete responds not only to the need for a more differentiated, bureaucratically oriented space for the exercise of local government. As more and more areas of daily life are differentiated and financialized within these new regimes, local officials become not simply responsible for local development but also accountable for the monies that are being spent. In a context of meager resources, a politicized civil service, and, more significantly, entrenched dynamics of conflict and inequality, local officials are highly constrained with regard to what they can safely spend money on. They need to provide jobs for local people, act in ways that produce visible outputs and 'improvements', and take on short-term projects that can be delivered during the course of their period in office. Concrete is a great ally in such circumstances. It is cheap, malleable, and enduring, and it carries strong symbolic resonances of better, more civilized ways of living that serve to bolster the credibility of this new generation of local state officials.[2]

However, the social effects of concrete can be far-reaching, sometimes in unexpected ways. When I first began living in Ocongate in the mid-1980s, the central square was built on compacted, hardened earth. By the late 1990s, the earth had been concreted over, and the square is now more suitable for motor traffic and is cleaner in relation to the small restaurants and stalls selling food and drink to travelers. But one of the quiet changes—unremarked, as far as I am aware—relates to the ritual potential of this space at the heart of the village. In the past, the square was the site of many public ceremonies and rituals. Some of these continue as before, but some are no longer celebrated, especially those that refer most directly to the forces of the earth and the deep relationship between farmers and the elements on which they depend—earth and water, most particularly.

The local bullfights are an interesting case in point. Held twice a year, the bullfights are state-sponsored festivals (Harvey 1997). Young men from the town used to urge herders from the hinterland to bring their bulls down to the village to fight, and they would contract ritual specialists to entice a condor down from the snow-capped mountain Ausangate to join in the play. On these occasions, the center of the town was turned over to those sectors of the population that were least likely ever to control this civic space. In classic rituals of reversal, the town re-energized itself through the fictive ritual enactment of a powerful yet ultimately playful engagement between the forces of the animate landscape and the local state. Furthermore, the town hall appeared in this ritual as the body that integrated the region. Each of the four *ayllus*, or broad community/kinship/land-holding groups representing the rural populations of the district, would take responsibility for closing off sections of the square, effectively holding the bulls and the condor in the heart of the village for the duration of the bullfight. Once the square was paved, it was no longer safe to hold the fight there. The owners of the bulls jealously guard the well-being of their animals. The bulls and condors should not be harmed in these encounters, they hold; it is the young men who should take the risk, those who seek out the engagement. A new coliseum was built on the outskirts of the town, and the bullfights are now held there instead. No longer at the heart of the settlement and no longer requiring the participation of the four *ayllus*, the local state and the young men of the town now simply contract wild bulls for the fight, often bringing them in trucks from other regions of Peru altogether. The paving of the square thus coincided with a subtle move away from an event that enacted the charged display of interdependence between educated elites and those more closely connected to the forces of the local environment. In the new coliseum, the bullfight has been quietly transformed into a folkloric spectacle.

Then there are radical and deliberate transformations, such as those connected to the two-lane asphalt highway that is currently being built to connect Brazil's relatively buoyant export economy to the enticing markets of China via Peru's Pacific ports.[3] This construction project is a major international collaboration, backed by resources from international development banks. The result of a huge capital investment, this swath of asphalt concrete that now connects the town of Ocongate to the departmental capital of Cusco makes a different kind of distinction. The temporal and spatial coordinates of the Peruvian state are now reconfigured by the changed modes and speeds of connectivity that this road affords. Ten years ago, the journey time was around 10 hours on a good day. The capital city is now just 2 hours away, allowing officials and public servants to come and go with ease. There is thus a more continuous state presence in the town, and public works are a powerful component of this local state activity. However, the opening up of this town to other lived modernities has also generated demand for a more adequate and fulfilling relation with the modern state. Technical expertise might be more readily available via the new personnel employed by the town council, but at the same time such 'expertise' has simultaneously become somewhat less convincing and less trustworthy.

Concrete affords a way to explore these dynamics. It is a substance that binds the material and ideational promises of modernity and also allows us to observe how and where fractures appear. In the next section of the chapter,

I explore the social potential of concrete through a case study of the small Amazonian town of Nauta. I then turn to look in more detail at the materiality of concrete itself—the demands it makes and the relations in which it embroils the engineers who are contracted to deliver state projects. Finally, in the concluding section I frame some questions with respect to how these understandings of the complex entanglements of the technical and the political might inflect our perceptions of the social order of the state and the concretization of state power.

The Social Potentiality of Concrete: Idioms of Connectivity and Modernity

Nauta, a small town in the northern Peruvian Amazon, has longed for modernity for the best part of a century. Local people tell of how the town was cheated of its destiny by the fickle move of the powerful river on which all commercial activity depends. Poised in the 1930s to become the center of the growing trading zone on the borders of Brazil, Ecuador, and Colombia, Nauta quite suddenly found itself stranded by the cloying mud and shifting sand that prevented the development of its port when the river changed course. Only 100 kilometers south of the booming city of Iquitos, a place that has thrived due to the consequences of Nauta's demise, the people of Nauta have conducted a long campaign to create and maintain an overtly modern civic space in the jungle.

Tourists who pass through Nauta are usually unimpressed by the dusty, sleepy—and very concrete—environment (fig. 2.2). The forest vegetation threatens to burst through at every point despite an overt attempt to keep it at bay. The central square makes some concessions to the notion of a 'garden environment', with trees and plants providing shade and color, but elsewhere the concrete is pretty much unadorned. It is as if the residents of Nauta resolutely, and very gradually, urbanized everything that they could in their immediate environment while waiting for the road that would eventually connect them to Iquitos. Some of these modifications have yet to come into use. There is concrete, but much of it is concrete in waiting. For example, a new fish market is now located down by the river in an area that might become the new dock—and it has yet to be opened. And by the old dock, there is the new tourist information booth, which has not yet welcomed any tourists.

Concrete pathways connect the center of Nauta to the outlying areas of town (fig. 2.3). In places you can almost feel the forest pushing back as cracks and bulges appear with alarming speed after the concrete is laid. This omnipresent but somehow insufficient concrete can disappoint environmentalists and modernizers alike. The environmentalists are still witnessing the brutal imposition of external and damaging values and materials, while the modernizers are frustrated by the fragility of the concrete skin that never fully manages to curb the forces of the forest.

Nonetheless, the concrete does provide a relatively stable surface, a possibility for movement and connectivity. It offers a modicum of predictability

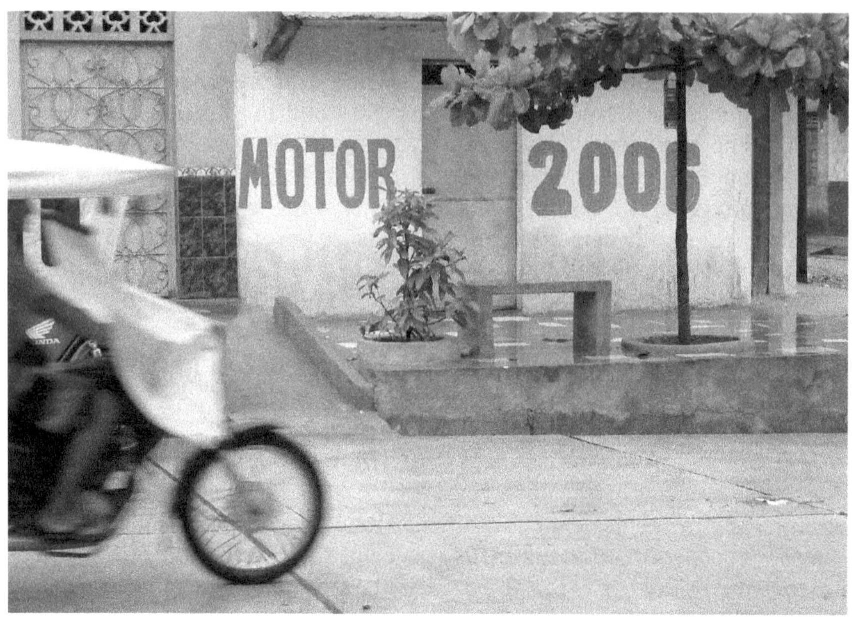

FIGURE 2.2 Concrete in Nauta

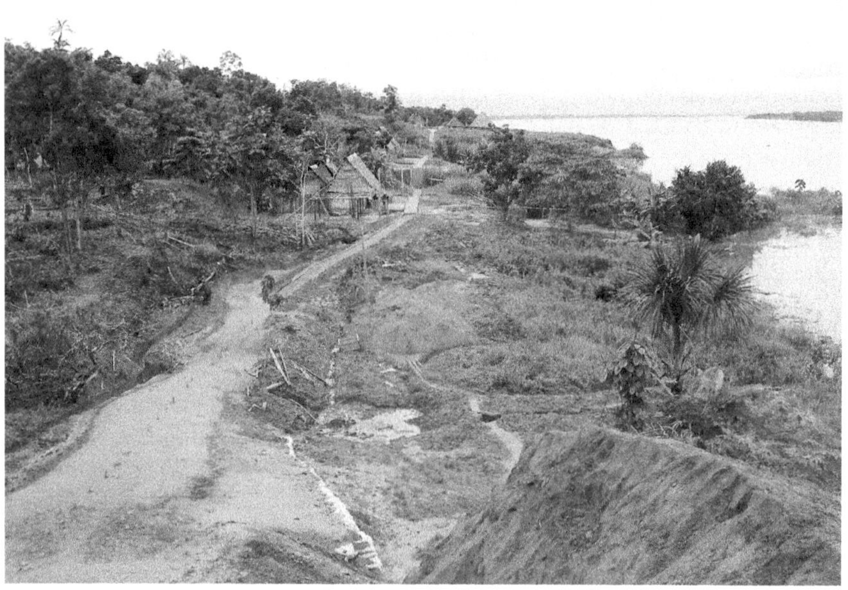

FIGURE 2.3 Concrete moving into the outlying areas

and bolsters aspirations for new markets, for a future in which tourists and traders might revive the stagnant economy of the town. And nowhere was this more keenly felt than in relation to the road that—I was told when I first went to Nauta in 2005—the residents had been waiting for for over 70 years. Most specifically, in this area the road was desired as a way of turning away from the river that had betrayed them. The Amazon River, which starts where the Ucayali joins the Marañon just 1 kilometer south of Nauta, is an energetic and unpredictable force that defies control. River transport is known to be dangerous and unreliable, and those who navigate have to learn the ways and the moods of the river. Even powerful motorized boats require skillful handling to deal with fast-moving debris, changing currents, and sudden squalls. Peruvian President Belaúnde Terry was somewhat disingenuous when in the 1980s he declared that the rivers were the highways of eastern Peru. These waterways certainly provide an effective communications network for forest peoples. However, Belaúnde's subsequent ambitious schemes to build the Trans-Amazonian Highway, thereby enabling the landless Andean peasants to colonize the eastern territories of the state, implicitly acknowledged that transportation networks requiring expertise and skill are incompatible with the kind of radical social transformation that he was aiming to engineer.

In this tropical forest environment, concrete often fails to live up to its promise of stability and strength. As residents watched the road slowly appear, they also witnessed how this supposedly predictable and autonomous material was continually undermined by the complex and tense relations in which it was embroiled. The story of the emergence of this road is long and complex. There were other twists and turns of fate beyond the original abandonment by the river, including fluctuations in international markets, border wars with Ecuador, and a weak central state that sought favors from oil-rich regional authorities. But by 2005, after several false starts and a fair measure of incompetence and criminality, the 100-kilometer stretch connecting Nauta to Iquitos was almost completed. The central government had provided the crucial funding to finish the work. I watched as the last in a long line of construction companies attempted to complete the road. The final 5 kilometers was all that remained—and this stretch was in dispute. The regional government had initiated legal proceedings against the contractor, which was itself a consortium composed of several sub-contracted companies. The problem was that the surface was already breaking up. One woman complained to me that it was simply crumbling—"like cake." Materials were impounded, and the people of Nauta waited for the resolution.

A year later, some months after the road was fully completed, we went to talk to the engineer who had directed the completion phase of the project. He told us of his "troubles" with that road and of his fears that the surface was again not going to last. But this time, instead of citing the malpractice and corruption of the previous contractors, he joked about the "savages," the ordinary people who did not know how to take care of what they had. He had driven down the road in order to document the diverse ways in which everyday negligence was prejudicial to the surface that he had laid. The townspeople were effectively putting their own mundane needs before the needs of the road surface, blocking drainage ditches by leaving heavy loads in them or failing to clear away accumulated debris.

This brief description of concrete surfaces in an Amazonian town shows how attention to such spaces can reveal the material traces of state intervention and withdrawal. Our inquiries into the background of the Nauta road opened up the layered histories of incursion into the area, the early trading and tax interests in relation to the rubber boom of the nineteenth century, the arrival of the national army to protect the frontier with Ecuador, the scramble to extract valuable hardwoods, the campaigns to establish national parks and nature reserves, the arrival and departure of oil companies, the gradual development of the infrastructures of state facilities, and the growing number of houses and small settlements along the emerging road. This road was thus not simply another icon of oppressive state presence—equivalent to the imposed concrete structures of the church, the bank, and the prison that Taussig (2004) describes in relation to small towns in Colombia. In Nauta, the hospital, the school, the town hall, and the post office were manifestations of state presence that, like the road itself, were actively sought after by local people.

Nevertheless, as suggested above, the 'social ordering' of Nauta and its integration into wider state structures remain unsatisfactory to most residents. For some, the connectivity is still inadequate as the new road has emptied the town of the relatively wealthy professional classes who can now commute with ease to the city of Iquitos. And while the majority of teachers and health workers no longer live in Nauta, the tourists have yet to arrive. There are no seductive infrastructures of comfortable but exotic locations for wealthy travelers who are keen to get away from the concrete and into other kinds of more eco-friendly, controlled spaces farther into the forest. Conditions have improved for those seeking to extract resources from the region. It is now easier to reach and remove hardwoods, to sell charcoal, and to get sparse agricultural goods and forest products to market than it was previously. But these traders now find themselves in open conflict with environmentalists and internationally backed campaigns that attempt to protect the flora and fauna of the forest made vulnerable by the road.

Concrete thus manifests an unstable power. To be sure, on the surface we note the visible reconfiguration of public spaces in small towns. But neither in the Amazon nor in the Andes did I find people particularly satisfied with what they had received beyond the rhetorical speeches made at the moment of unveiling a new structure. Back in Ocongate, people said that the concrete condor decorating the center of their town square looks more like a chicken. The statue fails to conjure up the majestic bird that they used to bring down from the mountain to take part in the bullfights. Still, it is also worth noting that there is no indigenous tradition of producing representational forms of this kind. The forms that people do make—often (but not necessarily) with great precision—are miniatures. These miniatures are nowadays most commonly produced as clay models in the context of appeals to the earth powers to bring good fortune. Ideally, the model operates as a prototype that can help to generate that which it depicts

(Allen 1997). There are long traditions of miniaturization in the Andes in which the model is understood to condense the force and vital energy of whatever is being represented. The Inka, for example, used to plant miniature ears of corn, crafted in gold, in their fields to draw forth a rich golden harvest from the earth.[4] Indeed, it is this notion of condensed force that links the powerful mountain spirits to the earth powers. The pebbles and small stones that, together with the compacted earth, constitute the paths and tracks over which people travel on a daily basis are condensations of the great power of the Andean mountain range (ibid.). The failure of the concrete condor thus has an added resonance: not only does it fail as a decorative image, but it is clearly seen as failing to activate any vital energies. The concrete from which it is made appears as inert matter, and the understandable disappointment relates to the reminder that this statue is thus always less than that which it purports to portray or invoke.

A parallel effect occurs in relation to many development projects, producing general skepticism with respect to the perception of benefits for local people. For some, there is even the sense that the town has somehow been marginalized by the road that now skirts around one of its edges. Despite the new connectivity, it becomes evident that what is more important is who travels, where, and for what reason. Many people sit and watch as others speed by in their fancy four-by-fours. These travelers no longer need to buy things locally since they are now not far from the wider range of goods and services available in the city.

Thus far, I have suggested that concrete mediates relations between civil society and the state. It furnishes the places where people and state officials meet, designates healthy and sanitized sites for trade, and promises efficiency, reliability, neutrality, and modernity. All of these things appear to work elsewhere for others but do not quite deliver during the here and now for the people I spoke to in Nauta and in Ocongate. Perhaps this connects to the sense in which concrete is quite literally a surface form and, as such, seems to preclude any deeper engagement with the relations and problems that it is brought in to solve. The vulnerability of local technicians and state officeholders in relation to these public works is exposed, for in their attempts to render visible their activity and intervention, they also reveal their inability to make a difference. The image of local government is thus tarnished by the inevitable accusations of corruption and ineptitude. Nevertheless, the enduring appeal of concrete is firmly lodged in its promise of strength and stability. In the following section, I consider the material potentiality of concrete and its capacities and limits in relation to images of power.

The Material Potentiality of Concrete: Aggregation and Process

Concrete is a composite material, made from the mixing of cement, water, and aggregates, which are typically sand and crushed stone. Additional additives can increase the strength of the concrete by reducing the amount of water required. The relative strength of the final product will depend on the ratio of cement to water and on the type of aggregate used. The mixing processes are thus crucial and require close control, as contaminants will affect the end result. The purity of the aggregates is tightly controlled since organic matter brought in with the sand and stones will adversely affect the strength and reliability of the concrete. The water also needs to be of a dependable and consistent level of purity.

The particularity of concrete as a building material derives primarily from the chemical reaction produced by mixing cement and water, which effects an irreversible process of gradual hardening. Indeed, it is this feature of being able to set hard in water that makes cement indispensable to many construction projects. This relationship between cement and water can appear counter-intuitive in contexts where most solid building materials gain their strength and durability through a process of dehydration. In the Andean region, techniques of dehydration have been central to local understandings of stored vitality. The Inka are renowned for their mummification practices whereby the vitality of the dead was preserved and reactivated through ritual libation, and where the annual cycles of rain and drought marked the release and the retention of life-giving forces (Gose 1994). In contemporary times, these techniques are still used for the storage of potatoes and meat, which are dried, stored, and rehydrated to release their energies as food.

In his book *My Cocaine Museum*, Michael Taussig (2004) has a chapter entitled "Cement & Speed" in which he reproduces a wonderful characterization of cement, its qualities and capacities, as well as the basic procedures of its production. He points out that the interesting and counter-intuitive relationship between cement and water has been known since ancient times, although the material was understood in very different terms and through very different relations than those that pertain today. Taussig reproduces the account of Vitruvius, a first-century Roman architect and builder whose name is closely linked to the first documentation of the nature of concrete (ibid.: 161):

> Vitruvius understood stone as composed of four elements: air, earth, fire, and water. As a builder, he wanted a substance like stone but malleable ... Smashing up limestone into small particles and mixing them with sand was not good enough, for there was neither unification nor hardening. That could only come with intense heat, which left the stone porous: [now quoting from ancient sources] "The water and air, therefore, which are in the substance of the stones, being thus discharged and expelled, and the latent heat only remaining, upon being replenished with water, which repels the fire, they recover their vigor and the water entering the vacuities occasions a fermentation; the substance of the lime is thus refrigerated and the superabundant heat ejected."

Builders and engineers have always attended to the capacities of specific materials. Concrete was valued for its ability to negotiate the tensions between solid and fluid matter, but this capacity had to be nurtured and drawn out from what was the more basic relational potential of its constituent elements. A successful resolution required the enactment or materialization of a theory of the cosmos in which the power of divine rulers was necessarily implicated. The pre-Socratic model of integration that Taussig outlines refers back to alchemical understandings of matter, where the challenge to the builder was to know how to activate the materials appropriately.

As discussed above, attention to the vital properties of matter was equally important to the builders of the Inka Empire. Like the Romans, the Inkas were an imperial power who invested heavily in road building and in the construction of monumental state palaces and temples. The rulers exercised divine power, but they did so in conjunction with advanced, pre-modern scientific experimentation. The Inkas are renowned today for their enduring architecture and specifically for their ability to erect monumental structures by working stone with such precision that they did not need to use mortar.[5] However, the point that I want to emphasize here is simply that, whether we are talking of stone or mortar, these materials were treated as vital entities that required skilled, often ritualized engagement, as well as a huge investment of resources and labor, which the fine Inka stonework is also famous for. The structures thus reveal not simply the political capacity to control other people, but the ability to shape and to accommodate to the forces of matter that ultimately contained and manifested Inka state power.

In relation to this account, it is easier to see how the claim that cement was 'invented' in the eighteenth century could in fact be credible. Chandra Mukerji (2006) has quite rightly disputed this claim, demonstrating that concrete was clearly known about, used, and supplied in seventeenth-century France and Italy. However, she also tells us that knowledge of these materials pertained to the skilled and secretive guilds of artisanal builders and, furthermore, that such knowledge was explicitly mistrusted in elite circles. She depicts a time of fascinating tension between the court, the artisan guilds, and the new technicians of the emerging fields of professional engineering and experimental science. The literary and courtly foundations of modern science played their part in severing the link between scientific and vernacular knowledge—and while this outcome was decidedly shaky in seventeenth-century France, eighteenth-century England provided a very different scenario. Here, in the context of emergent industrial production, concrete could be more definitively moved away from the occult associations with alchemical knowledge to form the basis of what was to become an axiomatically modern, mass-produced, and standardized material—one that was predictable and self-evident in its own terms, no longer requiring the kind of attention that would have been necessary in ancient Rome.[6]

Peter Jones (2006: 24–25) offers a standard account of the 'invention' of modern cement that supports Mukerji's point:

> The chemistry of concrete was of course unknown to the Romans, but they did know that small variations in the mixture altered its strength … Pozzolana was well known to Renaissance French architects, who recommended it for foundations in water or marshy soil, and pozzolanic substitutes … were commonly used in northern Europe from the seventeenth century onwards. But the most rapid developments took place during the nineteenth century, after the publication in 1791 of Smeaton's research since the late 1750s into mortars. The manufacture of artificial cements by burning materials at higher temperatures, from the 1820s, accelerated the development of modern concrete; the best known of these was 'Portland cement', invented in 1824, which soon became the basis of cement and concrete mixes.

Thus, while cement was known about and used since ancient times, it was effectively 're-invented' as the product of modern chemical knowledge in the eighteenth century. In the process, it became a different kind of material, understood to manifest relational powers quite unlike the concrete of ancient Rome or of seventeenth-century France.

The industrial context of cement production is crucial to the images of power that this material projects in the contemporary Peruvian environment. The cement industry requires high levels of capital investment in mineral extraction, factory production, and the transportation of the bulky and heavy finished product. It is an industry in which huge profits can be realized by those companies that are able to operate economies of scale; thus, there tends to be little competition (Dumez and Jeunemaître 1998). By the beginning of the twenty-first century, 96 percent of Peruvian cement was produced by only five companies (Gurmendi 2001). A century earlier, this tendency to concentration favored producers in Europe and the United States. Attempts by European businessmen to site production in Latin America (originally in Cuba and subsequently in Brazil and Argentina) failed to take off, due to the difficulties they faced in producing a competitive and sufficiently 'uniform' product. As a result of the disrupted supply lines during World War I, the Latin American states gained greater autonomy, and regional control of the industry was definitively established by 1918. The industry grew throughout the twentieth century in relation to the increasing demand for concrete generated by state-backed development programs, and it was further boosted by US intervention after World War II. Peru's cement industry was late to emerge: the first factories did not enter into production until 1922 (Tafunell 2007).

Most significantly, in relation to the current analysis, cement is an industrial product that was thoroughly entangled with foreign capital and technological expertise when it appeared in the first decades of the twentieth century. Its production was directly linked to the development of state infrastructures and the building of national economies. Indeed, there is a direct correlation between the size of the cement industry across the Latin American states, the relative indices of poverty, and the level of state investment in public works. In Peru, which has never competed with the economies of Brazil, Mexico, and Argentina, concrete was a material that they had waited for, a material that powerfully drove state investment, modernization, and prosperity (Tafunell 2007).

Thus far my discussion has focused on how concrete, this malleable stone, has been and continues to be deployed by modern states to manifest an enduring presence, a technical capacity, and a modernizing, transformative ambition. Taussig's allusion to the concrete of ancient Rome reminds us, however, that such projects require builders—people with theories and understandings of the social and material worlds that they seek to transform. In the previous section of this chapter, I argued that people from all walks of life in Peru actively welcome concrete into their worlds as a manifestation of state capacity and care. It is also the case, however, that the minerals and clays that are combined in the production of cement, as well as the water, sand, and stones that are added to produce the concrete, are far from neutral substances in the Andean world, and people struggle to integrate concrete with existing understandings of the material world and its inherent relations.

Concrete is a material that requires attention, but it is not understood by Andean people to be a form of matter that draws on the foundational cosmological principles that consider earth, rocks, and mountains to be a source of vital energy. It is in this sense that concrete became a properly modern and technical substance, achieving that most magical dimension of the material fact—the exclusion of its inherent sociality. However, in the mundane practices of building and engineering, these dimensions have a habit of reappearing. The issue of the components of concrete tends not to arise in small construction projects, since they use ready-mixed cement that arrives from elsewhere, packaged and thoroughly detached from the lived environment. In these circumstances, the concrete can stand for itself. Its industrial provenance successfully severs the ties to other kinds of matter. However, in the context of the major road construction project mentioned earlier, the state needed to call up its own resources and to assemble on site the aggregates for the production of concrete and asphalt. In the process, it is not simply that the component parts are revealed, but that their source is also identifiable. Thus, the competing claims of diverse materialities was made explicit.

In Ocongate, there is grave concern about the river that runs alongside the town. The river has its source in Ausangate, the snow-capped mountain that dominates the local landscape and is considered to be one of the most powerful spiritual forces in the region. The local people believe that the vitality of the land and of all human enterprise depends on the force of this mountain. The Peruvian state maintains that it owns all water courses, and it has given permission to the construction company to dredge the river for sand and stones. Both the river and the mountain have reacted to this process. According to some, the snows from the mountain are receding in direct proportion to the traffic flows. The river, submitted to a violent process of extraction that is literally painful for people to watch, has become unrecognizable (fig. 2.4). Local people now question the relationships that the extraction process has made explicit: Whose stone is it? Whose river? How have these been wrested away from local authorities? What is the relationship between the local state and the national state? What part does the regional state play in cutting across these tensions? How are such resources identified, located, channeled?

In the case of the Nauta road, a similar problem arose. Finding stone is one of the key dilemmas for road building in the Amazonian region. The construction company had identified a possible local source and, via the state, had established its right to extract the material. However, the people objected so strongly that the company calculated it would cost more in security, reparation, and negotiating time than it would to go farther afield. The stone for the Nauta road was eventually brought from a site located seven days up the river, a situation that created considerable logistical problems for the engineering company but at least prevented an explosion of the kind of social conflict that notoriously (and expensively) blocks progress in such projects.

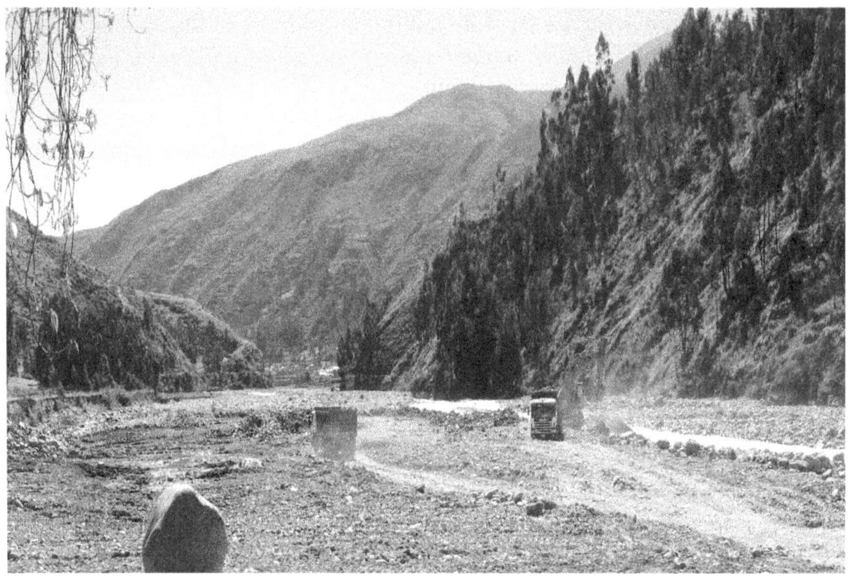

FIGURE 2.4 Extracting stones from the river

Conclusions: Cementing the Material and the Social

I have argued that concrete—a substance that binds and fixes—is a form of matter with overt potential for both social and material transformation. It also combines the qualities of water with those of stone, being able to take any shape and fit any form. However, unlike water, it sets hard. Its fluidity and adaptive capacity is only temporary. I have also discussed how the combinations and purifications that are intrinsic to the process of making concrete themselves entail particular ontological orientations to matter. In the Andean ethnography, the crucial distinction in play is in relation to the earth itself (the minerals, clays, rocks, and sand that constitute the earth) with respect to divergent understandings of vitality and of inert matter.

In the context of state-sponsored public works that are entrusted to the engineering skills of the modern professional, concrete affords a reliable, predictable, flexible, and strong material, perfectly suited to the molding of the generic, homogeneous space of a national road network—a space that in its very materiality connects a disparate and dispersed population. And there is no doubt that in some ways this scenario is achieved. Roads do provide consistent surfaces for travel so that vehicles from all over the country and beyond can move, at speed, without having to adapt in any particular way to the local landscape. And roads channel flows, for better or worse, directing and ordering the key lines of trade, the sites of regulation, the settlements that grow up to service this movement.

Yet, as is plainly evident, while concrete does unite and bind disparate social and material realities in some respects, it is also characterized by a fundamental fragility in relation to its connective capacity in both the material and social domains. The singularity of concrete is easily disrupted: it is vulnerable to water, temperature, heavy loads, and neglect. It is also exceptionally inflexible and brittle, and its strength becomes a weakness over time. As the earth continues to move and grow underneath and around it, the liquid stone, now set, cannot adapt or grow with it. Although it contains earth, concrete is not *of* the earth, and in that sense, unlike the earth, it is not alive. For some, this is the reason that concrete is important. It offers a resistance to the specificity of local conditions, but only if properly maintained and supported. For others, there is the hope that concrete might, through neglect, become more integrated into the general landscape—but, crucially, only to the extent that it becomes useless as a generic space. Through abandonment and repossession, the material might then become integrated with the living earth that surrounds it.

Contemporary road-building engineers pay considerable attention to the pre-existing fabric of the worlds that they seek to transform, but their focus resolutely separates the material and social worlds. Stones and soils are taken to laboratories where they are analyzed, tested, modeled, modified, and retested. Then they are taken out into the world and used, constantly under surveillance. Concrete receives exemplary attention in this respect: systems of maintenance are devised in order continually to control, measure, and evaluate. Water, identified as concrete's prime enemy, is carefully diverted, with the camber and drainage all minutely calculated to ensure its protection. Efforts to protect concrete from society result in all kinds of regulatory practices, including state officials who monitor the weight of vehicles and the spread of that weight over the axles in order to prevent unnecessary wear and tear on the road. Good citizens do not act like the 'savages' who threaten the integrity of the Nauta road. An ethnographic focus on the building process thus reveals the ways in which material and social relations are entwined (despite the best intentions of technocratic planners), and also how tense, frictional accommodations of divergent notions of the material and social orders are worked out (Tsing 2005).

Following this substance in action reveals various kinds of scalar discontinuity, such as between the promises and the limits of modernity; the potentialities of material and social arrangements and the actualities that they produce; the surfaces and appearances of things and the underlying conditions that sustain or disrupt them. This ethnographic attention to concrete also reveals fractures in the social order of the state, specifically, the conflicting domains of national, regional, and local government, as well as the limits to state sovereignty in relation to the flows of capital, people, ideas, and materials that do not respect or even acknowledge national borders.

In the engineering of public space, concrete is co-opted as an important material ally in the high-stakes business of ordering the world, but in practice it also brings the engineers up against the fractures and scalar disjunctions that modernist planning usually fails to take into account. It is in the negotiation of these tensions—between fixity and fluidity, between generic and specific materials, between autonomous and relational matter—that concrete offers us a way of thinking about society, aesthetics, and the state. Engineers find themselves drawn into pragmatic negotiations between specific material and social conditions and the general principles that motivate and structure their attempts to engage the specificity. The promise of concrete to operate as a generic, homogeneous, and, above all, predictable material is constantly challenged by the specificity of the terrains to which it is applied—terrains that are intrinsically unstable and heterogeneous. The image of power that concrete affords is thus a compromised one, as the stability and predictability of this material are secure only insofar as it is surrounded by and embedded in specific relationships of care.

Acknowledgments

My thanks to Hannah Knox for her intellectual companionship on our joint study of Peruvian roads, and to my friends in Ocongate and Cusco for teaching me so many things about life in the Andes. The seminars at CRESC, the Anthropology Department at the University of California, Davis, and the Sociology Department in Lancaster were all very helpful. Particular thanks go to Marisol de la Cadena, Amanda Ravetz, and Celia Lury for their support and inspiration, and to Celia Blondet, who continues to introduce me to Peru and who helped me to think about concrete and the state in a new way.

Penny Harvey is Professor of Social Anthropology at the University of Manchester and Co-Director of the ESRC Centre for Research on Socio-Cultural Change. She has done ethnographic research in Peru, the UK, and Spain on a range of topics (linguistic, technological, and exhibitionary). She is currently writing a book, with Hannah Knox, about road construction in Peru, tracking the material, moral, and social controversies produced by the volatile mix of engineering expertise, transnational capital, and territorial politics. Recent publications include *Anthropology and Science: Epistemologies in Practice* (2007) and *Technologized Images, Technologized Bodies* (2010), both co-edited with Jeanette Edwards and Peter Wade.

Notes

1. These ideas about municipal, regional, and central government relations are embedded in long conversations with Deborah Poole, with whom I am currently conducting research on the Peruvian regional state. Our project development was supported by the Economic and Social Research Council (ESRC) and the Social Science Research Council (SSRC) through a collaborative fellowship held at the Centre for Research on Socio-Cultural Change (CRESC) at the University of Manchester.
2. See Orlove (1998) and Colloredo-Mansfeld (1994) for detailed discussions of the relative value of earthen structures (adobe bricks, dirt roads, clay pots) and concrete. Both authors stress the ambiguous yet dichotomized values that these materials convey in the Andes.

3. I am carrying out research on this road, the Interoceanic Highway, with my colleague Hannah Knox. We are grateful for funding from CRESC and for a further grant from the ESRC, both of which have subsidized the fieldwork for this project.
4. For a more detailed discussion of this topic, see Harvey and Knox (2009).
5. I was amused to find the following comment from the president of the American Concrete Institute in the context of a report to the industry on her visit to South America (Coke 1999): "A visit to Peru wouldn't be complete without time spent at Machu Picchu, the ruins of the last Inka city, on top of a mountain in the Andes. But that's another story, and the ruins are not concrete. (In fact, no mortar was used at all, but you can't get even a business card between the stones!)."
6. See Bensaude-Vincent and Stengers (1996) for a fascinating account of the emergence of modern chemistry as a practice that constantly questioned its foundations, its knowledge, its practices, its status—a history of intellectual adventures rather than a singular enterprise with a sole telos.

References

Allen, Catherine J. 1997. "When Pebbles Move Mountains: Iconicity and Symbolism in Quechua Ritual." Pp. 73–84 in Howard-Malverde 1997.

Bensaude-Vincent, Bernadette, and Isabelle Stengers. 1996. *A History of Chemistry*. Trans. Deborah van Dam. Cambridge, MA: Harvard University Press.

Cohen, Jean-Louis, and G. Martin Moeller, Jr., eds. 2006. *Liquid Stone: New Architecture in Concrete*. New York: Princeton Architectural Press.

Coke, Jo. 1999. "President's Memo: South America Visit." American Concrete Industry. http://www.concrete.org/about/ab_presmemo_coke11.htm (accessed 24 February 2009).

Colloredo-Mansfeld, Rudolf. 1994. "Architectural Conspicuous Consumption and Economic Change in the Andes." *American Anthropologist* 96, no. 4: 845–865.

Dumez, Hervé, and Alain Jeunemaître. 1998. "The Unlikely Encounter between Economics and a Market: The Case of the Cement Industry." Pp. 222–243 in *The Laws of the Markets*, ed. Michel Callon. Oxford: Basic Blackwell.

Gandy, Matthew. 2002. *Concrete and Clay: Reworking Nature in New York City*. Cambridge, MA: MIT Press.

Gose, Peter. 1994. *Deathly Waters and Hungry Mountains: Agrarian Ritual and Class Formation in an Andean Town*. Toronto: University of Toronto Press.

Gurmendi, Alfredo C. 2001. "The Mineral Industry of Peru." US Geological Survey Minerals Yearbook. http://minerals.usgs.gov/minerals/pubs/country/2001/pemyb01.pdf (accessed 24 February 2009).

Harvey, Penelope. 1997. "Peruvian Independence Day: Ritual, Memory, and the Erasure of Narrative." Pp. 21–44 in Howard-Malverde 1997.

Harvey, Penelope, and Hannah Knox. 2009. "Abstraction, Materiality and the 'Science of the Concrete' in Engineering Practice." Pp. 124–141 in *Material Powers: Cultural Studies, History and the Material Turn*, ed. Tony Bennett and Patrick Joyce. London: Routledge.

Howard-Malverde, Rosaleen, ed. 1997. *Creating Context in Andean Cultures*. Oxford: Oxford University Press.

Jones, Peter. 2006. *Ove Arup: Masterbuilder of the Twentieth Century*. New Haven, CT: Yale University Press.

Mukerji, Chandra. 2006. "Tacit Knowledge and Classical Technique in Seventeenth-Century France: Hydraulic Cement as Living Practice among Masons and Military Engineers." *Technology and Culture* 47, no. 4: 713–733.

Orlove, Benjamin. 1998. "Down to Earth: Race and Substance in the Andes." *Bulletin of Latin American Research* 17, no. 2: 207–222.
Tafunell, Xavier. 2007. "On the Origins of ISI: The Latin American Cement Industry, 1900–30." *Journal of Latin American Studies* 39: 299–328.
Taussig, Michael. 2004. *My Cocaine Museum*. Chicago, IL: University of Chicago Press
Tsing, Anna Lowenhaupt. 2005. *Friction: An Ethnography of Global Connection*. Princeton, NJ: Princeton University Press.
Wagenaar, Cor, and Mieke Dings, eds. 2005. *Ideals in Concrete: Exploring Central and Eastern Europe*. Rotterdam: NAi Publishers.

❀ Chapter 3 ❀

Multifaceted Monolith

The Hidden Diversity of Mass Housing

MILES GLENDINNING

Many of the chapters in this book are concerned with the most recent phase of state power and its visual expression, namely, the revival of international capitalism that has seen governments and states around the world increasingly being reduced to the status of assistants and facilitators for forces that, fundamentally, hold them in little regard. In the post-war years covered by this chapter, the role of the state could not have been more different: dominant and proud rather than weak and apologetic, pushing forward rather than drawing back.[1] This contrast has had a corresponding effect on today's perspective of those years, which are now widely branded as alienating and homogeneous, as logical offshoots of a gray, mechanistic socialism. The surviving landscape of the post-war Modernist mass housing program, still vast in extent in many countries, is usually treated, at best, with benign neglect or, at worst, with active denigration and mass demolition—even, ironically, as the motifs of more individualistic set pieces of modern architecture are 'revived' and modified for capitalist commodification and consumption (see, e.g., Begg 1996).

Notes for this chapter are located on page 58.

Arguably, however, this portrayal of post-war mass housing as gray and monotonous is mischievous and anachronistic. Internationally speaking, a cursory comparative analysis reveals a kaleidoscopic variety of approaches to the organization and design of mass housing. Even within individual nations, there is a vast and little-known diversity of mass housing patterns. This chapter presents a brief overview of international mass housing, followed by a case study of Great Britain, where diversity came about due to tensions between municipal and national state agencies, and between professionals who were oriented either toward production or design. Many of these professionals were, in fact, also employed by the agencies of the state.

In post-war mass housing, we witness the relationship between aesthetics and the state in its most direct form, although it should be emphasized that 'aesthetics' in this instance is not a matter of elite 'art' but of the overall physical fabric of the built environment in which people live. In the post-war mass housing environment, the key issues were not those of individual design but of general characteristics, such as housing density (with a constant battle between advocates of low and high density and everything in between); house type (with the tension in many countries between the supposedly 'native' small, detached house and the 'alien' apartment block); architectural 'style' (with monumental, formal solutions often pitted against various versions of the Picturesque); and housing layout (with wildly fluctuating debates on how to manage the interaction of pedestrians and vehicles). In all these areas, there was great diversity between the views of administrative and professional elites and the direct perceptions and experiences of dwellers. The fervent debates of the early 1960s over how to apply factory pre-fabrication to the best effect in housing were followed, after a time lag of only 5 or 10 years, by a violent storm of inhabitants' protests against the alienation engendered by 'ugly concrete' housing.

Historians of the nineteenth-century built environment are well acquainted with the concept of local diversity within a modern, or modernizing, national society—as expressed, for example, through the strong and individual city cultures encouraged by the tradition of civic autonomy and power. My argument here is that even under the state umbrella in the post-war period, this tension between the local 'facts on the ground' and the 'wider picture' continued, albeit in much more complex, international patterns, with an almost limitless diversity of forms of definition—geographical, intellectual, social, political—all of which were constantly shifting and overlapping.

Context: The International Mosaic of Mass Housing

To trace this interplay between national/international and local, I intend to begin with the former, with the unifying concept of the 'national housing drive'—a collective term that itself would have been incomprehensible in the nineteenth century—and to put this briefly into a wider international comparative context. Post-war mass housing, in its stereotypical form—serried rows of multi-storey blocks, expansive garden suburb estates, or completely new towns, built mainly for low-income groups at the instigation of the state—was concentrated in limited areas of the world: Northern and Western Europe; the USSR and its immediate satellites; the city-states of Hong Kong and Singapore; and a few parts of the Northeast in the United States. Even in these areas, however, there are countries that have very little existent mass social housing, such as Norway and the Republic of Ireland.[2]

The 'heartland' of post-war social housing was undeniably Western Europe, where the balance of socialism and capitalism was reflected in an intricate mosaic of individualized state policies and solutions, both political and socio-architectural, that frequently featured dramatic clashes between intellectually high-flown initial aspirations and extreme rejection and/or alienation on the part of inhabitants. Vast projects included Amsterdam's Bijlmermeer, with its relentless landscape of interconnected 11-storey honeycomb blocks (built in 1965–1972 and containing 13,000 flats), which attracted ceaseless social controversy and physical degradation, culminating in the notorious crash of a jumbo jet into the blocks in 1992. Another is Emile Aillaud's famous Les Courtillières development near Paris, with its eccentric combination of undulating periphery blocks and tall, asterisk-like towers, which underwent ceaseless vicissitudes at the hands of a plethora of municipal and other public agencies.[3]

In the Soviet bloc, conversely, the more aggressively collectivist state attempted to impose a full-blooded standardization, especially in the massed pre-fabrication programs of the post-Khrushchev era in the USSR. Here, paradoxically, although

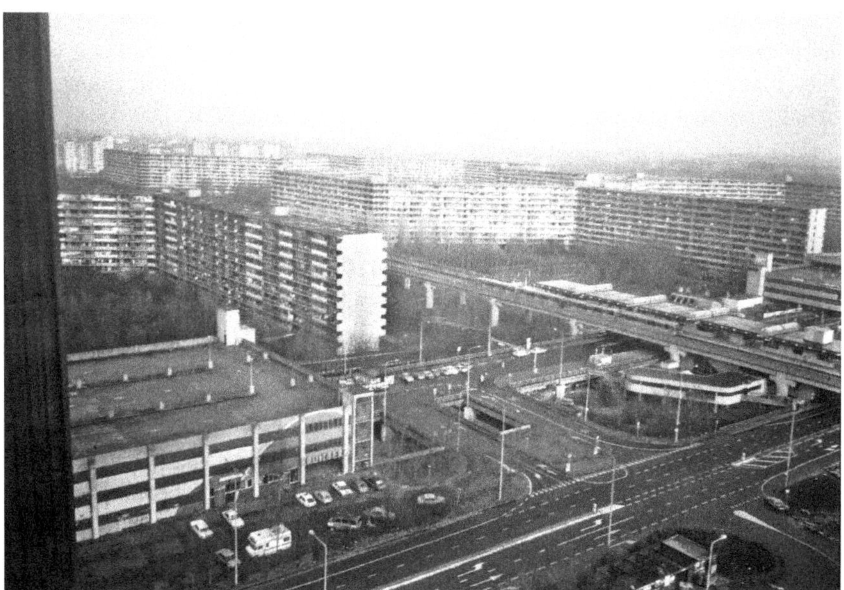

FIGURE 3.1 Panoramic view of Bijlmermeer in 1985, taken from the eighteenth floor of one of the towers (Kempering-Toren) and showing the original layout of deck blocks (Section E) and multi-level traffic infrastructure. © Miles Glendinning

there was extensive standardization and a drastic post-1991 economic polarization (especially in Moscow), the perpetuation of a wide social mix within
the Soviet mass housing legacy means that it today lacks the often wholesale
disrepute and radical regeneration/demolition experiences of its Western counterparts (see Kopp 1981; Morton 1984; Urban 2008).

In Europe, both East and West were in agreement that housing was a matter
of all-embracing community concern, reflecting a set of values that have never
been generally accepted in more thoroughly capitalist North America. There,
social housing is usually considered a peripheral concern of the state and is
often reserved for a residuum, with the largest-scale developments being built
by hybrid private-public or philanthropic agencies. This was prominently so
in the case of New York City's gigantic middle-income Mitchell-Lama housing program (initiated with federal funding from the 1949 Title One Housing
Act) and other similar programs of the 1950s–1970s, such as Co-op City in the
Bronx (built in 1965–1972 with over 15,000 apartments in 35 towers of 24–33
stories each) (see Ballon and Jackson 2007: 306–307). It was not in New York
but rather, starting in 1954, in the planned communities of another of the
continent's major metropolitan cities, Toronto, that North America's private
enterprise-dominated housing system—combined with a strong regional planning framework focused on high-density 'hot spots' in center and periphery—
was able to generate a vast built landscape of towers and slabs in open space
that almost rivaled the USSR for consistency and grandeur (McClelland and
Stewart 2007: 212–215; Stewart 2008). In South American countries, the private
sector was yet more dominant, excluding exceptional cases such as early post-
war Caracas, with its aggressive public housing programs. However, as in the
instance of the Brasilia superquadras, laid out as part of Lucio Costa's renowned
Pilot Plan, the private sector's operations could be reconciled at times with
strong planning and architectural frameworks (Williams 2007, 2008).

The most extreme juxtapositions of capitalism and welfare state housing
sprang up slightly later in those dynamic Asian city-states, Hong Kong and
Singapore. Beginning in the late 1950s, but only really gathering pace since
the mid-1970s, their free enterprise economies were complemented and supported by colossal programs of state-planned mass housing, including rental
blocks alongside publicly built home-ownership flats. In Singapore, a somewhat
authoritarian government system supported the program for over half a century
through highly structured regional planning and a consistent succession of fiscal
incentives, backed by a level of consensual political support that was unequaled
in any other twentieth-century public housing program. Hong Kong's public
housing drive followed a more exciting and radically fluctuating course over the
half-century that followed the building of the first Mark I resettlement blocks for
rehousing fire-displaced squatters, with sharp swings in emphasis from rental to
home ownership and back again and with multi-storey blocks and conglomera-
tions of often gigantic scale (Castells, Goh, and Kwok 1991).

Let us return now to look in more detail at the common chronological
and organizational characteristics of social housing in the Western European
heartland. Almost everywhere within it, 'informed' public opinion had come

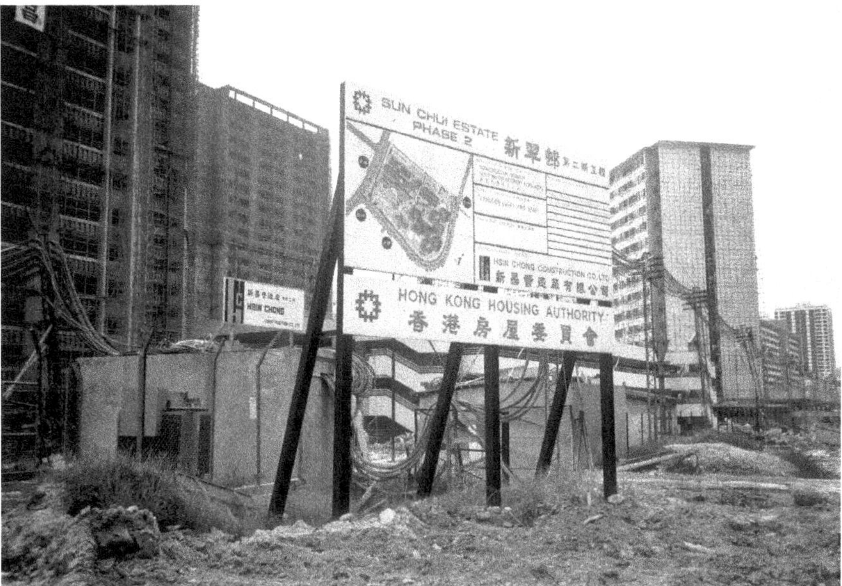

FIGURE 3.2 Hong Kong Housing Authority development notice board in Sha Tin New Town, seen in 1983. The Sun Chui Estate Phase 2 development, which comprised slab and tower blocks for mainstream rental housing, was built using a 'rationalized traditional' concrete construction. © Miles Glendinning

to believe by around 1910 that the private housing market had become incapable of providing enough low-income rental houses. In response, the state had put together national housing campaigns that required it to intervene in the workings of the private market and even, in some instances, to devise a full-fledged state system of housing provision. Depending partly on the level of international crisis, those national campaigns often varied between broad general needs campaigns, aimed at remedying wartime shortages and providing 'homes for all', and specialized campaigns such as the 'war against the slums' or the strategic dispersal of population and industry into planned new towns. The new collective social 'patrons' ranged from state agencies to philanthropic organizations and regulated private firms. But in contrast to the Soviet bloc, the system of production itself was organized almost exclusively through the private building industry, which shifted its orientation appropriately toward contracting as well as speculative work, although in some countries the speculative building sector stayed very prominent. Partly because of its close association with the passions of wartime, but also because of the traditions of polemical debate in architecture, mass housing in Europe also became bound up in a cycle of feverish advocacy and accelerated production followed by forcible rejection. Finally, from the late 1960s into the 1970s, all the variants of mass housing discourse were increasingly rejected in the face of trends away from centralization to more participatory processes and from social planning to market contexts (Denby 1938; Dufaux and Fourcaut 2004; Power 1993, 1997; Rowlands, Musterd, and van Kempen 2007).

One of the most prominent and consensually accepted aspects of these housing drives was their almost exclusive reliance on Modernist patterns of architecture, whose strikingly novel, free-flowing forms and layouts were intellectually buttressed by a complex ideology of scientific humanism, which combined a rationalistic concern for method and standardization with a utopian search for community-based salvation. This approach applied in Western Europe throughout the whole period and in the socialist bloc from around 1958, following Khrushchev's denunciation of Stalinism. In both cases, mass housing was a special focus of concern, being the building type that was widely viewed as *the* key arena for putting into practice the Modern Movement's values of mass provision based on scientific research and standards. This ascendancy of the Modern Movement in effect applied only since 1945, when inter-war experiments and aspirations provided the impetus for sweeping state-led efforts to implement modern mass housing production on a nationwide scale. Prior to World War II, traditionalist styles of various sorts had been generally dominant. In some ways, the Modern Movement was actually a very diverse movement, with strong creative tensions between science and humanism, between different layout types and styles of housing, between the brand new and the 'rooted', the particular and the international, the politically committed and the artistic-poetic, the mass-produced and the 'individual genius'. Yet all these had a lot in common, envisaging the task of the designer as that of "solving, architecturally, the most difficult of social problems," in the words of the eminent British Modernist architect Robert Matthew (Cleeve Barr 1958: foreword).

And there was a lot in common in the physical environment of the new housing—above all, through the stress on a striking, separate newness, sharply distinguished from the old environments left behind. The most prolific types of Modernist mass housing were cleanly geometrical blocks in flowing space and greenery, although other phases and approaches, especially in the 1960s, emphasized lower and denser patterns. Almost all previous housing, even in garden suburbs, had been built along streets, with a front and a back. The Modern Movement did away with overt architectural hierarchies and degrees of stateliness and monumentality: there was no front or back, no grander or humbler houses. Everything was equal—an approach exemplified in the so-called *Zeilenbau*, a rather horizontal pattern of slab blocks arranged in parallel to maximize sunlight orientation, without any regard for existing streets or context, and all evenly spaced out and the same, like the lines on a page. The 1950s and 1960s saw a greater stress on more variegated combinations, including high tower blocks to symbolize the radical break from the old horizontal street city and to provide a new type of landmark punctuation (Mumford 2003: 201ff.).

In the later 1960s and the 1970s, there was generally a reaction against these very high and markedly different patterns toward more 'traditional' scales and designs, including a degree of rejection even of newness itself and an embrace of preserving the previously reviled nineteenth-century capitalist-built housing environments. But just as universally Modernist, as we will see, was the

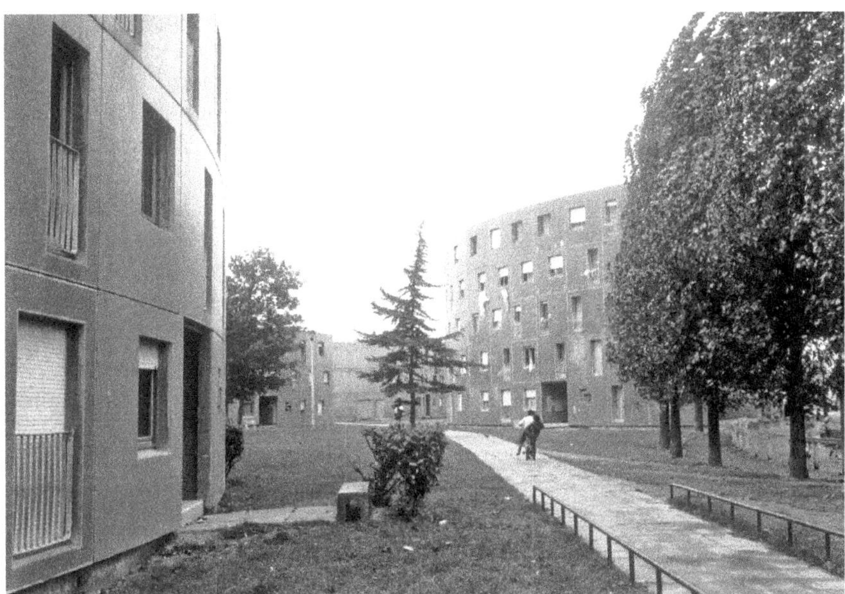

Figure 3.3 La Grande Borne housing project, Grigny and Viry-Chatillon (near Paris), a 3,685-dwelling development built in 1967–1971 for OPIEVOY (Office Publique de l'Habitat de l'Essonne, du Val d'Oise et des Yvelines), one of France's powerful local low-income housing agencies. This project, mingling medium-rise *Zeilenbau* and more sinuous blocks, was one of the innovative designs of architect Emile Aillaud, and, despite severe social problems, it still survives largely intact. © Miles Glendinning

insistence on debate and on constant diversity and change—even (from around the mid-1930s onward within the International Modern Movement) on the search for local or vernacular-influenced solutions (Bullock 2002; Gold 1997, 2007).

Case Study: Post-war Mass Housing in Great Britain

Let us now move on to our national case study, that of Great Britain, examining its distinctive place within this European context and also teasing out the local variety within its own 'national umbrella'. In Britain, the period after World War I saw the construction of a very distinctive system of public intervention in housing that focused overwhelmingly on municipal local authorities, traditionally very strong in the big industrial cities of England and Scotland: city councils began not only to regulate and subsidize low-rent houses, as in many countries, but actually to build and manage them (Daunton 1984). As a result, housing became closely associated with local politics and local pride, and parties competed to build up strong and self-perpetuating housing drives. Spurred on by a utopian political rhetoric, many city councils by the 1940s saw it as their duty to build 'for all'. In the big cities, the 'numbers game' became dominant, with pressure for the construction of new homes outpacing all else. This highly unified 'council housing' strongly contrasted, even within Western Europe, with the rather fragmented or arms-length social housing systems of countries such as West Germany or France, and even more with the reliance on tax breaks for private builders in countries like Belgium. In some parts of Britain, private speculative building remained prominent, but elsewhere council housing became predominant in new building: in Scotland, throughout the 1950s and 1960s, around 75 percent of all new housing was in council schemes (in Glasgow, as much as 96 percent) (Harwood and Powers 2008).

Architecturally, mass housing in Britain was marked by a strong intellectual tradition of concentration in London and a polarization against 'the rest'. The London pattern of intense intellectualization was diffused through a variety of innovative public authorities and city councils, as well as private firms staffed by bright ex-public sector people, and through the powerful and variegated architectural press. This intellectual-cum-journalistic ferment was shaped by the polarized traditions of English architectural debate that had developed after the publication in 1836 of A. W. N. Pugin's *Contrasts*, which interpreted architecture as a field of clashing utopias, fighting to displace each other (Hill 2007). Mass housing, with its incessant socio-political conflicts, was an ideal area for this kind of approach. In England and London, far from a stale homogeneity, different passionate fads of building type, density, and layout followed each other with a bewildering speed from the 1940s to the 1960s. Each of these phases, or fashions, was generally invented by London elites and then disseminated and mass-built in the 'provinces' until this form of mass building became the dystopia for the next phase (Annan 1990; Esher 1981; Saint 1983, 1987).

At first, though, during the 1940s and early 1950s, this constant intellectual warfare over housing, along with the polarization between intellectuals and 'the rest', was slightly put in abeyance. What predominated at this stage was a sense of disciplined national consensus among the architects and engineering designers of the first blocks of Modernist construction and the municipal agents who commissioned them. Everyone was motivated by the immensely strong, somewhat utopian mission of building the 'welfare state'. It was one of the chief boasts of the welfare state system of architecture that the cream of the Modernist elite devoted themselves not to private housing but to public housing. The architectural expression of this phase gradually shifted from a strict Functionalist demand for pure white flat-roofed blocks dictated by scientific standards and modern conveniences, laid out in the strict *Zeilenbau* pattern, toward more variegated ways of expressing newness and open space. The influential London County Council (LCC) pointed to two new ways of expressing this: a 'mixed development' of cottages, low flats, and slender, high point-blocks, visually more Picturesque and socially supposedly encouraging community; and a more rhetorically monumental approach, emphasizing massive concrete slab blocks influenced by the post-war work of Le Corbusier.

But even at this time of greatest unity, the British (especially English) tradition of polarization and debate between intellectual factions soon re-emerged. No sooner was the Modernist pattern of open space and high blocks established than, from around 1950, a new storm of controversy arose over English public housing. Rejecting the rationalist tenets of CIAM (International Congress of Modern Architecture) planning, avant-garde groups led by Alison and Peter Smithson rejected tower blocks in open space as crude and alienating. They advocated lower, denser, 'community intensive' or 'clustered' agglomerations of blocks—most notably at the massive late-1950s complex of Park Hill in Sheffield, with its 'deck access' system linking up a chain of slab blocks. From the late 1950s until the late 1960s, London authorities built a great number of immensely complex high-density estates—such as Bonamy, Lillington Street, and North Peckham—that featured a bewildering maze of lanes, internal courts, and split levels. Similar patterns were found in some post-1946 New Towns, such as Cumbernauld in Central Scotland (Glendinning and Muthesius 1994: 146).[4]

But the pattern of municipal autonomy in Britain was bound up with this hierarchical intellectual-architectural discourse in a rather antagonistic way. Here we pass from the national to the local story, finding in the process that the two grated sharply against each other. The enormous national output of public housing was not the work of gurus or professionals but rather that of a plethora of political, administrative, and industrial agents in municipal authorities across the country, or rather within the two national sub-units—England/ Wales and Scotland—each of which had its own separate housing legislation and national civil service administrative apparatus. In practice, under these national umbrellas there was a wide variation in the governing ethos of housing among individual municipal or public house-building authorities: between, on the one hand, the most intellectually elitist approaches (usually in authorities insulated from the most driving local political pressures) and, on the other, the most utilitarian or politically driven projects. The relative power of the two extremes of approaches with regard to output and design changed radically over time: the output grouping's time of ascendancy generally followed that of the architectural intellectuals, so that the story of mass housing in Britain was one of sharp disjunction: from the 1950s as the phase dominated by national architects to the 1960s as the decade dominated by municipal political and industrial forces. 'Package deal' (design and build) contracts with large builders were increasingly the rule in the 1960s, although some authorities also brought local employment into the political equation of municipal housing by founding a direct labor organization to build or maintain their houses.

Paradigmatic of the 1950s was the work of the LCC as the regional authority in the two-tier system of the County of London (now known as Inner London) up to 1965. A rather grand, supra-municipal body, its status came not just from its power but from its policies, which were shaped by the somewhat enlightened, intellectual Fabian ethos of many of its councilors (Jackson 1965). The LCC was in the forefront of the advanced design tendencies of the early 1950s, when the department of its chief architect, Robert Matthew, developed a highly creative, multi-branched organization encompassing both advocates of communist, Picturesque 'people's detailing', who favored 'mixed developments' of point-blocks and low housing, and a faction of heroic Corbusian aesthetes, who advocated monumental concrete slab blocks.

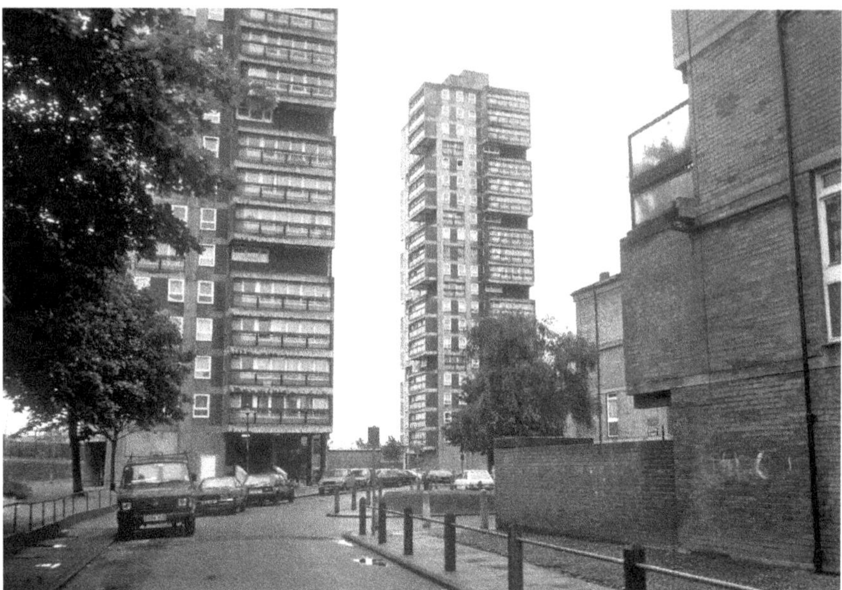

Figure 3.4 Neptune Street. A typical 'artistic' inner-city high-density redevelopment by the LCC. The Brandrams Works (Neptune Street) project in Bermondsey, built in 1962–1964, was a mixed development designed by the LCC's architects that included two 'sculptural' 21-storey towers; 1988 view. © Miles Glendinning

The other redoubts of the design-dominated approach were the post-1946 New Towns. Governed by the quasi-colonial administrative Development Corporation, their chief architect/planners, such as Frederick Gibberd in Harlow or Hugh Wilson in Cumbernauld, had almost total autonomy from political output pressures and were able to develop consistent patterns of advanced housing design and community planning (Glendinning 2008).

Typical of the 1960s, by contrast, was the work of large-city authorities, which focused on the local political demand for high output of new housing, either in closely packed developments of high flats largely dictated by engineers, or in projects designed by city architects who were sensitive to the need to balance design with output. Britain's two largest 'provincial' cities, Glasgow and Birmingham, were contrasting examples of the two approaches. Since the 1940s, the Corporation of the City of Glasgow had tried to fight off a 'threat' of planner-led overspill through the utilitarian mass building of dense flats—tenements in the early- to mid-1950s, tower blocks in the 1960s. The architects and planners in the Glasgow Corporation—despite having devised vast proposals for 'comprehensive developments'—were very much an endangered species. The finding and completely ad hoc exploitation of sites with massive blocks were controlled by the 'crusading' Housing Committee convener, David Gibson, and his engineer sidekick, Lewis Cross. In Birmingham in the 1950s, a new, young city architect, A. G. Sheppard Fidler, introduced a range of up-to-date LCC-inspired patterns. Ultimately, he was forced out by councilors looking for higher output and replaced by a less imaginative but much more efficient city architect, Alan Maudsley, who simply used Sheppard Fidler's most recent types and layouts in endless permutations of pleasant mixed developments of tower blocks and terraced houses, most notably at the huge peripheral project of Chelmsley Wood (Glendinning and Muthesius 1994: chaps. 25 and 26).

Conclusion

By the mid-1960s, the gulf between art and business that had dominated the history of British architecture and building in the nineteenth century now once again seemed as wide as ever, despite the shift from capitalist to state socialist initiative. However, notwithstanding the apparently vast scale and power of the national housing drive and its local supporters, this situation would prove short-lived. By the 1970s, all Modernist attempts to build community through new special housing environments of whatever pattern had fallen from fashion, discredited in the public mind by the frightening scale and pace of redevelopment. Instead, the notion of community was seen especially as something most inherent in the previously reviled nineteenth-century terraces and tenements. In these chastened years, people argued that, in places like Milton Keynes, new housing should be uncomplicated and should simply aspire to reflect 'traditional' values (Esher 1981; Taylor 1973).

Of course, the sharp decline in the status of Modernist mass housing in Britain, as in the rest of Western Europe, was also bound up with the beginnings of a wider retrenchment with regard to the fortunes and power of the interventionist welfare state. The complex relationship between aesthetics and the state now became viewed in almost purely negative terms, with the older *dirigiste* welfare state seen as directly represented in a homogeneous, alienating environment of concrete towers and slabs scattered in empty space. All of the past debates between different housing formulae of low, medium, and high density or between monumental and Picturesque solutions now seemed not just obsolete but incomprehensible.

This brings us full circle, back to today's position of the state being 'at bay', subject to the buffetings of our present-day market-driven society. Whether the recent crises of neo-capitalism hold out any hope of a brighter future for the built legacy of the *trente glorieuses* of welfare state power, including mass social housing, is unclear.

Miles Glendinning is a historian and critic based at Edinburgh College of Art in Scotland, where he is Reader in Architecture. He is Director of the Scottish Centre for Conservation Studies and recently served as Head of Architecture at the Royal Commission on the Ancient and Historical Monuments of Scotland. Specializing in the modern built environment of the twentieth and twenty-first centuries, he has written or contributed to a series of books and articles on this subject, as well as on the broader field of Scottish architecture since the earliest times. Recent titles include *Modern Architect: The Life and Times of Robert Matthew* (2008), and *Architecture's Evil Empire? The Triumph and Tragedy of Global Modernism* (2010).

Notes

1. For an analysis of earlier twentieth-century expressions of state power in city planning schemes, see Sonne (2003).
2. For a general international overview of the post-war mass social housing legacy, see *Docomomo International Journal* 39, September 2008 (themed issue: "Postwar Mass Housing"). See also the electronic proceedings of the 2007 DOCOMOMO Conference on mass housing, "Trash or Treasure: Towards a Rescue Archaeology of Modernist Mass Housing" at http://www.archi.fr/DOCOMOMO/docomomo_electronic_newsletter7.htm.
3. For discussions on this topic, see Landauer and Pouvreau (2007); Menzel (1989); Michel, Derainne, and Léger (2005); and Tomas, Blanc, and Bonilla (2003).
4. New Towns refer to those towns created under various Acts of Parliament to house populations relocated from overcrowded urban areas.

References

Annan, Noel. 1990. *Our Age: English Intellectuals between the World Wars*. London: Weidenfeld & Nicholson.

Ballon, Hilary, and Kenneth T. Jackson, eds. 2007. *Robert Moses and the Modern City*. New York: W.W. Norton.

Begg, Tom. 1996. *Housing Policy in Scotland*. Edinburgh: John Donald Publishers.

Bullock, Nicholas. 2002. *Building the Post-war World*. London: Routledge.

Castells, Manuel, Lee Goh, and R. Yin-Wang Kwok. 1991. *The Shek Kip Mei Syndrome: Economic Development and Public Housing in Hong Kong and Singapore*. London: Pion.

Cleeve Barr, A. W. 1958. *Public Authority Housing*. Preface by Robert H. Matthew. London: B.T. Batsford.

Daunton, Martin J. 1984. *Councillors and Tenants*. London: Leicester University Press.

Denby, Elizabeth. 1938. *Europe Re-housed*. London: George Allen & Unwin.

Dufaux, Frédéric, and Annie Fourcaut, eds. 2004. *Le monde des grands ensembles*. Paris: Editions Créaphis.

Esher, Lionel. 1981. *A Broken Wave: The Rebuilding of England, 1940–1980*. London: Allen Lane.

Glendinning, Miles. 2008. *Modern Architect: The Life and Times of Robert Matthew*. London: Royal Institute of British Architects.

Glendinning, Miles, and Stefan Muthesius. 1994. *Tower Block: Modern Public Housing in England, Scotland, Wales, and Northern Ireland*. New Haven, CT: Yale University Press.

Gold, John R. 1997. *The Experience of Modernism: Modern Architects and the Future City, 1928–1853*. Cambridge: Cambridge University Press.

______. 2007. *The Practice of Modernism: Modern Architects and Urban Transformation, 1954–1972*. London: Routledge.

Harwood, Elain, and Alan Powers, eds. 2008. *Housing the Twentieth Century Nation*. London: Twentieth Century Society.

Hill, Rosemary. 2007. *God's Architect*. London: Allen Lane.

Jackson, W. Eric. 1965. *Achievement: A Short History of the London County Council*. London: Longmans.

Kopp, Anatole. 1981. "Housing for the Masses," Working Paper no. 149, Conference on the Origins of Soviet Culture. Washington, DC: Wilson Center, Kennan Institute for Advanced Russian Studies.

Landauer, Paul, and Benoît Pouvreau. 2007. "Les Courtillières, cité ordinaire, histoire singulière?" *Espaces et Sociétés* 130, no. 3: 71–86.

McClelland, Michael, and Graeme Stewart, eds. 2007. *Concrete Toronto*. Toronto: Coach House Books.

Menzel, M. A. 1989. *Bijlmermeer als grensverleggend ideal*. Delft: Delft University Press.

Michel, Geneviève, Pierre-Jacques Derainne, and Jean-Michel Léger. 2005. *Aux Courtillières: Histoires singulières et exemplaires*. Paris: Editions Créaphis.

Morton, Henry W. 1984. "Housing in the Soviet Union." *Proceedings of the Academy of Political Science* 35, no. 3: 69–80.

Mumford, Eric. 2003. *The CIAM Discourse on Urbanism, 1928–1960*. Cambridge, MA: MIT Press.

Power, Anne. 1993. *Hovels to High-Rise: State Housing in Europe since 1850*. London: Routledge.

______. 1997. *Estates on the Edge: The Social Consequences of Mass Housing in Northern Europe*. London: St Martin's Press.

Rowlands, Rob, Sako Musterd, and Ronald van Kempen, eds. 2007. *Mass Housing in Europe*. Basingstoke: Palgrave Macmillan.

Saint, Andrew. 1983. *The Image of the Architect*. New Haven, CT: Yale University Press.

______. 1987. *Towards a Social Architecture: The Role of School-Building in Post-War England*. New Haven, CT: Yale University Press.

Sonne, Wolfgang, 2003. *Representing the State*. Munich: Prestel.

Stewart, Graeme. 2008. "The Suburban Tower and Toronto's Modern Legacy." *Docomomo International Journal* 39: 23–29.

Taylor, Nicholas. 1973. *The Village in the City*. London: Maurice Temple Smith.

Tomas, François, Jean-Noël Blanc, and Mario Bonilla. 2003. *Les grands ensembles: Une histoire qui continue*. Paris: Publications de l'Université de Saint-Etienne.

Urban, Florian. 2008. "Prefab Russia." *Docomomo International Journal* 39: 18–22.

Williams, Richard J. 2007. "Brasilia after Brasilia." *Progress in Planning* 67, no. 4: 301–366.

______. 2008. "Brasilia's Superquadras." *Docomomo International Journal* 39: 30–35.

Chapter 4

Folding and Enfolding Walls

*Statist Imperatives and Bureaucratic Aesthetics
in Divided Jerusalem*

DON HANDELMAN

> You should not try to find whether an idea is just or correct. You should look
> for a completely different idea, elsewhere, in another area, so that something
> passes between the two which is neither in one nor the other … You don't
> have to be learned, to know or be familiar with a particular area, but to pick
> up this or that in areas which are very different.
>
> — Gilles Deleuze, *Dialogues II*

After the 1948 Arab-Israeli War, the armistice line ran through Jerusalem on
a roughly north-south axis. That line developed into a dilapidated no man's
land, with ongoing back-and-forth sniper fire. The ancient Old City remained in
Jordan, its western Ottoman walls lying alongside the armistice line. After the
1967 June War, the Israeli government annexed an area that included Jordanian

Notes for this chapter begin on page 77.

Jerusalem, together with a large area of the adjacent West Bank, all of which was made part of a single municipal territory. The Israeli state declared this new entity to be "United Jerusalem, the Eternal Capital of Israel" (Klein 2005: 55). Ever since, actualizing a single Jerusalem, united through conquest under Israeli rule (although quite divided in mundane life), has been a statist imperative. In this state project, architecture has a prominent role. According to Nitzan-Shiftan (2005: 231), architecture "as a technique of execution ... is not transparent—it is neither devoid of ideology, nor is it readily accessible to political dictates, particularly not in sites saturated with national and religious symbolism. On the contrary, politicians are largely dependent on professionals who have privileged access to the spatial tools of architecture." Given the powerful presence of Jerusalem in the symbolism of each of the monotheisms and in the religious and secular cultures that emerged from these religions—and, no less, the prominence of Jerusalem in the Arab-Israeli conflict—the making and shaping of built forms there are often perceived through synecdoche, that is, the parts are seen as standing for the whole. Often changes in built form are a felt aesthetic presence that is immediately plumbed, analytically, commonsensically, for its significance in relation to the city-as-whole.

Since 1967, after seizing the heights surrounding the Palestinian city, Israel has been building a wide, dense arc of housing for Israeli Jews, without giving building permits to Palestinians. Residential building has been accompanied by a variety of physical barriers. The most recent, dubbed officially the 'separation fence', is intended to wall off much of the Palestinian city from its hinterland in the occupied West Bank, territory that might be given to the Palestinian-state-in-the-making, should this ever be actualized. Israel controls the Palestinian city with a bureaucratic and militaristic iron hand, while minimally investing in infrastructure for its Palestinian inhabitants, even as Israeli governance insists that the entire city is a seamless unity (Benvenisti 1995).

It is in this Israel-controlled cityscape that I discuss one vector of statist-related physical forms that have qualities of walls. Although here I consider only official and quasi-official forming of space, my intention is to bring out the dynamic of folding and enfolding space through the shaping of walls as a transforming vector of control. The term 'vector' comes from the Latin *vehere*, to carry. The vector as carrier refers to a line in space that has both the magnitude and direction of a quantity. Since I use the word 'vector' in a loosely topological way, the line of space becomes one of connectivities that need not be linear and may well be recursive. In my usage, the vector carries value through space, value that is enhanced, augmented, made more powerful as it moves into and through the enfoldings I discuss. In traversing these enfoldings, value turns into force, that of the state and its imperatives.

The architectural forms I discuss are new, ostensibly without relation to one another, yet together they create this vector of force, as the cityscape shifts from west to east. The first is a bridge pylon, while the others I refer to as walls, although only the last ordinarily would be understood as such. The first of these walls is a new historical museum of the Holocaust (the 'museum-wall'). The second is a massive continuous stretch of new buildings (the 'mall-wall') that crosses the former no man's land between Jewish West Jerusalem and the southwestern walls of the Old City. The third is the 'separation barrier' between Palestinian East Jerusalem and its hinterland. Together, these four constructions are one topological vector shaping the cityscape. Using the idea of topology in a broad way enables all four constructions to be implicated together in how the city is being shaped and practiced in accordance with statist imperatives. Crucially, this vector is self-referential. Therefore, what I will call its 'beginning' (the bridge pylon) and its 'end' (the separation fence) fold into one another, transforming the force of directionality into the totalizing of recursive energy.

I return to topological thinking in relation to that which Gilles Deleuze referred to as 'folding', a dynamic especially relevant to discussing the forming of form, in both social and material terms (Handelman 2005). By describing three of the constructions as walls, I imply that they partake of an aesthetics that I regard as bureaucratic, a topic that will be addressed in the concluding remarks.

In terms of their aesthetic form, cityscapes usually are analyzed by social scientists in terms of topography—the ways in which forms are situated on surfaces and through the lines on these surfaces that connect the forms. Topography relates more to material and social positioning in four-dimensional space. It is less concerned with the dynamics that actively shape forms and relations among forms through different scales and intensities, through vectors that come into being as forms are being formed, and that give direction and impetus to these vectorial thrusts. Topography is passive in that it can be presented as a given of things, natural or human-made. This sense of passivity easily enables social scientists to use features of topography as containers of representations of social and historical formations. Representation reflects, presents, reflects—but does nothing through itself. Topographies are representations; they, too, do nothing through themselves. They reflect forces (political, economic, ideological, architectural) that originate elsewhere. Thus, sites in the cityscape may be perceived as dense mappings of meaning, yet these are passive receptacles whose significance is to be deciphered.[1] As Deleuze (1994: 67) comments, "Representation has only a single centre, a unique and receding perspective, and in consequence a false depth. It mediates everything, but mobilises and moves nothing."[2]

The dominant use of aesthetics continues to link this to representation. For the pre-Socratic Greeks, *aisthesis*, or sense perception, was not separated from *logos*, and "physical sensory perception was trusted as knowledge" (Kane 2007: 83). The metaphysical project of the Age of Reason was to separate *aisthesis* from *logos* and to tie aesthetics to representation. I use aesthetics in a somewhat combined way as 'sensuous knowledge' (Goldman 2001: 255), as knowledge that is trusted but largely tacit and taken for granted. My usage of the aesthetic refers to something more like the 'feel' that one has for what one is doing or seeing or moving through kinesthetically (or perceiving through other of the senses)—the feel for the 'rightness' of how one is doing what one is doing, or how this is done in concert, the feel of the senses forming form through practice. The aesthetic in mundane living is related to Bergson's notion of 'habit memory', of attending kinesthetically to one's own body, monitoring what one is doing; but, I add, attending kinesthetically no less to the surround, including of course the built environment. In this regard, movement itself is a sense, as the body continuously changes position, revising the information it takes in from the environment, as do other of the senses in their own ways. Therefore, this is also a haptic aesthetics of practicing formed and forming space, of 'memory etched in movement', of the body, of the surround.[3]

These mundane aesthetics are an indwelling of largely tacit knowledge that always seems to include more than we can tell, were we able to relate this knowingly (Polanyi 1962: 314; 1966: 17–23). Tacit knowing is the feeling of disattending to ourselves that moves us beyond ourselves, enabling the exterior world of practice and the interior world of experience to be unified as the exterior world of experience and the interior world of practice (see Dufrenne 1973: 446; Katz 1999: 314). Indeed, the aesthetics of practice lead us to "an appreciation of the essential place of aesthetics in all behaviors, however mundane or esoteric" (Katz 1999: 314). No less, the aesthetics of practice lead us to all surrounds and, I emphasize, to vectors of force that connect through these surrounds in and during multiple dimensions.

In trying to consider how an aesthetics of statist practice forms the constructions to be addressed here, I will perhaps escape to a degree from the passive receptacles of representational symbolism, away from topographical thinking and more toward the topological, toward a dynamic of the relational among forms. Each of the four new constructions is in its own right a separate venue of statist imperatives for Jerusalem. Nonetheless, each is a variation of the dynamic of folding, and the vector of these variations intensifies its wall-ish qualities as it thrusts from west to east.

The Beginning—the Calatrava Pylon-Parabola

Driving up to Jerusalem (to a height of some 800 meters) from the coast in the west, the highway enters the lip of the city at a busy intersection and continues into the west-east axis that begins the major thoroughfare, Jaffa Road, which runs through the city all the way to the Ottoman-period walls of the Old City, the border of the Palestinian city. Traversing the intersection, roughly from north to south, is a cable-stayed bridge, some 360 meters in length, designed by Spanish architect Santiago Calatrava (see fig. 4.1). When it becomes fully operational in 2011, the bridge is intended to carry light-rail lines above the intersection. Part of the support system of the bridge is a slender steel pylon, some 118 meters in height, inclining toward the east. From either side of the pylon, steel cables in the shape of a parabola hold the bridge in place.[4] The parabolic imparts a sense of three-dimensionality to the pylon and its steel cables. Inaugurated in June 2008, the pylon is considered by Israeli authorities to be the major visual landmark at the entry to the Jewish city. The pylon-parabola quickly acquired a biblical referent, the harp of King David (the mythical founder of the Israelite city), and is referred to as the Chords Bridge or the Bridge of (musical) Strings—a giant harp embedded in the city's western entrance.

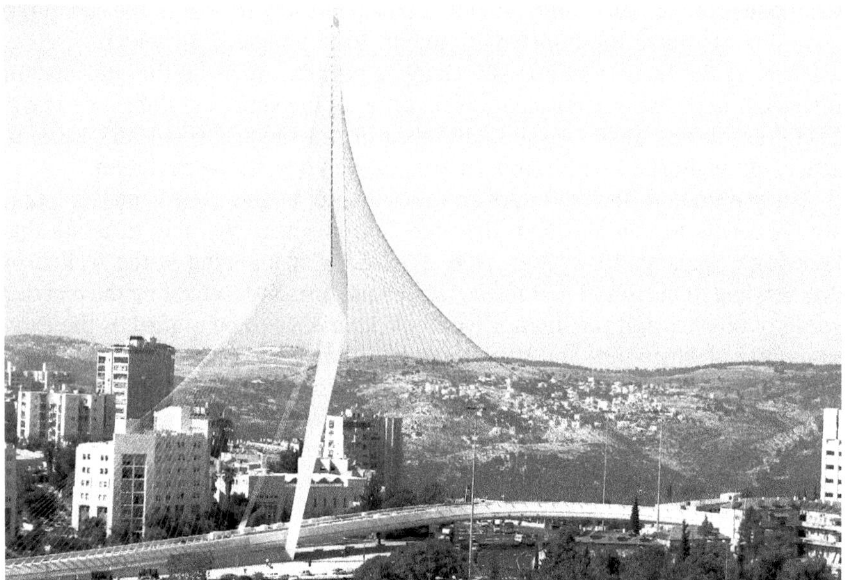

FIGURE 4.1 The Calatrava pylon-parabola at the western entrance to Jerusalem. Courtesy of Einat Bar-On Cohen

Since the founding of the State of Israel in 1948 with Jerusalem as the capital, the Jewish city has welcomed Jews to its precincts from the westerly direction with its dense concentration of finance, business, and industry on the coastal plain. The most striking feature of this pylon positioned at the edge of the mountain is its openness in multiple dimensions. It is quite transparent, concealing nothing, as it were, yet with quite extensive presence, visible from numerous points on the ridges around the city. The pylon leans into the city, opening the way, beginning an enfoldment. It soars into the heaven from different perspectives, sometimes shaping a great bird with outstretched wings, sometimes a feathery embracing cloak, sometimes the mythical harp of the love poetry and psalms of the ancient David.

The parabolic form of the pylon imparts a complexity to the open air, to open space through which it moves. In his discussion of Leibniz and the Baroque, Deleuze takes in the fold, the folding of space-time that is the opening of a different forming, a forming of difference that had not existed before in that space and time. Folding may be conceptualized as the forming of a pocket (of space, of time, of social action, and of their intersections)—a folding in of structures, of movements of living, articulating persons within these curving self-enclosures in certain ways and not in others. As it curves, the fold or pocket opens the depths of space-time where/when no opening had existed a moment before. The opening itself is a curving of space-time, since the movement of living is neither stopped nor blocked, but shifted into itself, enfolded, reorganized, and thereby made different, minimally, partially, utterly, from the movements in whose courses the opening is but a moment (Handelman 2005: 14). The fold or pocket inflects and involutes (Deleuze 1993: 14–26), entailing variable degrees of the emergence of autopoietic propensities for self-organization that follow from the self-closing that is the curve. The fold curves recursively because its forming in itself is anti-lineal, anti-Cartesian, turning over, upending. Of especial interest here is that Deleuze (ibid.: 16) cites Paul Klee as calling a point—the (pure) event that is a point of inflection—"'a site of cosmogenesis' … 'between dimensions.'"[5]

Consider the pylon-parabolic. It begins a curve, soaring as its curve leans and swerves into the city. This curvature has an axis, the pylon, yet it does not have a center that is centering itself, since its movement is upward, outward, reaching beyond the physical extension of the cables themselves. It is a folding dynamic, but one just beginning, the folding reaching toward, into, the city even as it soars into the heavens, gently, openly, enfolding both together. The point of inflection, the beginning, is the point of cosmogenesis for the vector (continuously emerging into being, here, elsewhere) that I am beginning to discuss—a point of cosmogenesis whose parabolic extension seems to modulate space harmonically (resonating with the metaphor of David's harp), imparting a rhythm to the ether.[6] Looked at this way, the pylon-parabola begins to take on the forming of a net, one that is in movement, leaning transparently, benignly, into its catchment area.

A net, not yet a wall. I problematize this beginning by shifting to the new Holocaust History Museum at the national Holocaust memorial, Yad Vashem (which means 'A Place and a Name'). As I noted at the outset, the relationality of spaces that I am connecting is more topological, less topographical. So although Yad Vashem is not quite on the west-east trajectory that begins here with the pylon-parabola, it is undoubtedly on that trajectory once temporality is added to the vector.

The Museum-Wall—Folding History into the State

Today the Israeli state is sieved through the Holocaust. During the state's early years, its representatives rarely raised the likelihood that its foundation emerged from the Holocaust or that the United Nations vote in 1947 in favor of this founding was a response to genocide. Israel's political leadership presented the establishment of the state as its own accomplishment. Nonetheless, statist imperative demanded commemoration of the Holocaust. Yet the end of European Jewry and the beginning of the new Jews of Palestine and then Israel were presented as two separate narrative trajectories—one buried into near extinction as the other was rising into prominence. In these narratives the fate of European Jewry was the inevitable dead-ended outcome of Diaspora living. Only as an independent nation-state could Jews have a future in a world of states.

In the present-day political realities of Israel, which have powerfully revived the presence of the religious Judaic as the cultural grounds for the existence of the Jewish people inside and outside the state, these two historical narratives have merged to the point that the state is now the direct consequence of the Holocaust. This causal relationship must be honored and sanctified continuously with respect and vigilance, since the conditions of the Holocaust are everywhere anew.[7] Most immediately, the Israeli people and state are threatened by the enmity of Palestinians and, more generally, of Muslims (perceived independently of Israeli occupation and settlement of the territories). It is in these senses that the trajectory of beginning (the open, although directional, folding of the pylon-parabola) has on its existential horizon the historical museum of Yad Vashem, through which it must pass.

The old Holocaust museum was located in a squarish, nondescript building, one of the cluster that make up the core of the Yad Vashem memorial complex (see fig. 4.2, the building in the left background). All of the buildings in this complex offer a blank exterior visage, the horrific realities of the genocide being hidden from external view (Handelman and Shamgar-Handelman 1997). Despite being concealed deep inside and far away, those horrors are immediately here and now. The exhibition in the old museum, which had been in place for about 30 years, was designed by historians and resembled a musty illustrated book of Holocaust history. Over the years since it opened, the Israeli political leadership had begun to emphasize Israel's role as the natural leader in Holocaust commemoration. The new Holocaust History Museum is a response to the tremendous rise in Holocaust commemoration among world Jewry, especially in the United States, culminating in the political success of placing the United States Holocaust Memorial Museum on the National Mall

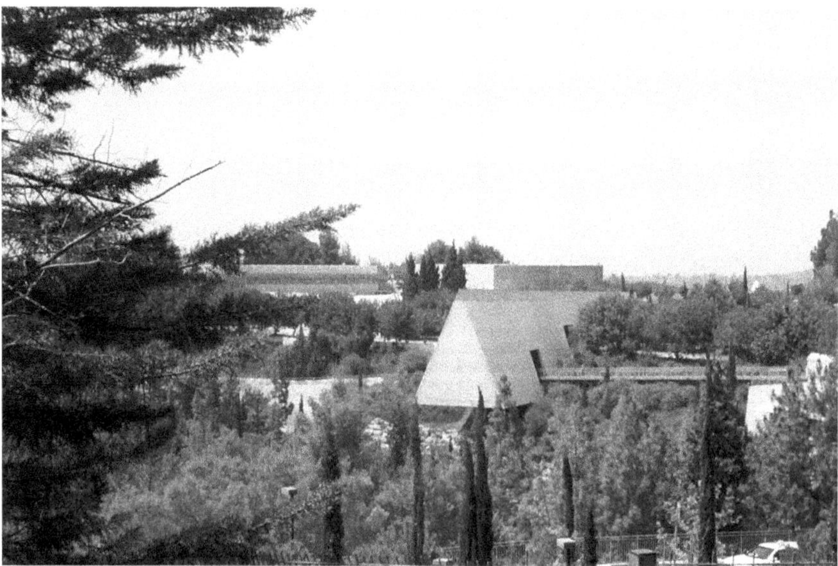

FIGURE 4.2 The Yad Vashem memorial complex with the old Holocaust museum in the background and the new Holocaust museum in the foreground

in Washington, DC, in the heart of American national symbolism. The new commemorative sites use innovative designs and aesthetics that had left Yad Vashem in their wake. The new Holocaust museum is intended to rectify this— or so its leaders imagine.

My focus here is only on the exterior of this building and its positioning within the national Holocaust memorial. The Yad Vashem complex is built along the top of a ridge, with most of the buildings fronting along its southern exposure. The outermost walkway along the circumference of the ridge is named the Avenue of the Righteous Among the Nations. On either side of the long walkway are carob trees dedicated to particular Gentiles who, at risk to their own lives, saved Jews during the Holocaust (see fig. 4.3). These trees, these dedications, are an outer bulwark, protective of the memories of elsewhen, elsewhere that are lodged within the complex. The three largest free-standing monuments of the complex are dedicated to the resistance and heroism of Jews during World War II. Open to the elements, they thrust abruptly upward from the land, dominating the perspective. The symmetric triangulation of these three monuments corresponds to the shape of the ridge and forms another bulwark within that of the Avenue of the Righteous. Within these two bulwarks are the major memorial buildings, protected by righteous Gentiles, by Jewish resistance and heroism (see Handelman and Shamgar-Handelman 1997: 101–110).

The positioning of the new museum reverses this patterning. The shape of the building is a long triangle, some 200 meters in length, positioned to intersect at a right angle with the Avenue of the Righteous. There are two openings set into the sloping wall of the building, facing outward toward the beginning of the complex. One is the entrance to the museum. The other opening is a larger

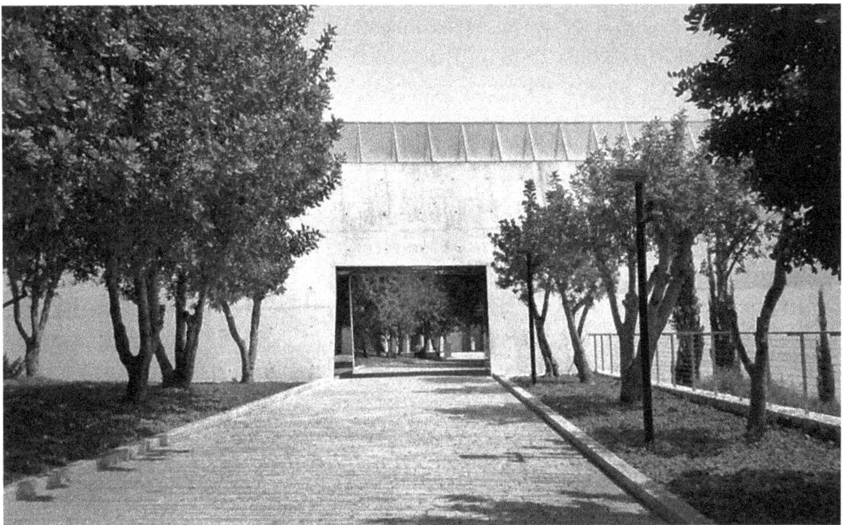

FIGURE 4.3 The Avenue of the Righteous passing through the new Holocaust museum

rectangle the width of the Avenue of the Righteous, continuing this walkway through the wall of the museum into the larger territory of the complex beyond. There are no windows or other apertures in the sloping side of the museum. But where the two sloping walls meet at their apex, there is a triangular skylight, a prism that runs the length of the building. On the northerly side of the Avenue, the museum triangle plunges into the mountain ridge of the complex, with the skylight above ground. At its northerly end the museum triangle emerges from the ridge, its sloping sides folding back and cantilevered to open into the space of large windows that frame an expansive view of the city below.

The exhibits of the museum's interior roughly correspond to the tripartition of the exterior walls. The first section of the exterior walls, including the entrance, corresponds to the first portion of the standard Israeli narrative of the Holocaust—the prologue, the rise to power of the Nazis, the setting of the trap, the condition of no exit. The second section of the exterior walls, buried in the earth of the ridge, corresponds to the second portion of the narrative— the extermination of European Jewry in concentration and death camps. Often these deaths are understood in religious terms as self-sacrifice, as dying in the name of God (*al Kiddush HaShem*). The third section of the exterior walls, emerging ("exploding," in the words of the architect [Safdie 2006: 94]) from their burial, opening into the light toward the vista of the living city below, corresponds to the narrative's third part—the liberation from the camps and emigration to the Israeli state-in-the-making, the pinnacle of freedom achieved through war and sacrifice (Handelman 2004: 171–199). Along the entire length of the museum its triangular skylight prism remains above ground, a honed, cutting-edge slicing open of the earth that exposes the sacrifices of the Holocaust beneath the ground to the redemption that illuminates this history with the light of the heavens over the State of Israel. One perceptive interpreter comments that "the architect's act of violence in slitting open the ground is felt viscerally, expressing itself as an archeological scar symbolically healed by the landscape itself" (Ockman 2006a: 21; see also Bennett 2005: 35).

The vector that begins with the ethereal innocence of the pylon-parabola breaks (explodes) out of the historical museum as a topos of enfolded force that has been transformed through sacrifice into the violence and redemption of war and destruction.[8] The motto 'Never forget' is no less that of 'Always remember', and nowadays the force of national remembering drives primarily eastward, striving to incorporate whatever it penetrates.

Astride the Avenue of the Righteous, the new historical museum becomes an integral part of the protective bulwarks around the other buildings and sites of the memorial complex. As noted previously, the old museum, huddled amid and deep within the configuration of Holocaust remembrance buildings, was enfolded by the protective bulwarks around it. The new museum comes forth, directly confronting the visitor, in his or her face, as it were. Its forming is a wall, severe in its absolutism of controlling passage. The building's exterior walls repel the climbing gaze, except through the permitted apertures. The architect of the new museum writes: "I was determined to cast the entire museum monolithically, jointless, unadorned—without any exterior waterproofing or cladding ... I wanted just the basic structure" (Safdie 2006: 98). Elsewhere he says, "I wanted something so primeval and archeological that you don't think about the architecture" (Dean 2005: 113). Yet the new museum is no less a fold. All buildings of course are folded materials and spaces that are enclosed and closed to varying degrees. Used banally in relation to material constructions, this could reduce Deleuzian folding to a non sequitur. Nonetheless, the Deleuzian fold is always a dynamic, constituted through other dynamics—the ways in which folding is done, the interactivity of exteriors and interiors, how folds are lived, the degrees of self-organizing within the fold, the contents that are shaped and shape. All these enable distinguishing among many varieties of folds and folds within folds (Deleuze 1999: 97). Moreover, from this perspective even folds in solids may become more textured rather than given as is, once and for all.

This site is a museum engulfed by a wall, a museum within a wall, a museum embedded in a wall, a museum-wall, a front-line enfolding of horrific history folded into itself, unlike the old museum, where the horrific was enfolded away anonymously, its vulnerability protected amid a cluster of memorial buildings. The new museum enfolds horrific memory on its very front line, thrusting it in the face of mundane life. This folding itself is powerful, since the fold in its forming regenerates the historical narrative of that which it enfolds. Thus, the standard Holocaust narrative of Israel is now on the front line (facing eastward toward the most immediate enemy) as it buttresses Holocaust memorialism. Simultaneously interiorizing/introverting and exteriorizing/extroverting, the museum-wall practices itself into existence from its outside and its inside—the self-fortifying wall of memory that unfolds history and memory within itself, even as it zealously guards yet opens the way to the parceling out of this history and memory through other buildings and sites in the memorial complex. No less, the museum-wall is dedicated to consumption—the consuming of history and memory.

The museum-wall is a fold in time-space of the topological variety that scientists refer to as "rubber sheet geometry" (Asad 1999: 41)—a fold through which any point in time-space may touch any other. The folding of the pylon-parabola touches the museum-wall—the embryonic openness of the parabola folding closes itself into the unyielding history of Holocaust that today enfolds and interiorizes so much memory work in Jewish Israel. In present-day Jewish Jerusalem, many journeys that meander eastward will touch Holocaust time, will pass into Holocaust time, into the time of the great sacrifice, becoming locked into the self-fortification of memory that the Holocaust has become, thereby emerging transformed, more self-protective, more defensive, more aggressive, more warlike. Today, this front line moves eastward. In the culture of the Jewish nation-state, in which memory and history are always on the way and always in the way, there is little choice but to go through memory and history and take them on the way, take them along, as our vector develops, involutes, expands, armoring itself with walls that are no less spears as it gathers force. This vector acquires the pointed desire to spear consumption as it moves eastward.

The Mall-Wall—Vector Becomes Vortex

Jaffa Road, with the pylon-parabola at its western end, runs eastward until it meets the Ottoman walls of the Old City and then runs alongside these in a southwesterly direction, along the 1949 armistice lines. After the 1967 war, much thought and argument went into planning how to relate architectonically to captured East Jerusalem and just what to build in this former no man's land between the Israeli and the Palestinian cities (Nitzan-Shiftan 2005).[9] It was unthinkable for the Jewish Israeli politicians, the army, and the general Jewish public to leave this as a (memory) scar running through the middle of the now joined city. Forty-three years later, the most dominant presence in this interstitial zone is almost complete, ramming across the former no man's land to the Old City. This project (designed by the architect who also did the new Holocaust history museum) stretches for about a quarter of a kilometer (likely longer) along the length of the slope of a hill, meeting Jaffa Road and the Old City walls at the Jaffa Gate, the only entry point into the Old City along the entirety of its southwesterly walls.

Perhaps the most striking feature of this project is that its entire length is uninterrupted, building abutting building, one after another (indeed reminiscent of the new Holocaust history museum). No less striking, the entire length of this built presence is bisected by a broad walkway with shops and restaurants on both sides,[10] intended for solidly upscale shoppers. Many stores are chain outlets, selling trendy brand-name clothes and shoes that fill shopping malls. Others sell jewelry a cut above the average, and one is a pipe and tobacco shop, a rarity in a country in which the imagery of the pipe harks back to a time perceived as more thoughtful, more intellectual. This mall, encased all the way to the Jaffa Gate, is almost entirely without perspectives to the outside environment.

At its Jewish city western end, this project is bulkier, with apartment buildings and a hotel reaching eight stories on both sides of the walkway. Farther east, the buildings are lower but still utterly obscure any view from the walkway of the nearby Old City walls (see fig. 4.4), unless one climbs out of the walkway on its northerly side onto an open promenade that runs alongside the walls.[11] Yet there is only one set of stairs on that side along the walkway's entire length. Along the other, southerly side of the walkway, there are nine flights of stairs that go downslope to the street below (called Valley [*HaEmek*] Road), where the entrances to the parking garages are located. At this lower level, these entrances run almost the full length of the project. Walking the mall toward the Jaffa Gate, the horizon of ancient city walls is constricted to a single image, that of the Tower of David next to the Jaffa Gate, since the nineteenth century a popular icon of Jerusalem for Jews. The rest of the vista is completely effaced. So, too, as one approaches the end of this shopping street, the elegant presence of the Jaffa Gate itself is blocked from view until one climbs the steep 30 or so steps to surface above the mall's encasing.

From the western end of the project, looking down Valley Road toward the Old City walls, the entrance to this street itself looks like a huge gateway. To one's left there are the buildings of the mall, and to one's right is a bulky, relatively new hotel, David's Citadel. With massive pillars supporting its entranceway (an

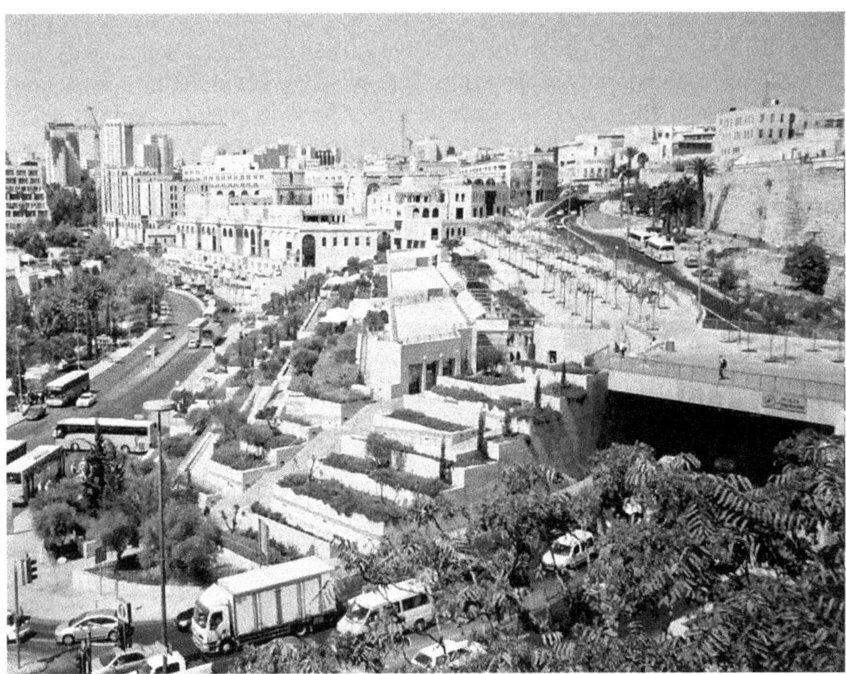

FIGURE 4.4 The mall-wall from the Old City wall, looking toward West Jerusalem

example of what I call 'Third Temple' architecture), it is a near parody of the modest symmetric proportions of the Ottoman period Jaffa Gate all the way at the far Old City end. When walking on Valley Road along the base of the mall-wall toward the Jaffa Gate, to one's left the Old City's southwesterly walls are completely obscured from view by the massive wall of continuous construction, with the linearity and instrumentality of its buying deeply embedded within.[12]

What does the mall-wall signify in terms of this discussion? This Jewish wall, a massive presence, blocks from view a section of the uninterrupted perspective of the Old City walls, which are integral to the grand presence of this ancient city and its history. Indeed, the mall-wall substitutes itself, a modern Jewish wall, one devoted to consumption, for a portion of the Old City Ottoman wall. Today, this is the only length of the Old City walls whose vista is obscured. Moreover, this meeting of the Jewish mall-wall and the largely Palestinian Old City is now the only location along the walls where the Jewish city threatens to penetrate the latter. Thus, I see the mall-wall driving toward the Old City, a bulwark of Jewish West Jerusalem that is no less a spear, or, more aptly, a battering ram, aimed at the Arab Jaffa Gate.

The mall-wall as a line of mass, as a projectile of the might of the Jewish state, propels itself at the ancient, deeply textured Old City walls and beyond.[13] No less, this projectile is the accelerating mass of consumer consumption and Israeli economic domination; indeed, the entirety of this line of force is justified in terms of, and is dedicated to, consumption. The mall-wall enfolds the capacity to consume—the long line of stores on either side, their windows full of separate items, the passers-by caught in the seductive gaze of objects-for-sale, one by one, all available to the desires of the buyer. The eye passes from item to item, from shop window to shop window, each of which has the potential to offer shoppers whatever they wish in order to stimulate their fantasies. These exchanges are embedded within the wall-mall, enclosed into itself without external perspectives—a closed single-purpose vessel with tunnel vision en route to the Old City. Within itself the mall-wall turns the vector into a vortical funnel, a vortex generated by and for desires of consumption, funneled through the recursive self-enclosure. Within this, the desire to acquire, to own, to consume is reified, accentuated, expanded, whirling through itself, augmenting itself as it is aimed at the Old City, which the state acquires, owns, and desires to consume over and over, altering its particular goals and strategies from time to time, yet never altering its need to make it its own. In this vector, the violence of sacrifice is whirled into another variety of absolutist violence—that of the commodity fetishism of ownership, certainly a prominent form of nationalist consumption.

The Impenetrable Block—the End Folding Back, into the Beginning

Beyond the Old City, on the eastern edges of Jerusalem, is the yet unfinished security barrier that Israel calls the separation fence, but which is intended to practice absolute division, domination, and sovereignty (Ben-Eliezer and Feinstein 2008). Planned during the Second Intifada, the entire length of the separation barrier, if completed, will span some 800 kilometers. Constituted in the main by networks of fences and trenches, with watchtowers, roadblocks, and gates distributed along its length, the barrier is legitimized in the name of 'security needs' (see Sorkin 2005; Weizman 2007: 161–182).[14] In the Jerusalem area, the barrier (see fig. 4.5) snakes up and down its ridges for some 170 kilometers, cutting off much of East Jerusalem from its Palestinian hinterlands. In neighborhoods of densely built housing, the fences become a wall of concrete slabs some 8 meters in height, splitting streets, chopping apart houses and social relations, separating farmers from their agricultural lands. The path of the fence/wall is quite arbitrary, based on army evaluations of security, but no less routed by the military, bureaucratic, and political establishments to include much additional land for settlements that will then be on the Israeli side of the barrier.[15]

Tens of thousands of Palestinians, official residents of 'united' Jerusalem, now find themselves on the other side of the barrier, unable to enter the city by any direct route, their neighborhoods receiving no municipal services (health, education, welfare, garbage collection, ambulance service, repairs to the water and electricity systems, etc.). The effect of the security barrier will be to destroy Palestinian metropolitan Jerusalem "and control it without annexing it" (Klein 2005: 71). In the words of Ehud Barak, a former Israeli prime minister and the current minister of defense, "They are over there, and we are over here." Stark concrete of brute force, slicing and slamming Zionist statist imperatives through Palestine, the wall is utterly without adornment, without

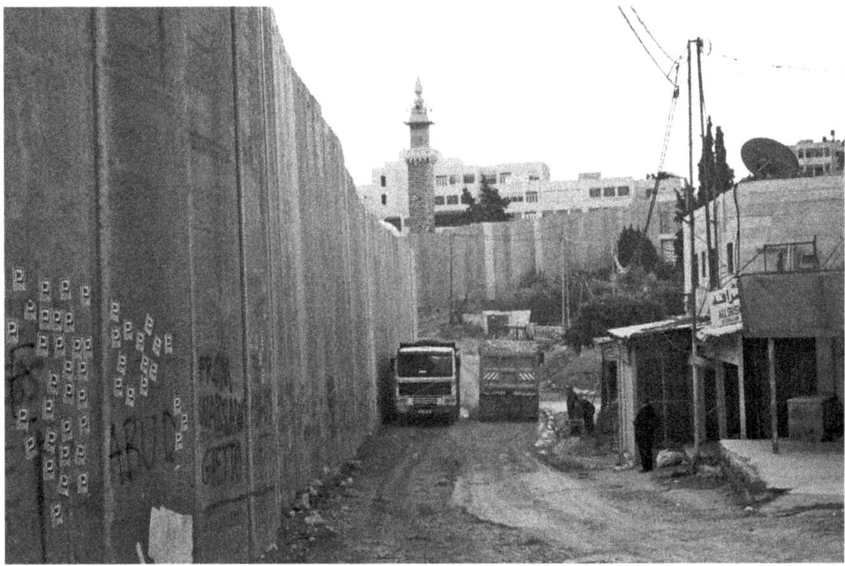

FIGURE 4.5 The security wall chopping through Palestinian Abu Dis

subtlety, containing nothing but its own impetus to do the violence of absolute difference. This is a Jewish wall reserved for Palestinians; for that matter, it is hardly intended for civilian Jewish eyes. At a distance from the Jewish city, the wall even appears abstract and pastoral as it meanders and curves up and down ridges. Up close, it is a row of huge blunt teeth sunk into the earth, their bite savage and unyielding. Horizons of living are blocked, perspective severely foreshortened. One cannot look over, under, or around. For many Israeli Jews, the civilized world ends here. Were we speaking of a cartography of Israeli Jewish consciousness, the eastern side of the security wall might well be inscribed by the Israeli state with the warning 'terra incognita' or 'here there be monsters'.

The security barrier may seem the termination of the vector I have laid out, but it is not. As it blocks movement, the barrier enfolds movement that may have been. By blocking movement, the barrier becomes different from the very block that it is. Put differently, in blocking movement the barrier does not repeat itself as just that which it was: it becomes different *in* itself even as it is identical *to* itself. Deleuze (1994: 57) argues provocatively, "It is always differences which resemble one another, which are analogous, opposed or identical: difference is behind everything, but behind difference there is nothing. Each difference passes through all the others; it must 'will' itself or find itself through all the others." As the barrier blocks movement, it is itself movement, a variation of itself. Sameness is a function of difference; without difference there is no sameness. Thus, sameness emerges through the *circulation* of difference—this is its re-petition, its repetition through itself, its 'willing' of itself that enables it to be that which it is and therefore other than it is. To wit,

Deleuze (ibid.) quotes the American poet Benjamin Paul Blood: "[T]he same returns not, save to bring the different. The slow round of the engraver's lathe gains but the breadth of a hair, but the difference is distributed back over the whole curve, never an instant true—ever not quite."[16]

Thus, the separation barrier enfolds whatever, whomever it blocks as it blocks. And as it blocks, the barrier curves back, enfolding, in the direction of the pylon-parabola from where we began and which I called the beginning of this vector. Reaching its apparent limits, its outside, the vector bends back, the outside becoming inside, the vector enfolding itself, its interaction with itself augmented, becoming more complex, its power emerging further, effecting itself. The vector is a great folding, an ongoing folding and re-folding, forming a spheroid of forces and sites that, enfolded, interact. At this juncture, I can say that the sites themselves are not crucial in these dynamics; it is the dynamics of their vectorization that are crucial, their *zeitgeist* diffusing through the spaces they organize as they do. In more topological terms, "[t]he most distant point becomes interior, by being converted into the nearest: life within the folds" (Deleuze 1999: 101). It is in this sense that the separation barrier is the transmogrification of the pylon-parabola. The bridge is inviting, poetic, soaring, graceful, opening into the Jewish city, encouraging horizons, a site of cosmogenesis, the beginning of an enfolding, while the barrier is forbidding, massive in its squatting, brutal in its starkness, an altar of sacrificial violence blocking the horizon from earth to sky, a site of cosmic closure, a folding back through itself to constrain, own, and sacrifice the Palestinian city in its containing.

Aesthetics, Fold, Vector

To appreciate the role of an aesthetics of power and control in urban form, it is insufficient to consider particular or singular forms or even their comparisons based primarily on symbolic and architectural criteria. The most powerful aesthetics are those that are lived mundanely. Without the aesthetic experiencing of power as practice, there is no feel that this is how doing is doing, how doing is done, how done continues as doing. But I also can invert this to say that this is how surrounds naturalize us into the practices of power. Aesthetics—the synesthetic, sensuous feel of things fitting together (and not fitting together)— enable us to proceed formatively, coherently, perspectively, and prospectively in the nowness of here. The aesthetics of practice are the persuasive grounds of practice, persuading that practice is in the process of being done as the kind of practice it is (and is becoming). In this sense, aesthetics may be more of a gestalt, a 'coherent entity' (Polanyi 1966), or an entity whose coherence is continuously coming into being, emerging, fitting itself together self-persuasively, even as that which it fits together erodes, ruptures, breaks. This is no less the aesthetics of the vector I have discussed. An aesthetics of power is distributed, circulated, transformed, and practiced throughout the vector rather than through connections between sites. In my terms, the aesthetics of control are those of an aesthetics continually practiced and augmented as a commonsense given.

More than four decades after the capture of Palestinian Jerusalem and the other Occupied Territories, despite two intifadas and numerous acts of resistance and protest, the conquest is fully naturalized in the most quotidian way for Israeli Jews. This is practiced into existence on a daily basis in ways far too numerous to enter into here—and likewise for the vector I have discussed. Beginning with the harmonic pylon-parabola as the entry to the historic and holy capital, gathering sacrificial empowerment through the museum-wall, its velocity becoming more directional, the vector accelerates through the mall-wall, gathering the power to own and fetishize, pinning Palestinians-as-objects against the security barrier with Holocaust history, squeezing, flattening, and sacrificing them with the power to consume against its unyielding, brute form. This form folds back toward the pylon-parabola, creating a multi-dimensional spheroid of forces to contain and imprison Palestinians' hopes and aspirations. Integral to this practice of power are the aesthetics that I call bureaucratic.

I argued at the outset that aesthetics enable the fitting together of people, things, places, worlds through practice. Aesthetics are crucial to all practice in mundane living. Historically, bureaucratic aesthetics are tied closely to the emergence of the modern state. This state-form (after Deleuze and Guattari 1988: 385), tree-like, is deeply rooted, centered stably around an axis mundi that opens in all directions and planes, vertical, tall, hierarchical, protective under the cover of its shading. Branching and reproducing clearly, exactly, this logic of forming expands by capture, by taking space, by reproducing its form in additional spaces, by making over these spaces into places. The state-form extends itself lineally, a design for quantitative growth of space and population (Patton 2000), giving especial regard to shaping and controlling its own interiority. Deleuze and Guattari (1988: 397) write: "The law of the State is ... that of interior and exterior. The State is sovereignty. But sovereignty only reigns over what it is capable of internalizing, of appropriating locally." The aesthetics of doing this are in large measure the bureaucratic.

The bureaucratic aesthetics of what the state-form does are related to closing up space, dividing it into determinate intervals, establishing clear-cut breaks and absolutist boundaries. An integral component of this is mono-thetic classification (Bowker and Star 1999). This system demands that every classified item be put into a category with exact boundaries and explicit distinctions that set it apart from all other categories on the same level of classification, without fuzziness, overlap, confusion. This is the kind of classification that Foucault (1973) traced historically in Europe. This is how Western bureaucracy has desired to be practiced. This feels right aesthetically in the practice of bureaucracy, in its commonsensical self-persuasions. Everything is in its proper place, with concomitant consequences in the actualization of power. In practicing the imperatives of the state-form, bureaucratic aesthetics shape and control the social and spatial surfaces of expanding space by capturing new territory for the deployment of power. The aesthetics of bureaucratic classification enable the creation of space that simultaneously is captured, contained, and accounted for. Moreover, new classifications create their own raison d'être for expansion and self-totalization. Bureaucratic aesthetics enable the bureaucratic state to expand through a kind of cellular division of difference yet sameness.

In the modern state, the bureaucratic aesthetics of capture, containment, and taxonomic division are given the formidable impetus and coercion of law. Analyzing the mutual exclusiveness in law of categories such as law-ful/unlawful and legal/illegal, King (1993: 223) argues that, through such social codes, wherever absolute categorical distinctions are made, they will be regarded as part of the legal system—and I emphasize that they will be *felt* aesthetically as part of the legal system. In my terms, phenomenal forms created through or enabled by an aesthetics of monothetic classification will have embedded in them something of the feel and force of legal mandate that stems from inclusion and exclusion. Through bureaucratic aesthetics, truth is a singular, not a multiple.[17]

Bureaucratic aesthetics are those of the making of walls, the walls of capture and containment, of lawfulness, the walls of an absolutist classification that strives to banish overlap, fuzziness, fluctuation, uncertainty—the walls discussed in this work. The wall that folds and enfolds (unlike so many other potentialities of folding) resonates with the lawful feel of bureaucratic aesthetics. The wall that folds and enfolds encloses by constraining access, perspective, exit, by striving to totalize everything it contains to make all of this homogeneous—in this way, whatever is within is self-fortifying and protected within itself. This is the vector that I have discussed, itself one of bureaucratic aesthetics. A vector connecting walls otherwise distant in topographical space from one another, in part through connectivities that resonate with bureaucratic aesthetics. A vector within which these folding and enfolding walls give through themselves a push, a *phusis* (Castoriades 1997: 331), toward the completion of the self-fortification of the city that they (and numerous other vectors) have helped set in motion.

Don Handelman is Shaine Professor Emeritus of Anthropology at the Hebrew University and a member of the Israel Academy of Sciences and Humanities. Recent and forthcoming publications include *Models and Mirrors: Towards an Anthropology of Public Events* (1998); *Nationalism and the Israeli State: Bureaucratic Logic in Public Events* (2004); *Siva in the Forest of Pines: An Essay on Sorcery and Self-Knowledge* (2004), co-authored with David Shulman; *Ritual in Its Own Right: Exploring the Dynamics of Transformation* (2005), co-edited with Galina Lindquist†; *The Manchester School: Practice and Ethnographic Praxis in Anthropology* (2006), co-edited with Terry Evens; *Religion, Politics, and Globalization: Anthropological Approaches* (2011), co-edited with senior editor Galina Lindquist†; and "Self-Exploders, Self-Sacrifice, and the Rhizomic Organization of Terrorism" (2011).

Notes

1. A classic modern exposition that reflects this perspective on the meaning of buildings is that of Goodman (1985).
2. Deleuze has influenced theorists of architecture in developing computer models of what they call 'folding architecture', characterized by "a more fluid logic of connectivity" that integrates "unrelated elements within a new continuous mixture" (Greg Lynn, cited in Harris 2005: 37).
3. The term 'haptic', according to Alois Riegl, refers to a kind of vision distinct from the optical, one in which the eye behaves as does the sense of touch (Deleuze 2003: 189). The haptic gaze is tactile, reaching out, touching, even shaping the textures of another surface and penetrating the contours of its depth (Handelman 2006: 66). See also Gandelman (1991: 5).
4. This is what we are told. In fact, the bridge stands on its own; the pylon and cables are decoration. Since the bridge is not weight-bearing, this vector begins with an illusion. My thanks to Allen Weiss for this observation.
5. This is in relation to Deleuze's arguments regarding singularity coming-into-being from virtuality; virtuality creating, but the creation not quite yet created.
6. In Deleuzian terms, this point of cosmogenesis, a singularity, can also be understood as a point of catastrophe, with the consequences of the oscillation of its waves yet to be known fully.
7. In addition to high school students sent in droves to visit Auschwitz-Birkenau and other extermination camps (see Feldman 2008), during the past few years the Israeli Army has developed its 'Witnesses in Uniform' program, which sends thousands of officers and soldiers annually to visit death camps.
8. In *The Feast of the Sorcerer*, Kapferer (1997) explicates this logic of sacrifice.
9. According to Meron Benvenisti, deputy mayor of Jerusalem at that time, "these plans were de facto a political tool, equal to government policy, in the light of the scarcity of symbolic land" (Nitzan-Shiftan 2005: 231).
10. This walkway, Alrov Mamilla Avenue, is named after the company developing the project, Alrov Properties and Lodgings, which is owned by the Israeli billionaire Alfred Akirov.
11. A recent advertisement aimed at foreign tourists describes the "shopping avenue" as overlooking the Old City—a "stretch of beautiful architecture, which *connects* the old and new city" (*International Herald Tribune*, 20 November 2008; emphasis added).
12. There is one angled turn in the mall walkway, about halfway along. It is here that the only steps leading up to the promenade alongside the Old City walls are located.
13. If we enter the Old City through the Jaffa Gate and continue straight on, downslope through markets and neighborhoods, we reach the ancient Israelite wall, the Western Wall, the last remnant of the outer walls of the Second Temple, which was destroyed in 70 CE. This is part of the wall that surrounds the Haram al Sherif mosque complex, enclosing the Dome of the Rock and the Al-Aksa Mosque. After the 1967 war, the state religion officially turned the Western Wall, long a traditional place of Jewish worship, into the holiest place in Judaism, but also into the *ur*-wall, iconic of Israeli control of all of Jerusalem from its Judaic religious center.
14. The phrase 'security needs' is stock-in-trade discourse for the military and security establishments and often should be understood as justification for undisguised statist and military interests. Apart from the Occupied Territories, Israel's military, defense, and security establishments have been estimated to control over half of the territory of the state (Oren 2008).
15. The original route of the barrier would have confiscated more than 20 percent of the occupied West Bank, but court-ordered alterations have reduced this to about 10 percent (Ben-Eliezer and Feinstein 2008: 178–179).
16. In this vein, Deleuze (1994: 57) argues: "The world is neither finite nor infinite as representation would have it: it is completed and unlimited. Eternal return is the unlimited

of the finished itself … Repetition is the formless being of all differences, the formless power of the ground which carries every object to that extreme 'form' in which its representation comes undone."

17. The above is discussed in Handelman (2004: 19–42) and elsewhere.

References

Asad, Maria. 1999. *Reading with Michel Serres: An Encounter with Time*. Albany: SUNY Press.

Ben-Eliezer, Uri, and Yuval Feinstein. 2008. "'The Battle over Our Homes': Reconstructing/ Deconstructing Sovereign Practices around Israel's Separation Barrier on the West Bank." *Israel Studies* 12, no. 1: 171–192.

Bennett, Barbara Horwitz. 2005. "For the Six Million." *Building Design & Construction* 46, no. 4: 34–41.

Benvenisti, Meron. 1995. *Intimate Enemies: Jews and Arabs in a Shared Land*. Berkeley: University of California Press.

Bowker, Geoffrey C., and Susan Leigh Star. 1999. *Sorting Things Out: Classification and Its Consequences*. Cambridge, MA: MIT Press.

Castoriades, Cornelius. 1997. *World in Fragments*. Ed. and trans. David Ames Curtis. Stanford, CA: Stanford University Press.

Dean, Andrea Oppenheimer. 2005. "Moshe Safdie Offers a Memorial Journey through the Depths of a Jerusalem Hillside with His Yad Vashem History Museum." *Architectural Record* 193, no. 7: 112–119.

Deleuze, Gilles. 1993. *The Fold: Leibniz and the Baroque*. London: Athlone Press.

______. 1994. *Difference and Repetition*. London: Athlone Press.

______. 1999. *Foucault*. London: Continuum.

______. 2003. *Francis Bacon: The Logic of Sensation*. London: Continuum.

Deleuze, Gilles, and Felix Guattari. 1988. *A Thousand Plateaus*. London: Athlone Press.

Dufrenne, Mikel. 1973. *The Phenomenology of Aesthetic Experience*. Evanston, IL: Northwestern University Press.

Feldman, Jackie. 2008. *Above the Death Pits, Beneath the Flag: Youth Voyages to Poland and the Performance of Israeli National Identity*. New York: Berghahn Books.

Foucault, Michel. 1973. *The Order of Things: An Archeology of the Human Sciences*. New York: Vintage.

Gandelman, Claude. 1991. *Reading Pictures, Viewing Texts*. Bloomington: Indiana University Press.

Goldman, Alan. 2001. "The Aesthetic." Pp. 181–192 in *The Routledge Companion to Aesthetics*, ed. Berys Gant and Dominic M. Lopes. London: Routledge.

Goodman, Nelson. 1985. "How Buildings Mean." *Critical Inquiry* 11, no. 4: 642–653.

Handelman, Don. 2004. *Nationalism and the Israeli State: Bureaucratic Logic in Public Events*. Oxford: Berg.

______. 2005. "Introduction: Why Ritual in Its Own Right? How So?" Pp. 1–32 in *Ritual in Its Own Right: Explorations in the Dynamics of Transformation*, ed. Don Handelman and Galina Lindquist. New York: Berghahn Books.

______. 2006. "Death and the Mask." Pp. 59–71 in *Behind the Mask: Dance, Healing, and Possession in South India*, ed. David Shulman and Deborah Thiagarajan. Ann Arbor: South and Southeast Asian Series, University of Michigan.

Handelman, Don, and Lea Shamgar-Handelman. 1997. "The Presence of Absence: The Memorialism of National Death in Israel." Pp. 85–128 in *Grasping Land: Space and Place in Contemporary Israeli Discourse and Experience*, ed. E. Ben-Ari and Y. Bilu. Albany: SUNY Press.

Harris, Paul A. 2005. "To See with the Mind and Think through the Eye: Deleuze, Folding Architecture and Simon Rodia's Watts Towers." Pp. 36–60 in *Deleuze and Space*, ed. Ian Buchanan and Gregg Lambert. Edinburgh: Edinburgh University Press.

Kane, Carolyn Lee. 2007. "*Aisthesis* and the Myth of Representation." *Minerva: An Internet Journal of Philosophy* 11: 83–100.

Kapferer, Bruce. 1997. *The Feast of the Sorcerer*. Chicago, IL: University of Chicago Press.

Katz, Jack. 1999. *How Emotions Work*. Chicago, IL: University of Chicago Press.

King, Michael. 1993. "The 'Truth' about Autopoiesis." *Journal of Law and Society* 20, no. 2: 218–236.

Klein, Menachem. 2005. "Old and New Walls in Jerusalem." *Political Geography* 24: 53–76.

Nitzan-Shiftan, Alona. 2005. "Capital City or Spiritual Center? The Politics of Architecture in Post-1967 Jerusalem." *Cities* 22, no. 3: 229–240.

Ockman, Joan. 2006a. "A Place in the World for a World Displaced." Pp. 19–26 in Ockman 2006b.

______, ed. 2006b. *Yad Vashem: Moshe Safdie—The Architecture of Memory*. Baden: Lars Muller Verlag.

Oren, Amiram. 2008. "Shadow Lands: The Use of Land Resources for Security Needs in Israel." *Israel Studies* 12, no. 1: 149–170.

Patton, Paul. 2000. *Deleuze and the Political*. London: Routledge.

Polanyi, Michael. 1962. *Personal Knowledge: Towards a Post-Critical Philosophy*. New York: Harper Torchbooks.

______. 1966. *The Tacit Dimension*. London: Routledge & Kegan Paul.

Safdie, Moshe. 2006. "The Architecture of Memory." Pp. 92–101 in Ockman 2006b.

Sorkin, Michael. 2005. "Introduction: Up against the Wall." Pp. vi–xx in *Against the Wall: Israel's Barrier to Peace,* ed. Michael Sorkin. New York: New Press.

Weizman, Eyal. 2007. *Hollow Land: Israel's Architecture of Occupation*. London: Verso.

Chapter 5

Body Shock

The Political Aesthetics of Death

ULI LINKE

Graphic images of death can be profoundly disturbing. The sight of human corpses captures attention, unsettles feelings, and fractures meanings. In a global media market, visual representations of dead bodies are trafficked with intent: political and commercial image makers rely on the shock-and-awe effect of death to propagate truth claims about war, nation, and security. Some images of death, however, may not be shown. In the United States and Europe, photographs of dead citizen soldiers are typically censured. Government intervention begins with the camera work at military sites. Visual access to dead bodies in war zones is restricted and tightly controlled. Since the 1990s, beginning with the first Gulf War, as Nicholas Mirzoeff (2005: 80) points out, "there has been a concerted effort to keep the visual representation of death off Western television screens and front pages." Images of US soldiers killed in action and pictographic evidence of dead civilians have been barred from circulation in political space. By contrast, the debased corpses of enemy soldiers or heads of state, such as Iraq's Saddam Hussein in 2006 or Libya's Muammar Gaddafi in 2011, have been publicly paraded as evidence of military victory. But such visual moments are also inherently dangerous. The graphic display of the dehumanized and blood-stained body of an enemy can serve to affirm the killing as a righteous act of justice or to evoke oppositional sentiments of pity, victimhood, and revenge. Visual records of the human casualties of war are therefore never entirely devoid of political signification.

References for this chapter begin on page 96.

The vanishing of dead military bodies, erased from visual space by the intervening power of the state, has created a new commodity fetish: the phantasmic realism of violent death as a fictional genre. Fantasy productions of dead bodies are circulated as popular entertainment throughout the domain of commercial culture: television, cinema, video games, art, and the museum. Simulated enactments of blood and pain belong to the theater of popular pleasure. While the real-world war dead are hidden from public view, global media industries have created ever more realistic spectacles of killing and dying for public consumption. These fantasy performances of the fake dead body as a commodity form are governed by an "exhibitionary apparatus" (Bennett 1994: 144), which is propelled by the collusion of media, military, corporate, and political interests. Governments promote specific forms of public entertainment to manufacture consent, that is, "to enlist popular support for the values and objectives enshrined in the state" (ibid.: 151). In this realm of entertainment, the corpse is rendered visible by a sensorial regime focused on public drama and popular pleasure. But the cultural industries that traffic images of death to national or transnational audiences also pursue a strategic negation of life. The political aesthetics of death and the commercial organization of visual space are founded on dehumanization—an increasing atrophy of empathy, a thinning of compassion for the suffering of others. While such affective dispositions may be symptomatic of a global capitalism, they are also socially produced and encoded by specific histories, discourses, and meanings.

Building on these schematic observations, my analysis of the political aesthetics of death proceeds by scrutinizing a state-sanctioned entertainment enterprise that commodifies corpses with promises of making visible and knowable the interior world of human bodies. I trace the entanglements of politics, visual culture, and capitalism to a concrete ethnographic site: the dramatic staging of Body Worlds (Körperwelten), an exhibition on human anatomy designed by a German anatomist, Gunther von Hagens. Endorsed as a scientific exhibit on the art of preserving human remains, the installation opened its doors to the German public in 1997 in Mannheim. The exhibit then toured through Germany, Europe, Asia, and North America. According to media reports from Germany, the exhibit's "dead body specimens" became "a peak attraction for the general public" (Roth 1998: 50). In Germany and Austria, the exhibition "was kept open twenty-four hours a day, seven days a week, to accommodate all visitors" (Dijck 2005: 43). The immense popularity points to a new global market for the commoditization and optical consumption of human remains. My aim is to examine this fascination with corpses, which, I suggest, succeeds by unmaking empathy and memory. In this chapter, I am specifically concerned with the German cultural dimensions of Body Worlds, without, however, ignoring its global significance. In contrast to previous studies (Dijck 2005; Jespersen, Rodríguez, and Starr 2008; Walter 2004), my analysis is focused on the problematic of exhibiting human cadavers in Germany, a country in which public culture, despite its affinities to a global modernity, is succinctly framed by issues of genocide and conflicted memories of a violent history.

My goal is to analyze the anatomical exhibit Body Worlds as both medical spectacle and popular entertainment in a society that continues to struggle with the aftermath of the Holocaust. As I argue in the following, a multiplicity of themes associated with the atrocities of the National Socialist regime are uncannily played out by the exhibit: the negation of humanity, the objectification of embodied subjects, medical experimentation, anatomy as a site of anthropological truth, judicial decisions leading to dehumanization, the sexualized appropriation of bodies, the recycling of body parts, the public complicity in state violence through spectatorship, and the indifference and lack of empathy displayed by onlookers. Although my analysis situates these regimes of violence in the context of Germany's history, such practices and discourses are also relevant for our understanding of other histories of war and genocide. Looking beyond the German case, comparative studies reveal that dehumanization and empathic failure are integral to the industrial, military, and political apparatuses of mass murder in other parts of the world (see Hinton 2002, 2005). In all such instances, 'forensic violence' (which is applied to the corpse) emerges as a logical extension of social violence. An additional theme that comes to light concerns the social labor of forgetting: in the aftermath of trauma and genocide, collective remembrance tends to become constricted by an imposition of silence. Following World War II, the prolonged attempts in Germany to silence and to forget the past have been linked to denial and shame (Dean 2005; Linke 1999, 2002). Already in 1945, Allied soldiers were implementing countermeasures against the presumed German indifference to the atrocities. Committed to the belief that direct contact with the murdered victims would awaken German feelings of remorse or compassion, Allied soldiers began to use shock therapy: at gunpoint, local townspeople were forced to tour the killing fields. The aim was "to make them see" (Barnouw 1996) through mandatory contact with the corpses. But, as historians observed, this compulsory contact-shock practice produced neither remorse nor empathy for the dead. Rather, it promoted the Germans' assertion of their own status as victims.

These observations are crucial for my analysis of an installation that I examine through the voids of memory and empathy in a post-Holocaust society. In light of German history, what accounts for the immense popularity of the Body Worlds exhibit in Germany? Although the installation of human bodies was deemed controversial and received enormous media attention, German public discourse was curiously silent on the pertinent connections between genocide, memory, and the dissected corpses. As C. Nadia Seremetakis (2001: 119) points out, in Germany "church and cultural critics have criticized this usage of the dead [in the exhibit] as exploitative and disrespectful." Such criticisms, however, avoided engagement with the specters of violence in historical time: where did these dead bodies come from and how had these once living human beings died? For almost 10 years, critics and supporters were content to reiterate the curator's comforting assurances that the bodies on display had been legitimately harvested from deceased German donors. Until 2004, spectators believed that they were looking at German bodies. But, as I suggest here, a multi-layered remembrance of violence, with attention to the humanity and life histories of the dead, would soon have uncovered the exhibit's link to a global traffic in corpses and to the requisition of bodies from the Third World.

In this chapter, my aim is to enter these zones of silence by inquiring how emotional anesthesia, in the context of a popular fascination with mutilated bodies, is produced by discourse, image, and representation. My analysis is structured by the following questions: What propels German spectators to look at aestheticized, albeit mutilated, corpses? What representational mechanism does the exhibit use to enable such a viewing in present-day, post-Holocaust Germany? What is the role of the state in the formation of a political aesthetics of death?

Corpses in the Museum

In the Body Worlds exhibit, the objects on display, unlike most specimens at a conventional science museum, are real human corpses—cadavers. The bodies are arranged in various stages of dissection, albeit without showing any signs of decomposition. The corporal remains have undergone a process of preservation, a procedure called 'plastination': the plasticized corpses "do not rot or smell, and they maintain the structure, color, and texture of the original tissue and organs down to the microscopic level" (Herscovitch 2003: 828). Salvaged from decay with an "unprecedented measure of realism" (Clewing 1998: 16), the dead are forever preserved in corporal forms that bear the mark of deep anatomical intrusions. The bodies have been skinned, cut open, dismembered, and sectioned to expose the interior world of human physiology—muscles, bones, blood vessels, and organs—including fetuses, wombs, and penises. In the exhibit, surreal visuality and hyper-realism work in tandem to promote the relentless consumption of the dead. While Body Worlds does rely on optics and visuality to annihilate compassion, it simultaneously endows its displays with a tangible, sensuous, even tactile quality that proffers, as I show in this chapter, an unmediated realism and an authentic facticity as a sensationalist allure. The global attraction of the unmitigated contact with dead bodies rests on machinations of authenticity that are sanctioned by the state and commodified by the museum.

In this era of globalization, which is governed by a perpetual 'simulation of the sensual' through new media and communication technologies, the materiality of dead bodies clearly takes on new meanings. For under the impact of global capitalism, the non-virtual presence of corpses in the museum seems to accommodate a yearning for the 'thingness' of things—the permanent, the tangible, the concrete. As such, the sensorial access to corpses might nourish a longing for an authentic reality, for a perceptual realism without simulation, without simulacra or copies. From this perspective, it is understandable why the Body Worlds' exhibit "implores the cult of the 'authentic'" (Roth 1998: 51–52). The display of dead bodies is promoted by a discourse that foregrounds the realism of the cadavers. German exhibit reviews insist that the displays are stocked with genuine human specimens, "actual corpses" (Nissen 1998: 36), whose "naked reality" (Vorpahl 1997: 8) and "authenticity is fascinating" (Becker 1999: 15). The exhibited objects are "not artificial anatomy models, but real dead people" (Budde 1997: 11), "not instructional models, but genuine corpses, presented to the museum visitors openly, in public, and in closest proximity, without the protective glass of the showcase" (Schmitz 1997: 8). But the titillating charge that emanates from dead bodies, this fascinating allure of the authentic, needs to be understood in terms of a more general social dynamic.

Under global capitalism, the quest for anchorage and authenticity is intimately connected to the currency of the corporal turn. Such a reading is in part confirmed by the exhibit's visitor statistics. More than 20 million people worldwide have attended the Body Worlds exhibit, including 8 million in Europe and of these 6 million in Germany. Journalists have hailed a "German record for a museum exhibit" (Nissen 1998: 36) with "up to 20,000 people per day" (*Frankfurter Rundschau* 1998a: 33). The body museum deploys the semiotics of the corpse to appeal to a global consumer public, while, at the same time, signifying, explaining, and representing the dead in a culturally specific manner. The exhibit, as I will show in the following, utilizes an aesthetic that not only disguises the brutality of death and dismemberment but also deflects memories of historical violence.

The 'Living' Corpse

The public display of the corpse, which inspires both morbid curiosity and scientific interest, appears at first glance to be part of a more general history of human exhibitions. But the German exhibit Body Worlds presents something quite different: it explicitly distances itself from this trajectory of the human museum by placing an emphasis on unemotional and dispassionate anatomical displays. The galleries of plastinated corpses are not intended to inspire fear or revulsion by dramatizing death. On the contrary, this collection of dead bodies, which contains more than 200 specimens, wants to create the illusion of life after death. According to Hagens (1997: 214), the preservation of the corpse with silicon and plastic makes possible "a new form of post mortem existence"—namely, "the 'resurrection' of the enfleshed body" (in Roth 1998: 52). What are we to make of such statements?

In the exhibit, human anatomy is staged by means of dramatic visions of the normal, ordinary, and everyday body. The exhibitors strive for "an aesthetic that strips the dead of their estranging rigidity and instead emphasizes their affinity with the living" (*Der Spiegel* 1997: 214). Many of these life-sized plastinated corpses are posed to simulate familiar activities: running, standing, walking, and sitting.

> The man appears to be running: he stands there—as if moving in a fast stride. He is naked, and moreover: he has been stripped of his skin, the muscle tissue detached from the bone. Shreds of flesh trail down. (Clewing 1998: 16)

> [We see] a basketball player caught mid-dribble ... a human rider mounted nobly on a plastinated horse ... a seated chess player concentrating intently on his game ... A pregnant woman reclining. (Herscovitch 2003: 828)

The bodies on display are set up as if taking part in social activities from the mundane world—sports, play, and recreation. In this menagerie of corpses, human remains are presented as 'ballerina', 'horse rider', 'chess player', 'swimmer', 'cyclist', 'runner', and 'sword fighter'. These dissected and cut-open bodies, which are posed in typified representations to "give the impression that they are forever alive" (Zoschke 1994: 12), are depicted as skillfully crafted installations—"the 'living corpses'" (Roth 1998: 52) or "human-flesh sculptures" (*Der Spiegel* 1998: 184). The exhibitors describe their galleries of dead bodies as works of "living anatomy," not "stiff corpses lying prostrate on the dissecting table," but rather "entire bodies positioned upright ... standing in life-like poses" that "create anatomical individuality" and replicate "a living being" (Hagens 1997: 203–204).

What does this persistent invocation of authenticity signify? The presumed works "of authenticity, of living realism in death" (Schmitz 1997: 8) are in fact synthetically produced artifacts, mimetic objects. They are designed to simulate the anatomy of live human beings. And this vital anatomy is the end product of a series of machinations: reconstructed, fabricated, aestheticized, and mimetically staged. Nonetheless, the exhibitor emphatically insists on the authentic realism of his displays. By circumventing the use of conventional media, such as stone, plaster, or wax, he claims to have fashioned human figures directly from organic substances: tissue, muscle, and bone. In this regard, the exhibited objects are deemed to be "authentic anatomical specimens" (Hagens 2004: 260). But "the plastinated cadaver," as José van Dijck (2005: 47) points out, "is as much an organic artifact as it is the result of technological tooling ... The cadavers are manipulated with chemicals to such an extent that that they can hardly be regarded as real bodies." Moreover, in the process of manufacture, the organic substances are instrumentalized as mere raw material: "Even a body saturated with silicone rubber must be shaped into the desired pose before the preservatives can polymerize" (Roth 1998: 50–51). The human body, the dead flesh, is treated, transfigured, and sculpted: "[T]he corpses are worked on without restraint and set in poses" (Becker 1999: 15). Dead human flesh has been reshaped to take on certain physiognomic characteristics: white skin, blue eyes, European facial features. This ethnic modification of the dead was a fabricated truth claim, intended to support visually the assertion that the corpses had been harvested from German donors. As we now know, this is a fiction. But the authenticity of the corpses can be called into question further. Each plastinated figure consists of a collage of different bodies: thus the baby in the belly of the pregnant woman, for example, may not actually be hers; indeed, the woman's pregnancy is a simulacrum, a fiction of flesh created by the anatomist's artistic intervention. Hagens "freely admits to taking artistic license in the preparation of his corpses, swapping organs and tissues between bodies as he deems necessary, justifying this by noting [that] organ exchanges are also done for the living" (Hessel 2005: 31). The exhibit is a postmodern assembly of "human flesh sculptures" manufactured by the self-proclaimed "anatomy-artist" (*Frankfurter Rundschau* 1998b: 8).

These sculptures or artifactual corpses transcend any markers of death. The bodies assume lifelike postures, perform everyday activities, and display facial expressions that convey pleasure and contentment or concentrated attention. These depictions of vitality are representational strategies that divert the spectators' attention from the domains of terror and death. The lively appearance of the dead negates awareness of the circumstances of their death, of the prolonged procedures of medical intervention, and of the enabling power of the state. The installations create a world of living corpses that is devoid of trauma, historicity, and violence. Anatomical realism works to annul memory: historical consciousness recedes into a blind zone. With this dissociative strategy, the plastinated figures are presented and come into view as sites of transparent scientific truth, as surfaces for the inscription of medical fact that, in turn, "eradicat[es] all mediation between object and representation" and "render[s] all subjective intervention—inherent to representation—obsolete" (Dijck 2005: 56). The exhibition of 'living' corpses incarcerates the spectators' interpretative capacity within the self-referential field of anatomical realism. This erasure of critical perception, which is encoded into the displays, is further enhanced by the erotic appeal of the artifacts, as I discuss in the following.

Sexualizing the Corpse

The installations create a self-referential field of anatomical realism, which in turn accentuates the figures' sexual characteristics. The German body museum, however, goes beyond simply articulating the naked sexuality of the corpse; instead, it renders sex iconographically hyper-visible. With a few exceptions, the exhibited whole-body specimens are male. Every male figure, regardless of its anatomical disarray, has been equipped with an intact penis, emphasizing its sex—its manhood. Even the 'deep' body specimens, which have pared down to their muscular or skeletal system, show an accentuated display of unharmed male genitalia, enlarged, engorged, and oversized. Although this observation is rarely made by journalists, regular exhibit visitors do not leave these genitalia details unremarked. Their comments on the Internet, in blogs or archives, and in guest book entries include critical assessments about the unveiling of the male organ:

> Be prepared to see lots of penises but other than that it's all good ... That guy's penis was really gross! (Drcharles 2006)

> Yes, you do see penises, yes, you do see breasts, yes, you see reproductive organs, but just because you see them, does it mean it's pornographic? (Arts & Faith 2005)

> You too can have an eight-inch penis! I thought the specimens in the show were hung like Clydesdales. Hey, if I had equipment like that, I'd want my body preserved for posterity too. (TrashCity 2002)

> The plastinated men ... their bodies are all muscle [with] increased penis size ... So many men fret about cock-size—pumps, pills, and faulty measuring techniques

will never prove as effective as letting Germans embalm your unit with plastic. (Sass 2004)

In any case, most of the plastinated figures are men. Is that just because the lengthened penises enhance the craving for spectatorship? (Treffpunkt-Ethik 2004)

The prominence of oversized male genitalia is perceived as eye-catching: displays of the enhanced penis are registered as both titillating and disturbing. By contrast, the nakedness of female bodies with their upturned silicone breasts provokes less of a stir. Yet the exhibition of female corpses likewise shows sexualized bodies and poses: the women's breasts are prominently accentuated, and although the bodies are stripped of all skin, the nipples are placed erectly on prosthetic tissue plates. Whereas the male corpses are equipped with enlarged genitalia, the women's bodies are given postures that visually accentuate their erogenous zones. As one visitor remarked: "[T]here was a ten year old kid standing beside me … We're both gawking at Yoga girl, [who is] bent over in a back handstand, her sex exposed for the world" (Hessel 2005: 31). Even the pregnant figures are positioned in seductive poses. The reclining pregnant woman seems to stretch backwards casually and pleasurably in order to permit a look at her firmly enhanced breasts, her open abdomen, and her crotch (see Hagens and Whalley 2004: 176). A female visitor asserts: "One was pregnant, reclining on one side with a hand behind the head, a pose taken straight from pornographic cliché" (Stern 2003). There is the striking standing woman, with full lips and high cheekbones, who is displayed in her fifth month of pregnancy. The exhibit catalogue describes this installation in the following manner: "The pregnant figure shields the genital area with her arm, while at the same time framing the fetus in her womb" (Hagens 1997: 214). Yet when we re-examine the image, we observe that she actually points to and even touches her genitalia with one hand (an auto-erotic movement), while her other hand extends to the side, its palm open in a beckoning gesture, inviting us to look at her. This woman's curved breasts are prominently accentuated: although her body has no skin, her nipples are visually enhanced. Indeed, following the exhibition in Mannheim in 1997, this figure was replaced by another female corpse. Although staged in an almost identical pose, her breasts had been conspicuously enlarged.

The exhibition of corpses or anatomical "object-bodies," as Horkheimer and Adorno (1981: 277) phrased it, requires sexualization, a libidinal charge, in order "to be at once desired as that which is forbidden." The display of corpses operates with an eroticization of vision, a sexualized optical regime, for in the center of these visual productions stands the voyeuristic exposure of naked corpses—"the body's anatomical nudity" (Whalley 1997: 161). But this nakedness of the corpse is accentuated by an ideographic sexualization, for the flayed bodies are endowed with either an enlarged penis or voluptuous breasts and are placed in erotic poses.

The transfiguration of human cadavers into sexual objects received nationwide attention in Germany when the exhibit moved into Hamburg's Erotic

Art Museum in 2003. The choice of this site not only points to an enhanced appetite for libidinal signs, but also reveals the installation's pornographic appeal. German media headlines celebrated the "striptease of corpses," the "well-endowed bodies" shown "ultra-nude and uncensored" (Assheuer 2003). As a tribute to the museum's location, prostitutes and taxi drivers were invited to visit the show free of charge. Not surprisingly, the Erotic Art Museum exhibit was synchronized with the curator's decision to expand the installation's section on sex and reproduction and to move pertinent objects, including "the erect penis of one of the dead, a clitoris, and a fetus in the mother's womb," into the center of the exhibit (ibid.). In Germany, death and sex—or corpses with sex appeal—have market value.

Nearly half a million visitors attended this Hamburg showing, an erotic spectacle that the German media subsequently termed "event-anatomy with erection" (Ahrens 2003: 25). On the day of the opening, Hagens announced at a news conference that his newest creation—a pair of copulating corpses—could unfortunately not be completed in time (ibid.). Instead, however, he was pleased to present the 'The Early Riser' (*Der Frühaufsteher*), a German circumlocution that captures the erectile activity of the male genital on awakening in the morning (Knür 2003). Especially designed for the Erotic Art Museum exhibit, this installation shows an arterial male corpse sitting up on a modulated bed, with a stiff upright penis rising from between his outstretched legs—a dead man forever preserved with this icon of "sexual arousal" (Kopp 2003). The corpses are thereby made to perform in a pornographic spectacle: their vulvas, breasts, nipples, and penises are exhibited, and they are forced to enact intercourse, sexual excitement, and pregnancy. In this human museum, as one commentator phrased it, "dead bodies are turned into obedient cadavers: they wear their skin over their arm, twist, turn, dance, and become erect, just as it pleases him [the exhibitor]" (Köhler 2003). It is an "amassment of corpses," remarked the well-known German cultural critic Günter Wallraff, where human beings "are prostituted in cheap poses" for popular entertainment in a "voyeuristic and exhibitionist society" (in Sauer 2000).

After the dead had been "allowed to strip" at the Erotic Art Museum in Hamburg (Assheuer 2003: 1), Hagens further augmented the exhibit's sexual appeal by infusing the exposition of corpses with additional pornographic accessories and erotic events. Whereas in other European countries the exhibit's publicity stunts had been limited to anatomical demonstrations, such as the public dissection of a corpse in London or the performance of circus acrobats in Vienna, who "gave a show amidst the plastinated cadavers, in order to 'emphasize the remarkable similarities between the muscular structures of the corpses and the acrobats'" (Dijck 2005: 58, 59), in Germany, by contrast, these undertakings were thoroughly sexualized. By insisting on the German public's "civil right to an uncensored body showing" (McGuffin Foundation 2004: 6), Hagens proceeded to stage live shows featuring topless models among the dissected corpses. In this manner, the traveling exhibit concluded its European tour in the city of Frankfurt in 2004 with a week-long program titled "Naked Nights" (Pressemitteilungen 2004), a promotional event that combined anatomy and sex in a spectacular body performance. In this show, described as an act of "extreme denuding" by the exhibitor (McGuffin Foundation 2004: 6), a cast of female strippers, male bodybuilders, and a transvestite performed naked on stage among the dead. These "live specimens," with their "anatomically perfect body form" and "well-developed musculature," as Hagens phrased it, had been hired as models for anatomical demonstrations—for a comparative showing of physiological surfaces by visually juxtaposing the naked dead and the nude live bodies (Pressemitteilungen 2004; *Spiegel Online* 2004). According to the exhibitor: "The vitality that is thereby achieved turns anatomy into a real experience" (HAI-Lights 2004).

During the promotional event, the nude models who exhibited their bodies among the corpses were objectified and turned into commodities just like their dead counterparts: "Like the plastinated bodies, the models have been rendered anonymous: in addition to wearing a mask, they have been given names like 'Arteria', 'Veina', or 'Musculus'" (*Spiegel Online* 2004). The week-long program was cut short by an injunction issued by the city: Frankfurt city officials did not share the German popular enthusiasm for "show effect," declaring the exhibit to be an "impermissible instrumentalization of corpses" (Pressemitteilungen 2004). Nevertheless, this performance ultimately reveals the making of the exhibit as a sexual images industry: dead bodies are conscripted to labor in a pornographic spectacle, which is a "form of commodification" (Stern 2003). In Germany, the exhibit turned mutilated corpses into erotic fetishes and presented necrophilia for public consumption. The corpses' intense libidinal charge seems to mute critical historical awareness: the pornographic spectacle anchors emotions in the present, in the erotic pleasure of visual consumption. The optical consumption of the dead, whose bodies are presented as libidinous objects, encoded by nakedness and sex, diverts attention from the body as a site of suffering.

Corpse Art

The erotic appeal of the dead belongs to a commercial venture that makes contact with corpses exciting but safe. For museum visitors, the optical intimacy with lifeless figures becomes something of a fairground adventure. In this world of sex and eroticism, dead bodies are successfully transformed into consumable objects—eroticized action figures. "The exhibition," says philosopher Megan Stern (2003), "represents, in the most dramatic terms, the redefinition of the human body within consumer culture." All bodies, even mutilated cadavers, can be packaged as marketable commodities, especially when they are beautified, sexualized, and rendered sensually appealing. The fabrication of anatomical truth is furthermore obfuscated by the aestheticized figuration of the exhibited objects, thereby circumventing the possibility of critical reflection.

The exhibit of human bodies is encoded by an aesthetic that seeks to commodify corpses as sculptures, as artistic figures. What visitors supposedly see is the "art of anatomy: the aesthetically instructive presentation of the body's interior" (Hagens 1997: 214, 216). In Germany, the plastinated specimens are praised as an "intellectual and creative achievement" by an "anatomy-artist," who works on bodies "just like a sculptor" (Roth 1998: 51). According to media reports, the "remarkable success of the current Body Worlds exhibition" is linked to the fact that "dissected human cadavers are ... presented as works of art" (Smith 2003: 829). Museumgoers can view "strangely disfigured corpses as art" (*Frankfurter Rundschau* 1998b: 8). Artistic intervention is a critical aspect of the presentations. As Hagens notes: "The corpse must be displayed artistically; otherwise, it becomes an object of revulsion and obstructs the unemotional gaze" (in Fonseca 1999: 50). Furthermore, "the aesthetic pose helps to dispel disgust" (Hagens 1997: 205). The aesthetic dimension enables viewers to "see" the corpse as a "natural" object (Fonseca 1999: 50); the installations are supposed to instruct without eliciting any emotions. The dead, who are "here shown in a highly artistic form of preservation," are "beautiful and educational ... artistic and instructive" (Kriz 1997: 9–10). As one visitor remarked: "Some of the displays were undeniably beautiful, especially the lacy circulatory system of a rabbit, a hand, an adult, and a child" (Herscovitch 2003: 828). Moreover, "no offensive odors disturb the viewing," because plastination stops the lifeless bodies from entering decomposition (Hagens 1997: 205, 216). The corpses on display are "dry, hard, and scent free" (Vorpahl 1997: 8), "clean," and "non-infectious," and "one can touch them ... with one's own hands ... as often as one likes" (Roth 1998: 50), "even without gloves" (Rothschild 1998: 3). Indeed, the exhibition explicitly extends "an invitation to touch and to look into the bodily interior" (Schmitz 1997: 8). Since the individual exhibits are strategically "placed in the very center of the walkway, the tactile contact with the artful dead is in fact palpably provoked" (Roth 1998: 51).

Such a fabricated proximity to the corpse is suggestive of a "democratization of anatomy" (*Frankfurter Rundschau* 1998a: 33), for the exhibited objects—being "resilient, enduring, and realistic" (Zoschke 1994: 12)—offer the visiting public "seemingly direct access" to the cadavers (Becker 1999: 15). The museum display is designed to facilitate "a sensory awareness of the world of the body through the immediacy of visual contact by the eye and the comprehending touch of the hand" (Bauer 1997: 199). Such a sensual exhibit undoubtedly reinforces the feeling of a material presence of real and authentic corpses—a presumed intimacy with death. Of course, this contact with death is a staged illusion, a museum effect, because the displayed objects are not stinking corpses but rather synthetically sanitized bodies that are "dry and odorless," "graspable," lacking "decomposition and desiccation so completely that the bodily interior ceases to be an object of revulsion" (Hagens 1997: 204). The show is supposed "to diminish the horror of death" (Kriz 1997: 9). But the installations retreat precisely from this reality, insofar as they exhibit living corpses that have been normalized and eroticized. The prominent characteristics through which death might be experienced, the sensually apprehensible signs of putrefaction, have been intentionally excised from the exhibited objects. These staged encounters with dead bodies, while granting sensual immediacy, also furnish the necessary emotional distance.

Central to this museum exhibit is "the aestheticization of corpses. By means of the plastination technique, the exhibited objects become in large part unrecognizable as real bodies; this art form promotes a forgetting of the fact that these are indeed dead human beings" (Emmrich 1998: 6). One "has to repeatedly remind oneself that this is not an artificial panopticon, but true anatomy. There are absolutely no detectable odors either … [T]he dissected bodies look … so deceptively lifelike that they indeed appear to be works of art" (Schmitz 1997: 8). These observations are important, for they are suggestive of the fact that the effect of the installation intentionally negates the propagated proximity to death. The cadavers are presented in such a way that they appear to be undead. The figure of the 'Muscle Man', for instance, is described as "skillfully perform[ing] weight-lifting experiments" (Roth 1998: 51). The anatomical exhibit of corpses is "lively, active, and posed" (Hagens 1997: 204). The "beauty [of these corporal forms] displaces our revulsion" (Eggebrecht 1998: 1), and "aesthetics becomes a means for pushing away disgust" (Reimer 1998). Out of the raw material of human remains, new bodies have been fashioned: beautified, durable, and sensually accessible.

Plastination remakes the corpse into an aesthetic object: with his flesh preserved and rendered immortal, the 'Man with Skin' stands transfixed, focused only on himself. A set of motifs that typify the transfiguration of this corpse—white skin, classic (European) facial features, a muscular body and heroic pose—reveal a return to an uncanny fascination with fascist masculinity. Presented without reference to their personal biography, life history, or cause of death, the plastinated specimens perform an inverse symbolic function: the bodies are propelled out of historical time and social space. The corpses are aestheticized in such a way as to suppress any evocations of violence, victimhood, or history. The performative success of the specimens is inscribed in the amputation of feelings and the erasure of memory. Plastination renders the dead bodies "timeless and thereby removes the potential of forgetting or remembering" (Fonseca 1999: 58). The displayed objects, which are repeatedly described as "anatomical art works," "praiseworthy" "art objects," "artistic representations" and "skillfully" crafted "statues" or "sculptures" (in Eberhardt 1998a: 32; see also Roth 1998: 51), successfully evade the memory work of history: they possess neither an autobiographical memory nor a historical remembrance. The installation suppresses the commemoration of the dead subjects' life histories as much as it does Germany's problematic history (medical experiments, eugenics, racial hygiene) under National Socialism. Indeed, the refurbished corpses, crafted in the tradition of the white German body, are "eternal human monuments" in a "museum without forgetting, therefore without remembrance, which means without loss, without mourning, and, as such, without empathy" (Fonseca 1999: 56, 60).

Negations of Humanity

The practice of corpse art is grounded in a series of negations, in a negative dialectic that facilitates the public showing of corpses. The bodies are estranged, depersonalized, and reified. Dead people are morphologically transformed into 'living' corpses. Cadavers are turned into artistic sculptures. The motionless flesh is made to stand upright. Lifeless matter is sculpted into lifelike poses. Mortality is denied through the 'resurrection' of the dead body. Temporality is negated by means of synthetic preservatives. The inevitable deterioration of the body is pre-empted: the corpses remain forever "frozen" somewhere "between death and decay" (Hagens 1997: 201). In this manner, the dead come into view as an eternally enduring monumental body architecture.

But this kind of monumentalism uncannily consumes death in the same manner that "fascism feeds on bodies" (Wolbert 1982: 7). While claiming to uncover forensic truth beneath the human surface, the exhibit "offers up the interior of the body as a commodity-object and use-item": the panoptic penetration of the cadavers is at once also an "anatomical cannibalism" (Seremetakis 2001: 120). As in Germany's Nazi past, where the propagation of racial ideals was synchronized with a total apparatus of destruction and mass death, the exhibit's aestheticism, with its manufacture of beautified anatomical figures, is coordinated with the unscrupulous debasement of human remains. In this sense, the "eviscerated bodies are themselves expressions of a post-Holocaust embodiment" (ibid.: 128). The use of the dead as artistic raw material rests on dehumanization, which is, moreover, enabled by the state's collusion in this enterprise.

In the exhibit, the processed corpses have been rendered anonymous. The dead subject, the very identity of this formerly living human being, has been erased from the displays: "[T]he historical-biographical construct of the person of the deceased [is] excised from the plastinated objects" (Bauer 1997: 197). Moreover, the "age and cause of death are generally withheld in order to avoid a 'personification' of the specimens" (Hagens 1997: 201). Every remnant of subjectivity is destroyed, for the dead bodies have been "transfigured" beyond recognition (Clewing 1998: 16). "We do not know how these human beings lived, who they were, or how they died. We do not know their names, their age, their life story. Even their facial features, which have been altered by the dissection process, can no longer tell us very much" (Budde 1997: 11). The exhibit shows "peeled, perforated, opened, and halved ... dissected bodies, a 'corpse inside the corpse', as it were" (Roth 1998: 51, 52), which stands there, frozen in time, without personal identity and life history, robbed of its humanity.

Through the negative labor of medical intrusions, these dead bodies are not merely estranged and transfigured; they are also objectified. The "cut up, dismembered, and recombined three-dimensional 'living corpses'" (Roth 1998: 52) are no longer recognizable as human subjects. "As soon as the dissection process begins, the corpse becomes an anonymous specimen, which no longer reminds us in any aspect of the individuality of the deceased" (*Der Spiegel* 1997: 212). This process of dehumanization has concrete legal implications, for these subjectivity-deprived bodies have been stripped of their civil rights. The insistence on anonymity, the abrogation of identity, scientific objectification, and aesthetic figuration collude to neutralize any potential judicial concerns. In most German states, such as Baden-Württemberg, "burial regulations generally prohibit the public display of corpses ... But the Mannheim judiciary determined that plastinated bodies are not 'corpses in the eyes of the law'" (Eberhardt 1997: 18). From a juridical perspective, the exhibited specimens are not human bodies but lifeless matter, material objects. In a legal sense, "an anatomy corpse becomes a 'thing' that is no longer entitled to a peaceful death, if it remains anonymous, lacks any emotional attachment, and is no longer the object of commemoration" (*Der Spiegel* 1997: 214). Thus, legally defined as a 'thing', with no claim to personhood, the plastinated corpse loses its humanity. Affect and empathy are severed from the exhibited object: "It is indeed not the lifeless body or even the plastinated body saturated with synthetics that is the object of our compassionate remembrance" (Bauer 1997: 197). The corpses are empty, uninhabited figures, exhibited in a human museum that negates all signs of humanity. The dead bodies are dehistoricized and thereby also without remembrance. According to the curator, "corpses are after a certain point merely 'specimens' … 'An anatomical specimen ceases to be the object of reverence and human compassion'" (in Vorpahl 1997: 8). "The lasting effect of dignity accorded to the deceased by the work of mourning is thereby extinguished [and] the sense of emotional attachment to the deceased" has "come to an end" (Hagens 1997: 207). On display are dehumanized "subjectless bodies" (Fonseca 1999: 66), which are denied any affective attention. Thus rendered emotionless, the German body museum, in Helmut Lethen's words (1994: 6–7), "takes its leave from the culture of conscience" and the "drama of the culture of shame."

Recycling Death

The dead are redesigned to become thing-like figures. Legally dispossessed of the rights of personhood, they are not human subjects and thus not even corpses. By means of this negation of human subjectivity, the exhibit realizes "phantasms of disposition about the biomass" and, in doing so, "reduces the human subject to a functioning apparatus" (Becker 1999: 15). The human being "becomes a body, a physical device for study" (Budde 1997: 11). Thus, at the same time that the dead are emptied out of their individual subjectivities and rendered bare of empathic appeal, they are constructed into forensic types. Eviscerated and opened up for inspection, human beings are exhibited as categorical biological specimens: the 'Body Slice,' the 'Skeletal-Muscular Man', the 'Organ Presenter', the 'Autopsy Body', the 'Exploded Body', the 'Ligament Man', and the 'Female Arterial Bone Body'. Legally dehumanized yet displayed as sexually enhanced icons of human activity, the plastinated figures have been equipped with phantasmic identities "through a fusion of aesthetics and medical diagnostics" (Seremetakis 2001: 127). The anatomically bared bodies are variously dissected to reveal specific biological functions: the nervous system, the digestive tract, the circulatory system, and the respiratory apparatus. What is shown is the "human being as a construct" (Budde 1997: 11). Instrumentalized and objectified, these "nameless figures," as Hagens asserts, come on stage with "a decisive purpose," as "objects of knowledge" (in Fonseca 1999: 44; see also Hagens 1997: 207, 214). Within this operational scheme, in which the body is recognizable only as an apparatus, a system, or a tract, the dead are posed as task-oriented action figures. The installations attempt to create a functional death.

The curator, Gunther von Hagens, "wants to extract as much 'didactic profit' from the dead as possible" (*Frankfurter Rundschau* 1997: 22), to make the dead "serve an instrumental purpose" (Eberhardt 1997: 18). In this anatomical museum, the dead can be "disposed of" in "a meaningful way" (Vorpahl 1997: 8), because they are "used for educational ends" (Hagens 1997: 207). By such a "productive use" of the deceased, some additional benefit can be extracted from their bodies (Eberhardt 1998b: 40). But this "postmortem exhibitionism" (Rothschild 1998: 3), as it was called by the German media, operates rather more like a postmortem recycling procedure, a commercial enterprise that we recognize on principle from the Nazi era, which, in its horrifying dimensions, should have been burned into historical memory. The aspects of this venture that resonate with National Socialism include the attempts to profit from corpses, the recycling of the dead and their body parts, and the medical exploits with racialized human material.

According to Hagens, "the plastinated specimens ... are no longer objects of mourning, but instructional objects ... to remain useful even beyond death" (in Eberhardt 1997: 18). Through medical intervention, he asserts, the dead body undergoes "a shift in value from a useless corpse to a useful, aesthetically instructive ... plastinated specimen" (Hagens 1997: 215). This rational economy, which simultaneously devalues and reclaims value by recycling and which aims to extract surplus value from the bodies of the dead, was rarely acknowledged in German public discussions. And yet it is part of a cultural logic, a capitalist mode of thinking, whereby historical consciousness is repressed in favor of an instrumental rationality: not only the living but also the dead must be usefully productive. According to the exhibitor, compassion is an "intrusive" factor, a "digressive" obstacle, in this enterprise, for "mourning would interfere with learning" (ibid.: 203–207, 214).

The Global Traffic in Corpses

In this world of purposive rationality, anatomy and pedagogy, economy and medical science, pornography and consumer capitalism, and pathology and the state's denial of human rights are closely intertwined. In Germany, however, these linkages have been ignored for a long time. After the launch of the first Body Worlds exhibit, it took nearly a decade to uncover the origin of the plastinated specimens. Contrary to the exhibitor's claims, the corpses were not bequeathed by German donors. Research conducted by German journalists, complete with photographs, documents, and bank account transactions, exposes "an extensive trade in corpses," "a global enterprise that in near to industrial fashion utilizes and recycles dead human beings and their individual body parts" (*Der Spiegel* 2004a: 5). According to these investigative reports, the bodies were procured from Russia, Kyrgyzstan, and China (*Der Spiegel* 2004a; Schmidt 2004). "The dead," as Michael Sappol (2005) points out, who are "conscripted to perform for the amusement of the living," are obtained "from places where human rights are precariously non-existent and bioethical standards are not enforced—such as China and the central Asian former republics of the Soviet Union—and who therefore cannot honestly meet any ethical standard of informed consent." An inspection of the exhibitor's body factory in Dalian (China), where corpses are skinned and prepared for later use, reveals the inhumanity of this enterprise: "a truck unloads 27 dead men and 4 women, still fully clothed"; there are "647 corpses," "blood-drenched … stacked in piles," "some with bullet holes in their heads," and, moreover, "3,909 body parts, such as legs, hands, or penises, and 182 fetuses, embryos, and newborns, all catalogued with serial numbers by size, age, and sex" (*Der Spiegel* 2004b: 8). According to the inquiry's findings, some of the bodies derive from the purchase of executed Chinese prisoners (*Der Spiegel* 2004b, 2004c).

This business with corpses, a multi-million dollar enterprise, calls into question the exhibit's legitimacy. By remodeling the corpses to embody a Western European racial aesthetic, the exhibit conceals the acquisition of bodies from the Third World, from "the mentally ill, impoverished, and convicted Asians" (Stern 2003: 3). As a result of the exhibit's representational strategies, concerns about human rights abuses and victimhood appear less salient. But the purported 'art of anatomy', with its sanitized installations and clinical exposition, is in reality founded on a violent capitalism with human victims, whose bodies are sold and bought for profit. Not surprisingly, the exhibit stages a dehistoricized morphological landscape, wherein corpses are shown without memory and without compassion—as timeless artistic figures.

Such optical regimes, those vistas of visuality, which amputate emotions and remembrance in favor of recycling death, are characteristic of attempts to purge a violent history from memory. Given this context, it is not surprising that the German exhibit of corpses has remained silent about the historical trajectories of Nazi anatomy lessons. The curator, Gunther von Hagens, defines his work by detour to Renaissance art rather than fascist aesthetics (Linke 2005, 2006a, 2006b, 2009). In Germany, the public intimacy with corpses is indicative of a psychic economy which, with the return of the repressed, simultaneously moves in an eroticized void of remembering and forgetting.

Unlike the mummy, the embalmed body, or the venerated relic, the exhibit's plastinated corpses are supposed to be self-referential or auto-iconic—emptied of social meaning, emptied of symbolic content, and devoid of empathic appeal. The German museological management of the corpses presents an antithesis to the performative efficacy of the "political lives of dead bodies," as Katherine Verdery (1999) phrased it. Voided of representational, evocative power with regard to memory and history, the corpses signify a form of death that lacks emotional significance and political cosmology. Indeed, by annulling the humanity of the corpses, the German state distances itself from the exhibit and thereby denies moral accountability. In this human museum, dead bodies are *not* "a site of political profit" (ibid.: 33). The corporal displays, as shown here, have been invested with different meanings. Sanitized of death and violence, they conceal a history of victimization. Contact with mutilated corpses, previously evocative of war and genocide, has been rendered safe in the cocooned space of the anatomical museum.

Acknowledgments

This chapter emerges from a larger project concerning the politics of dehumanization and the political technology of the senses in capitalist states (see Linke 2003, 2005, 2006a, 2006b, 2009). Texts originally in German have been translated by the author.

Uli Linke is Professor of Anthropology at the Rochester Institute of Technology. Her principal areas of interest include the political anthropology of the body, visual culture, violence and genocide, and the politics of memory and suffering. She has conducted extensive fieldwork in Europe, with long-term projects in Germany. Linke has held academic positions at the University of Toronto, the Central European University in Budapest, Rutgers University, and the University of Tübingen, Germany. Her major publications include *Cultures of Fear* (2009, co-editor), *Blood and Nation* (1999), *German Bodies* (1999), and *Denying Biology* (1996, co-editor). She has written numerous essays and articles for scholarly journals, including recently "The Limits of Empathy" (2009) and "Contact Zones: Rethinking the Sensual Life of the State" (2006). Her current projects include border militarism and the black male body in contemporary Europe.

References

Ahrens, Peter. 2003. "Event-Anatomie mit Erektion." *Tageszeitung*, 30 August, 25.
Arts & Faith. 2005. "Body Worlds—von Hagens Plastination Exhibit," *Arts & Faith*, July. http://artsandfaith.com (accessed June 2006).
Assheuer, Thomas. 2003. "Die Olympiade der Leichen." *Die Zeit* 35 (Feuilleton), 21 August. http://www.zeit.de/2003/35/K_9arperwelten (accessed February 2007).
Barnouw, Dagmar. 1996. *Germany 1945: Views of War and Violence.* Bloomington: Indiana University Press.
Bauer, Axel W. 1997. "Anatomie und Öffentlichkeit—ein bioethischer Problemfall?" Pp. 195–200 in Landesmuseum für Technik und Arbeit in Mannheim and Institut für Plastination 1997.
Becker, Jürgen. 1999. "Zugriff auf die Biomasse." *Tageszeitung*, 11 October, 15.
Bennett, Tony. 1994. "The Exhibitionary Complex." Pp. 123–154 in *Culture, Power, History*, ed. Nicholas B. Dirks, Geoff Eley, and Sherry B. Ortner. Princeton, NJ: Princeton University Press.
Budde, Kai. 1997. "Der sezierte Tote—ein schreckliches Bild?" Pp. 11–28 in Landesmuseum für Technik und Arbeit in Mannheim and Institut für Plastination 1997.
Clewing, Ulrich. 1998. "Schneller Altern im Ideenkorsett." *Tageszeitung*, 7 September, 16.
Dean, Carolyn J. 2005. *The Fragility of Empathy after the Holocaust.* Ithaca, NY: Cornell University Press.
Der Spiegel. 1997. "Ausstellungen: Stachel im Fleisch." *Der Spiegel*, 6 October, 212–214.
______. 1998 "Mut zur Todesnähe." *Der Spiegel*, 31 August, 182–185.
______. 2004a. *Dr. Tod: Die horrenden Geschäfte des Leichen-Schaustellers Gunther von Hagens*, ed. Stefan Aust. *Der Spiegel*, 19 January.
______. 2004b. "Leichenhandel: Neue Vorwürfe gegen Leichen-Plastinator." *Der Spiegel*, 24 January, 8.

______. 2004c. "Leichen ohne Totenschein." *Der Spiegel* 10, 1 March, 56.

Dijck, José van. 2005. *The Transparent Body*. Seattle: University of Washington Press.

Drcharles. 2006. "Body Worlds." *The Examining Room of Dr. Charles*, March. http://drcharles.blogspot.com/2006/03/body-worlds.html (accessed June 2006).

Eberhardt, Johanna. 1997. "Leichen im Sinne des Gesetzes?" *Frankfurter Rundschau*, 17 December, 18.

______. 1998a. "'Körperwelten' sind Magnet." *Frankfurter Rundschau*, 21 July, 32.

______. 1998b. "Sie wollen nicht unsterblich, sondern nur nützlich sein." *Frankfurter Rundschau*, 18 February, 40.

Eggebrecht, Harald. 1998. "Mehr als nur Haut und Knochen." *Süddeutsche Zeitung*, 17 January, 1.

Emmrich, Michael. 1998. "Sich selbst begreifen." *Frankfurter Rundschau*, 28 February, 6.

Fonseca, Liselotte Hermes da. 1999. "Wachsfigur—Mensch—Plastinat." *Deutsche Vierteljahresschrift für Literaturwissenschaft und Geistesgeschichte* 73, no. 1: 43–68.

Frankfurter Rundschau. 1997. "Über das Sterben." *Frankfurter Rundschau*, 22 November, 22.

______. 1998a. "'Körperwelten' waren Magnet fürs Publikum." *Frankfurter Rundschau*, 3 March, 33.

______. 1998b. "Die Leichenshow," *Frankfurter Rundschau*, 16 April, 8.

Hagens, Gunther von. 1997. "Der plastinierte Mensch." Pp. 201–216 in Landesmuseum für Technik und Arbeit in Mannheim and Institut für Plastination 1997.

______. 2004. "On Gruesome Corpses, Gestalt Plastinates, and Mandatory Interment." Pp. 260–282 in Hagens and Whalley 2004.

Hagens, Gunther von, and Angelina Whalley, eds. 2004. *Body Worlds: The Anatomical Exhibition of Real Human Bodies*. Heidelberg: Institut für Plastination.

HAI-Lights. 2004 "'Nackte Nächte' in Frankfurt." *HAI-Lights: Die Stadtzeitung*. http://www.hailights.de/0604/buehne.html (accessed June 2006).

Herscovitch, Penny. 2003. "Anatomy: Rest in Plastic." *Science* 299, no. 5608: 828.

Hessel, Andrew. 2005. "Death as Design." *Mungbeing* 6: 31. http://www.mungbeing.com/issue_6.html?page=31#513 (accessed June 2006).

Hinton, Alexander Laban, ed. 2002. *Genocide: An Anthropological Reader*. Oxford: Blackwell.

______. 2005. *Why Did They Kill?* Berkeley: University of California Press.

Horkheimer, Max, and Theodor W. Adorno. 1981. "Interesse am Körper." Pp. 276–281 in *Dialektik der Aufklärung*. Frankfurt am Main: Suhrkamp.

Jespersen, T. Christine, Alicita Rodríguez, and Joseph Starr, eds. 2008. *The Anatomy of Body Worlds*. Jefferson, NC: McFarland Press.

Knür, Deborah. 2003. "Leichenschau im Blitzlichtgewitter." *Die Welt*, 30 August. http://www.welt.de/data/2003/08/30/161550.html (accessed June 2006).

Köhler, Otto. 2003. "Der Hamburger Totentanz." *Ossietzky: Zweiwochenschrift für Politik/Kultur/Wirtschaft* 19. http://sopos.org/aufsaetze/3f6b79819b138/1.phtml (accessed June 2006).

Kopp, Eduard. 2003. "Kommentar: Mit dem Leichenwagen zur Ausstellung 'Körperwelten'." *Chrismon*, 1 September. http://www.chrismon.de/ctexte/cmeldungen/01sep03_plastination.html (accessed June 2006).

Kriz, Wilhelm. 1997. "Einführung." Pp. 9–10 in Landesmuseum für Technik und Arbeit in Mannheim and Institut für Plastination 1997.

Landesmuseum für Technik und Arbeit in Mannheim and Institut für Plastination, eds. 1997. *Körperwelten: Einblicke in den menschlichen Körper*. Heidelberg: Institut für Plastination.

Lethen, Helmut. 1994. *Verhaltenslehren der Kälte*. Frankfurt am Main: Suhrkamp.

Linke, Uli. 1999. *German Bodies*. New York: Routledge.

______. 2002. "Archives of Violence." Pp. 229–271 in *Annihilating Difference*, ed. Alexander L. Hinton. Berkeley: University of California Press.

______. 2003 "Volks—Körper—Kunde." Pp. 65–94 in *Unterwelten der Kultur*, ed. Kaspar Maase and Bernd Jürgen Warneken. Cologne: Böhlau.

______. 2005. "Touching the Corpse." *Anthropology Today* 21, no. 5: 13–19.

______. 2006a. "Art for Art's Sake?" *Anthropology Today* 22, no. 6: 23.

______. 2006b. "Theatrum anatomicum." Pp. 140–182 in *Verführerische Leichen—Verbotener Verfall*, ed. Liselotte Hermes da Fonseca and Thomas Kliche. Berlin: Pabst Science Publishers.

______. 2009. "The Limits of Empathy." Pp. 147–191 in *Genocide: Truth, Memory, and Representation*, ed. Alexander L. Hinton and Kevin L. O' Neill. Durham, NC: Duke University Press.

McGuffin Foundation. 2004. "Barbarei in Scheiben." *Kassiber der McGuffin Foundation—Sektion Hamburg* 1: 1–10. http://www.antifa-hamburg.com/erklaerungen/mcguffin0104new.pdf (accessed June 2006).

Mirzoeff, Nicholas. 2005. *Watching Babylon*. New York: Routledge.

Nissen, Klaus. 1998. "Anatomie nach Mitternacht." *Frankfurter Rundschau*, 27 February, 36.

Pressemitteilungen. 2004. "Frankfurt unterbindet 'Nackte Nächte'." *Gunther von Hagens Körperwelten—Pressemitteilungen*, 28 May. http://www.körperwelten.de/de/pages/Pressemitteilungen_FFM_4.asp (accessed June 2006).

Reimer, Ulf. 1998. "Nächtliche Wallfahrt zu den Toten." *Süddeutsche Zeitung*, 2 March, 1, 2.

Roth, Jürgen. 1998. "Body Counts." *Konkret* 4 (April): 50–52.

Rothschild, Markus. 1998. "Das nennt man 'postmortalen Exhibitionismus'." *Tageszeitung*, 8 October, 3.

Sappol, Michael. 2005. "Why the Dead Are a Killer Act." *Los Angeles Times*, 12 June.

Sass, Roxy. 2004. "Sometimes All I Want from a Man Is His Bone—and Organs." *Stanford Daily-Online Edition*, 5 November. http://daily.stanford.edu/tempo?page = content&id = 15190&repository = 0001_article (accessed June 2006).

Sauer, Stefan. 2000. "Ein Geschäft auf Kosten der Toten: Ein Interview mit Günter Wallraff." *Kölner Stadt-Anzeiger*, 18 February. http://www.guenter-wallraff.com/ausstellungkorpe.html (accessed June 2006).

Schmidt, Thomas E. 2004. "Party der Plastinate." *Die Zeit*, 22 January. http://zeus.zeit.de/text/2004/05/Spitze_5 (accessed February 2006).

Schmitz, Helmut. 1997. "… was die Welt im Innersten zusammenhält." *Frankfurter Rundschau*, 12 November, 8.

Seremetakis, C. Nadia. 2001. "Toxic Beauties." *Social Text* 68: 115–129.

Smith, Orla. 2003. "Nota Bene: Anatomy." *Science* 299, no. 5608: 829.

Spiegel Online. 2004. "Körperwelten: Frankfurt verbietet von Hagens nackte Nächte." *Spiegel Online*, 28 May. http://www.spiegel.de/panorama/0,1518,302055,00.html (accessed June 2006).

Stern, Megan. 2003. "Shiny, Happy People: 'Body Worlds' and the Commodification of Health." *Radical Philosophy* 118 (March/April). http://www.radicalphilosophy.com/default.asp?channel_id = 2187&editorial_id = 11213 (accessed June 2006).

Treffpunkt-Ethik. 2004. "Geil auf Tote?" *Treffpunkt-Ethik.de*. http://www.treffpunkt-ethik.de/foren/post1.asp?id = 10305 (accessed June 2006).

Verdery, Katherine. 1999. *The Political Lives of Dead Bodies: Reburial and Postsocialist Change*. New York: Columbia University Press.

Vorpahl, Annette. 1997. "Der Tank für den Elefanten steht bereit." *Frankfurter Rundschau*, 25 October, 8.

Walter, Tony. 2004. "Body Worlds: Clinical Detachment and Anatomical Awe." *Sociology of Health and Illness* 26, no. 4: 464–488.

Whalley, Angelina. 1997. "Der menschliche Körper—Anatomie und Funktion." Pp. 49–194 in Landesmuseum für Technik und Arbeit in Mannheim and Institut für Plastination 1997.

Wolbert, Klaus. 1982. *Die Nackten und die Toten des "Dritten Reiches"*. Giessen: Anabas-Verlag.

Zoschke, Barbara. 1994. "Qual des letzten Willens." *Tageszeitung*, 13 April, 12.

Chapter 6

The Symbolic Body and the Rhetoric of Power

LAURA VERDI

It is becoming increasingly difficult to relate our forms of shared knowledge (social representations) to wide-ranging, if not long-lasting, symbolic and cultural universes. In many cases, the current crisis of the political model of democracy makes it very arduous, perhaps even impossible, to understand the extent to which these representations are the effect of an omnipervasive logic of spectacularization or, rather, new mythologies and passions elaborated according to a bottom-up rather than top-down logic, as most past history reminds us. The democratic model—never wholly implemented as the direct government of the people, but instead historically achieved through a representative system of empowerment—has been able to co-exist with the model of the nation-state, which incorporates the image of a law sovereignly exerted from above.

References for this chapter begin on page 114.

Lately, the crisis has intensified under the effect of telecommunication networks: their planetary diffusion has questioned and discredited the classic democratic model by introducing and spreading models that are more directly participatory. Capable of global visibility, cultural codes are used nowadays to express a form of 'liquid power'. Banking on empathy and affectivity, digital cultures allow cybernauts to enter public space directly and, through new virtual communities and urban tribes, enable them to participate in 'communicracy', as Susca and De Kerckhove (2008) call it, following in the track of Bauman's (2000) 'liquid modernity'—as if, from the organic solidarity model of modernity, we were returning to mechanical solidarity, not to mention Durkheim (1893). Individuals are once again gathered by their likeness, and the individual personality is absorbed into the collective personality. The aura of the tribe is re-created, with symbols, affects, and information being circulated and shared. Destined to dissolve in the immediacy of the *hic et nunc*, it is a form of horizontal sharing that does not imply the vertical, diachronic dimension. Also, it does not contemplate ideals to be achieved in the long term through repeated participation and political commitment. It creates new idols to consume, as if in cannibal rites; new kings' bodies to be transformed into symbols; new spaces in which to share emotions that have increasingly less to do with the spaces of everyday living and solidarity and increasingly more to do with virtuality. And yet we are still under the influence of a political and thus vertically exercised power, even if it arouses our enthusiasm less and less and can hardly stimulate our imagination. Here, indeed, lies the paradox of this effervescence, which reveals itself to be a 'nascent state' (Alberoni 1968) of digital more than political power. Here, no groups or movements with shared social goals are formalized; rather, an inner solidarity is created that is destined to dwindle when the network that links the members of the digital tribe— and with it 'communicracy'—dissolves.

However, in digital tribes, as in traditional communities, that which underlies interaction and the meaning of human relationships is always the body. It is the first object of observation and imitation through art, but also the first measure of space and the first form of active and passive power. It exerts power and suffers it through the construction of symbolic apparatuses, and it is soon distinguished into the physical body and the political-symbolic body.

The social perception of the body is always changing, diachronically and synchronically, according to the time and space where the body is inscribed, taking on different valences in the social. Within a more historicist than idealistic or materialistic-dialectic view, however, a background option emerges: the irreducibility of the 'mental equipment' of both traditional and contemporary societies. This notion has its roots in an almost motionless conception of history, often marked by the 'mental prisons' described by the historian Fernand Braudel (1963). It is from these premises and from the analysis of the contradictions that the body encounters, through the attempts of rationalization and imposition of social control, that I will discuss the body as an instrument of both active and passive political and aesthetic power and the processes of its social construction.

I will start with the image of *Corpus Mysticum Christi*—that is, the Christian belief that considers all of Christendom to be a holy, mystical body of Christ—as the metaphoric organizational structure of consensus to power from the Low Middle Ages to the early Modern Age. I will then move to the body as represented by present-day celebrities in show business and politics, who can well illustrate how the rhetorical exemplum enacted from time to time makes use of charisma. From classically conceived "concentrated stardom," which gives the star (*divus*) his or her extraordinariness and peculiarity of personal charisma, the shift is toward a conception of "diffused stardom" (Kermol and Tessarolo 1998: 136), in which charisma tends to generalize when the mechanisms of role separation weaken (Rein, Kotler, and Stoller 1987). Both models are given an aesthetic meaning and become images of power as an instrument of social control and rhetorical amplification. And so the charisma concentrated in the body of the thaumaturgical kings becomes charisma that is learned through exercises and behaviors and is then spread through the media to get visibility, as we will see below.

The Reasons of the Body

In bringing the body to reason, we address the root cause of the centuries-long focus on the body, which has attracted the interest of every type of society, from the most puritanical to the most liberal, simply because the body has reasons that reason often ignores. The discourse on the body has developed through all possible means: dialectical and philosophical, theological and medical, artistic and dietetic. However, it has oftentimes been a war waged against the body by other reasons (state, religion, health, etc.) to such an extent that even today a large part of the so-called advanced West has not yet resolved, if not in an extreme way, the *querelle* between the body and the mind, formerly between the body and the spirit. This *querelle* can be interpreted as the first example of social control exerted on the body through the mind. In history, however, opposite cases can be found whereby different value systems (usually seen by others as deviant) pertained. Removing the body from the subjugation of the mind and from mechanisms of social control has always meant giving unbounded satisfaction to body drives, as was the case in medieval heretical communities.

Today, the body is known to be, first of all, sexed and seeking to assert itself from either a male or female standpoint. It has also a gender, which is not so well defined by innate characteristics but rather is socially and culturally constructed—that is to say, it is defined through a weakening or strengthening of its sexed identity as a result of social roles, language, and behaviors. From Plato onward, a conflict has also arisen between 'geographically' distant parts of the same individual: the head and the belly, subsequently represented as the spirit (later as the mind) and the body, with the former nearer to heaven and thus more noble, and the latter nearer to earth and thus more prone to guilt. This corresponds with the different cultural perception of the body, the twofold meaning—semantic, as well—that both the Greeks and the Romans gave to the opposing pairs σῶμα/δέμας and *corpus/anima* (i.e., dead body/live body). In other words, like *bios* (the living being in its empiric individuality), which is inescapably tied to temporality and destined to structure itself through the body, the *soma* (the single specific form of life)—as opposed to *zoè*, which indicates life as a physical phenomenon—alludes to the vitality expressed and manifested in all organic beings. *Zoè* indicates life *qua vivimus* (*by which* we live), while *bios* signifies life *quam vivimus* (*that* we live) (Melchiorre 1989).

Defined by Descartes as the opposition between *res extensa* and *res cogitans* (i.e., the world of objects and the world of those who think of them), the *querelle* over the body was destined to arouse heated polemics within the very culture that, together with Greek classicism, was its source. The Platonic idea of the body as the prison of the spirit, as folly and, in a wider sense, denial of all values, has remained rooted in Western thought as an enduring, disjointing thought. The mind-body opposition—seemingly overcome by modernity and already forgotten by postmodernity—surfaces whenever the uncertainty and complexity of our culture bring up questions that we cannot answer. Again, we are unable to cope unless we resort to binary and opposing barriers that, in turn, consider the mind as the origin of rational, positive values and the body as the generator of disvalues.

Classic logic, with its *modus ponens* (which has an insurmountable foundation in the principles of identity, non-contradiction, and excluded middle), does not allow for any respite in our effort to construct a body with its own reasons, emotions, and feelings—a body that is not heteronomous but has its own power, one that is non-conflictual with the power of the mind. In Greek and, later, Latin thinking, knowledge is acquired by understanding causes, and the cause of the existence of the body, the *causa prima*, could only be God. Seventeenth-century deism, for instance, maintained that the universe had been deterministic from its creation: God may have started the process but had no further influence on subsequent events, which were determined by the cause-effect chain. Hence, the construction of a unilinear logic, far from supplying satisfactory cosmological justifications, was soon to lead to metaphysics. Only modern scientific thinking, in its rationalism, was then able to conceive the notion of an order to the universe in which a man, composed of both body and spirit, could finally act on nature to his own advantage. However, the anthropocentric rationalistic model, inaugurated in the Renaissance by demanding that the body be given back its own centrality, had to co-exist with models of social and pulsional control put forward by the Christian religion to bring the body to reason. Suffice it to recall the outbreak of Inquisition folly against witches, Jews, heretics, and Moors in the midst of the Renaissance (cf. Verdi 1980).

The body, then, is memory of the law (Galimberti 1983: 185), which expresses itself through marking, sexual differentiation, and the artificial creation of needs and desires—so much so that we could say that "the law cannot exist without bodies ... in the sense that without bodies the law would have no instincts to deviate from, no pleasures to postpone, no manifestations to repress" (ibid.:

212; see also Verdi 1991). However, the law is exactly what makes the *physical* body a living *social* body (Husserl [1931] 1950), giving life to those 'mental prisons' (Braudel 1963) that engender dichotomous conceptions of history (traditional societies/modern societies), which can be resolved only through huge changes in mentality. These same changes have generated new cultural models that have been widely addressed in the anthropological and then sociological literature (Benedict [1934] 1946), while the issue of collective attitudes toward great events is considered central by historians besides Braudel (e.g., Alberto Tenenti, Philippe Ariès, Pierre Chaunu, Michel Vovelle) and by scholars leaning toward historical anthropology (e.g., Carl Schmitt) who have analyzed the role of the body as a collective image.

The King's Two Bodies and the Metaphor of Power

Husserl's ([1931] 1950) distinction between the two models of the body—the mortal one that perishes with death (*Körper*) and the social, political one (*Leib*) that is made imperishable through the heightening of the space-temporal sense horizons—is the same as Kantorowicz's (1957) well-known distinction between the king's 'two bodies'. According to this notion, "a king is something more than his mere body; it is an imaginary presence in which the whole social body can recognize itself" (Furet 1997). Actually, as Ornaghi (1996) explains, "the theory of the king's two bodies is the main point of junction between the medieval community and the modern territorial state: similarly to how the former finds its collective body identity in the *ecclesia Christi* (church of Christ), the latter can replace it based on the new collective identification that can be found in the sovereign's body. Here, the thaumaturgical practices described by Marc Bloch … find their intrinsic justification: so that the monarch can be the body of the entire community he must arouse—as Kantorowicz himself says— a 'semi-religious emotion', like the one produced in the presence of a sovereign who is himself 'God's anointed.'"

Likewise, it appears credible that "the image of *Corpus Mysticum Christi* provided the fundamental metaphoric structure around which the consensus to power organized itself from the Low Middle Ages to the early Modern Age. In other words, the formula of the king's two bodies is the lay version of an ecclesiastical principle to which, in a transfigured way, jurists and writers resorted to guarantee the territorial state an everlasting *dignitas*, which 'will never die' … Indeed, what makes the theories on the political body obsolete will be the subsequent process of juridical abstraction through which the dignity of the *persona ficta* will be directly reserved, without bodily mediations, to the state as an artificial construction" (Ornaghi 1996). The sovereign's political body, a kind of *deus absconditus* (hidden god) within his physical body, is destined to dissolve inside the structures of the modern state. It becomes the 'total social fact' that Mauss (1923–1924) talked about.

Contemporary social systems can even "dream of and program the total takeover of their members' bodies … The socialization process does not have theoretical limits, only those of the body and of the flesh" (Pozzi 1994: 121). The social control, which Parsons's (1987) sociology assigns to centers of power and institutional sources that neglect a social body endowed with heavy bodies, carried by social actors understood as individuals, is no longer issued by a single recognizable source but rather by a plurality of sources. And so the outcome is what Pozzi (1994: 123) describes as a paradoxical result, as regards the disappearance of the mono-referential figure of the king: "In turn, the social is forced to mobilize massive structures and processes to hold at bay and bring to reason what it itself produces when it invests the bodies with sociality. This is a further ironic contradiction of the social that reflects again on the social."

Sociology keeps a prudent distance from such points of view, preferring a perspective that presents the body as abstract, if not as a pure organism (Pozzi 1994: 117). The great exception of the nineteenth century was certainly Simmel, who started his exploration of the body from the tangible image of things and thus referred to the unity of the individual in which body and soul are indivisible. With respect to the disorderly and chaotic instances expressed by the body and to its substantial asymmetry, the soul acts as a unifying principle through law, harmony, and symmetry. And so Flaubert's aphorism, 'Le bon Dieu est dans le détail' (which was later taken up by Warburg and his school), was also valid for Simmel (1985: 27). However, sociology seems to forget that the social appears as the dimension of the political-social-experiential body (*Leib*) and not the natural individual body (*Körper*), which is mortal and unrepeatable. The power of the former over the latter thus seems to be irreducible.

It is exactly starting from here that an attempt can be made to approach the complex reasons that, for 2,000 years, have guided figurative art along such diverse routes in the representation of the body subjected to social control. The example I will use is drawn from the Christian iconography of the body of Christ and of the saints. My goal is to review some of the steps that, from the first moment of construction and social control of the body as anti-physical body (and therefore as social body), originally divine (Christ's), led to the subsequent creation of a *deus absconditus* (sovereign) and ultimately to the state.

Holy Schizophrenia

We will need to return to the notion of *Corpus Mysticum Christi* mentioned above in order to try to understand the meaning that figurative art has given to this body, at once human and divine, which lives, dies, and is resurrected. Above all, we will try to understand how the Christological model has been the key to, and at the same time the origin of, the social and artistic representability of a suffering but paradoxically powerful body.

In the Middle Ages, *De Imitatione Christi* (The Imitation of Christ) became the principal exemplum, both in religious literature and in iconography. As such, it was constructed top down, starting with the Edict of Milan (AD 313), which gave Christians the freedom of professing their religion, and the Edict of Thessalonica (AD 380), which recognized Christianity as the official state religion of the Roman Empire. Flagrantly violating the faith's evangelical precepts, the temporal power of the Pope was theocratically exercised in an increasingly marked way (not as a means of autonomy but as a goal) for 1,500 years until 20 September 1870, when the Aurelian Walls were breached at Porta Pia and the Italian army subsequently captured the Vatican State.

However, if *De Imitatione Christi* was the exemplum, it was fairly easily manipulated. Focused on social control and integration and mirroring the widespread fear aroused by the fast approaching Day of Judgment (Delumeau 1987), the exemplum also promoted a millenarian siege mentality that held the ignorant masses of the Middle Ages in its power. Fear resulted in denial of the physical body—now looked on as a source of contamination and deviance (sin) since birth—and inspired belief in the divine precept of mortification to exalt the spirit. The denial of the body, then, involved punishment, flagellation, and mortification of the flesh. In addition, the body of Christ, the optimal model of the body that must suffer to redeem its sins and earn the happiness of Paradise, was increasingly represented as suffering rather than triumphant. It was the body that offered itself in a supreme "total performance of the agonistic type" or "total social fact" (Mauss 1923–1924)—an absolute 'feast' that was the donation of the self in the name of the schizophrenic annihilation of the physical body.

Theology and the interiorized notions of the Christological model were at the origin of the twofold iconography of *Christus triumphans* (triumphant Christ) and *Christus patiens* (suffering Christ). The image of the cross appeared at the end of the fourth century (thus, after the Edict of Milan), first in a bejeweled cross in Santa Pudenziana, a church in Rome, and then on the mosaics of the triumphal arch in Santa Maria Maggiore and on those in the mausoleum of Galla Placidia in Ravenna. The crucifix with the figure of Christ first appeared in the fifth century in Rome's Church of Santa Sabina sull'Aventino, where Jesus, open-eyed and without a nimbus, was placed between the good thief and the bad thief.

In the following centuries, wooden crucifixes also become popular in country churches or along pilgrims' routes as a memento to praying. However, it was from the twelfth century onward that the tradition of painted crucifixes began. On them, Christ was depicted in a frontal position, with his head held high and his eyes open, alive and triumphant over death. *Christus triumphans*, endowed with a social body (*Leib*), was recognized as the unifying *logos*, a far-away deity, alien to the other direct conditions that medieval men were subjected to. This was the king's body in its symbolic and anti-naturalistic form, later to be succeeded by its other form, that of the individual and physical body (*Körper*) in the iconography of *Christus patiens*. Depicted as dead from the thirteenth century, this model of Christ had first a Byzantine and then a Franciscan origin. The figure appeared in agony, his eyes downcast, his body contracted in a painful spasm. In this image of a suffering Christ, 'losing his life drop by drop' (*per stillicidia emittere animam*), lay all the negative power of the exemplum. One of the first of its kind was the lost crucifix by Giunta Pisano for the Basilica in Assisi (1236), which represented the twofold iconography with a cross on both sides. Still preserved to us is the crucifix of San Domenico in Bologna (from about 1250).

Obviously, the study of the origin of the iconography of the body of Christ does not end here. Greenhalgh (1985) examined the use of the social and political body of a triumphant Christ when he addressed the many similarities to the pagan use of the political body of emperors. This correspondence offered "a rich field from which to draw suggestions for the development of Christian ideas. As most iconography of the Roman emperors was generic rather than strictly personal, the same goes also for that used for Christ, who can be portrayed as a learned teacher as well as a god and a king" (ibid.: 168). The scholar made a list of several iconographic coincidences between the body of Christ and that of the Roman emperors, such as the theme of the Resurrection, corresponding to celestial apotheosis, or the triumph of Jesus over Satan in the form of a snake, similar to the image of the emperor who triumphed over his enemies by treading on them (ibid.: 169). All of these coincidences correlate with the model of 'concentrated stardom' mentioned above. However, no correspondences are found in pagan iconography for the theme of Passion, which remains wholly Christian. The symbols of the nimbus, the globe, the Tree of Life, and many others (which have nothing to do with the iconography of the body) are pagan-derived (Verdi 1996: 49). They survived for a few centuries, but they never became equal to the symbol of the crucifix. Ultimately, the great novelty lies in the representation of the sovereign body, the body of religious power, as no longer victorious (as it was with the emperors), but prey to suffering and death.

The Holy Body and the Salvation of the Soul

It is not only in the body of Christ but also in his iconographic simulacrum that Christianity identifies the source of all forms of salvation. However, when the concept is taken back to its original meaning, *salus* ($\sigma\omega\tau\eta\rho\iota\alpha$), it appears again in its semantic duality of both salvation and health. Invested in a cyclic conception of time, the Christian culture identifies itself in the body of Christ through the moment alternative to his death and resurrection, that is, the moment of his birth, which to the eyes of the world represents the hope for redemption. The body of the Divine Infant appears as the originator of a new order and, at the same time, of salvation and health for the social body of Christianity. The formal perfection and freshness of flesh found in the figurative reproduction of that body are forgiven for one reason only—because, despite being divine, it is predestined to suffer and die. This notion is central to the attempt to define a key to the representability of the body that gets to the core of contemporary Western culture. It does not then seem unreasonable to start from here in order to understand the generation of the social body from the physical body—of a carnal, individual body that generates the social one, just as Simmel intended.

Likewise, the exemplum of the body of Christ is followed by that of the saints, who, in the Christian-Catholic theology, represent the intermediation between humankind's insignificance and God's perfection. The integration of the body of the saint into the ecclesial body depends on how far it is removed from the social body. Like the physical body of Christ, that of the saint is also a source of scandal and transgression, of disorder and non-integration. Indeed, it goes against the fundamental (and pagan) precept of *amor sui* (self-love), again launching the obscene image of heroism of the flesh that opposes any project of integration due to the immense and chaotic disorderly strength it has at the symbolic level. This body is the image itself of the paradox of power: the indecent unacceptability of the physical body and its intrinsic violence have as a counterweight the social body, a model to be imitated and venerated, imposed by a power that always wants humans to be heteronomous.

The body of the drawn and quartered, the crucified and the beheaded, the roasted and the stoned, the drowned and the suffocated, the hungry and the sick is the body of total sanctity: in sum, the salvation (*salus*) of the soul is not through health and its deceiving seductions, but rather the consequence of giving up the health (again *salus*) of the body. Therefore, without God there is no possible salvation, but, we can add, without health there is certainty of salvation. In the paradox of the application of the ancient precept of *salus* lies the key that is essential to an understanding of the (figurative-preceptive-didascalic no less than theological) use of the body in Christianity (cf. Verdi 2006).

Actually, the figurative representation of the body is nothing but the other side of the social and mental representations of each epoch, the negotiated and then shared model of knowledge, which makes it a type of a priori category of vision. It is at the base not of our looking but rather of our seeing—that is, the collecting of information that the world affords us through intermediation, made collective but unconscious, or even preconscious, by images. It is that 'visual thinking' (*das bildhafte Denken*) that forms the "archetypal expression of all communicative behaviors," not conceptually or musically formulated, but expressed "as rhythm, proportion, atmosphere, in short … an 'image' not yet embodied in a specific medium," as Dorfles (2000) says, and that precedes the spoken language.

Holy images, in particular, have represented for centuries the exemplum of vision and behavior, the indication and paradigm of action. The body of 'holy anorexics' (Bell 1985), for instance, appears more subjected to social control and conditioned by a symbolic order that denies its natural dimension as a physical body (incorporating it into the social one). As a result, it is more capable of aberrations, renunciations, self-constriction to disgusting rituals, flagellations, the use of the cilice, and other such actions. Therefore, the more a body is physically obliged, the more socially constructed it is; it becomes the subject, one could say, of a rationalized irrational choice. Its cultural meaning, as Geertz (1973) summarizes, is in its use, that is to say, in its being a form of reproduction of a model of power and order and, at the same time, a guarantee of continuity and recognizability. Such a body is perfectly integrated within a social order aiming at *salus* and at the reproduction, yet again, of the mechanisms that perpetuate it. The paradox of the exemplum (at least following the classic Mertonian functionalistic typology) becomes more evident than ever: while on the one hand it puts forward salvation as a goal, on the other it uses every possible means to damage the health of the body. Giving up satisfaction with regard to the physical body leads to the triumph of the social body and its absolute symbolic power within the Christian, in particular Catholic, imaginary.

Let us also not forget the theodicy (vindication of divine goodness) developed by the Scholastic philosophy. Although it stated that when God created the world, He did the best thing of all, it never actually deduced the point that underlay Leibniz's theodicean theory a few centuries later—that ours is the best possible world because it was created by God. Like Boethius ("If God exists whence evil? But whence good if God does not exist?" *De consolatione philosophiae*), Plotinus, and Augustine of Hippo, medieval philosophers did not expect to rationalize the origin and explanation of evil and suffering. Paradoxically, Christ's suffering also remains unexplained and mysterious, the effect of the same inscrutability of the divine will that concerns humankind as a whole.

The body of the saints lends itself to further categorization, recalling a model I have established elsewhere (Verdi 1996) concerning the ever different forms that the body takes on in the history of art, but also in the history of ideas. I believe that it is recognizable in the first and second of five models of the body that I have outlined as follows (ibid.: 55):

> … the *angel-like* body, the *exceptional* body, the *everyday* body, the *deformed* body, the *missing* body. The first is mainly the body of the Paleochristian and Byzantine art up to Gothic art, in other words, the medieval body; the second is the body of deities (by now only Christian), the body of saints and heroes, but also the crazy body that inspired so many, especially northern paintings of the Renaissance, through to Mannerism, the Baroque, and the Age of Enlightenment. The *everyday* body appears with Naturalism and Verism in the nineteenth century, while the *deformed* body is created by the artistic avant-gardes of this century wishing to leave behind quickly Verism and the soppiness of Symbolism. Lastly, the *missing* body did not survive the excesses of its representations—an orgy of portrayals in the new 'anonymous depiction' of advertising—in the contemporary age.

The body of the saints, 'angel-like' or 'exceptional', belongs in any case to the wider category of the denied body, not in its portrayal, but in its health and physical integrity and in its being, once again, a social body that is deprived of a sexed and gendered body identity. To be a fully recognizable model, the body of the saint will always iconographically wear the stigmata of suffering and illness. Able to endure both of them, according to indicators of pain bearability or the threshold of pain (which was very high from the Middle Ages until the Industrial Revolution, which introduced new drugs), the body of the saint became an icon that, alongside the crucifix, accompanied the daily life of believers and was thought to be the way to salvation, if not to health. The body of the saint was petitioned for intercession and healing, miracles and special blessings. The saint was seen as a vicarious deity, closer to humans because he himself was human. In his name, shrines were built and pilgrimages organized, ex-votos were offered, and the monumental construction of the intermediation between God and the world, that is, between the social body and the physical body, which was totally absent in Protestantism, had its beginning.

The Body and the Discomfort of Modernity

At least until the Age of Enlightenment, art agreed with medicine, suggesting to politics the consonance between military and manly virtues. According to the stereotype of manly classicism, moral values were embodied and realized in ideal measures, any variations on which had to be seen as deviance (Mosse 1996). The social body, yet again, was reflected in a powerful and normative male body, both in the iconography of power and in medical theories, like those of Lavater (1803), of the second half of the eighteenth century. Drawing on the connection between Lavater's Christocentric theology and theories of physiognomics, which also gave God the body of a white man, the scholar's postulate of the eighteenth century was born: as Jesus Christ was the ideal man, he must also have been the most handsome. For another hundred years, the perception of the body—the result of widely shared social representations, filtered through painting and sculpture—kept alive the distinction between the holy body and the profane body. This distinction, which had long created very radical categorizations, started fading toward the end of the nineteenth century until it disappeared. As mentioned elsewhere (Verdi 1996), the model of the 'exceptional' body drifted toward the 'everyday' body, which no longer needed religious mediation to find reasons for its own representability.

After the Industrial Revolution, the new division of labor, the introduction of ordinary medical practices in the daily life of an increasingly greater number of people, the changes brought about by the improved eating habits of adults and babies, higher schooling levels, and women's participation in the production processes—all these allowed the body new visibility, which was also due to the now prevalent tendency toward rationalization. In the mid-nineteenth century, the body was represented according to the models and techniques typical of Verism and Naturalism, which reigned in all of the arts. Nudity was no longer looked upon negatively, nor was it removed through the conceit of the natural distance of mythological subjects (Gay 1984). A healthy body did not need to hide behind a sacred body to be portrayed or behind a sick body to become the object of public devotion. From then on, sickness and health became values (or disvalues) to be treated separately. The boundary between the two, however, remained the object of cultural definition.

The 'deformed' bodies created by the nineteenth-century avant-gardes were not simply artists' inventions; they actually responded to the diffusion of a new expressionistic explosion. The deformations reproduced the symptoms of a cultural and social discomfort that was already deeply felt in the first decade of the century and then increased in the wake of the first-ever world wars. Initially through Surrealism and then through an increasingly pervasive abstractionism that resulted in a desperate tendency to the materic and the informal, the image of the body was on its way to the representation (mediated by social construction processes) of the negative. One could indeed wonder if any body at all was contemplated in the imaginary of some artists and authors, or whether it had actually dissolved, along with the hope of recovering it to more human dimensions of life. This question arises vis-à-vis works by Picasso and

Schiele, Dix and Grosz, Dalì and Max Ernst, and many others. Only in the post-war years did that deformed, unrecognizable body reach the apex of its non-being, through the excess of being, of overexhibition through the amplifying mechanisms first of the mass media and then of the new media. By then, artists such as Frida Kahlo, Fernando Botero, Hans Hartung, Francis Bacon, Alberto Giacometti, Jean Fautrier, and Jean Dubuffet had already been noticed.

The tragedy of 'contemporary man'—destined to live, as Sartre says, with death in his soul in a vacuum crossed by the real—is expressed through bodies that are emaciated, ravaged and corroded, worn out by time and by life. It is indeed here, and not earlier, that the ascending course of overexhibition of the body reaches its climax and the body disappears, behind and within its media simulacra. A prisoner of excess, the body becomes invisible, almost transparent, as a social and symbolic, as well as individual, machine. In advertising, the body is everywhere and nowhere; it towers in the ads as it does on the walls, in the press, and on television. Lastly, the Internet robs the body of its weight, confines it to virtuality, devoid of space and time, because it is immersed in every space and every time all at once. Taking as the categorical imperative the duty of pleasure—"a manifest absurdity," according to Kant (1970: 49; see also Verdi 1991)—or, if we prefer, the duty of being healthy (Ariès 1975, 1977), the body denies death and sickness and disguises its insignificance before them. This view, held by Andy Warhol, Gina Pane, and Louise Bourgeois, is represented by present-day artists Orlan and Stelarc, Marina Abramović, Maurizio Cattelan, and Marc Quinn.

The body takes upon itself the stigmata of a sick and guilty culture, irresponsible but hugely powerful, forgetful and launched at full speed, no longer with goals or limits. Never so visible and at the same time so invisible, art has never understood the body so well. It refuses pain and death in a compulsive and definite way; it does not accept itself in the weakening of old age, as in the mirroring of other bodies that are totally devoid of their sexual markers. The body is a mere wrapper, better if beautiful. It no longer even resorts to *salus* as health but rather to a neurotic health consciousness misunderstood as beauty, which falls prey to extenuating aesthetic rites and to increasingly frequent surgery. Carried out on the body, such surgery removes evidence of the passage of time but also of any form of thought. Body art has—ironically and painfully—increased this neurotic aspect of body-mind schizophrenia by sometimes combining Baroque iconography, medical and computer technology, the theatre, and mass communications, as does the performance artist Stelarc when he challenges the traditional idea of beauty and the Western concept of identity and otherness.

However, at the same time, starting at the end of the twentieth century and continuing into the twenty-first century, a strengthening of the phenomenon that began in the United States at the time of the 'flower power' movement of the late 1960s and early 1970s has now converged into the phenomenon of the New Age movement. The religion-medicine relation that was solid in the Middle Ages but increasingly less so from the Humanism of the Renaissance onward now shows the novel result of a relation between medicine and religion and of a link between physical healing and inner healing (Guizzardi 2004: 151). In this instance, too, an artistic current exists alongside the issues of the body, in relation to an individual's psycho-physical well-being and the evocative potential of the environment on the body.

What is certain is that art (i.e., 'visual thinking') always manages to be the first to grasp and express the changes in communication paradigms and in the formalization of the codes of power, drawing from the development of medicine the manifestation of experiential and research elements that win over ideological and partisan ones. However, the end of the twentieth century has offered the body another instrument of technological expression—one so powerful that it will have an impact on all previous codes.

The New Community Body

Compared to a century ago, we are now happily free from the scandalousness of the physical body-social body union. Thanks to technology, the physical body has been liberated from the power of the social body: the former has been deified in order to make the latter a symbolic object of undisputed media power. In the process, the borders between high and popular culture have disappeared. Technology, still the art of *logos*, has rapidly transformed into what Susca and De Kerckhove (2008), with a delightful neologism, refer to as 'technomagic'. Within new emotional and symbolic ('affectual') communities that lack a project and are removed from the 'social contract', new forms of communication are being created that vibrate and coalesce around the community body. This results in a 'connective intelligence', triggered by the new media.

The crisis of religions and ideologies has sanctioned the success of this knowledge, which is incorporated within communities that find in electronic tribes a new path to an otherwise lost re-enchantment and 'aurization'. According to Susca and De Kerckhove (2008: xi), "the process of technical reproducibility of the work of art has not extinguished … the aura, but rather has displaced … it on the social body. It seems therefore pertinent to view the latter in terms of the 'social divine' proposed by Emile Durkheim." The social body reappears here in the shape of the aurization of new diasporic public spheres, in which, in terms of symbolic power, it has been reinvested. Buoyed by emotional exuberance, cognitive and aesthetic pleasures, and ludic impulses, 'technomagic'—in a concurrence of religiosity, magic, and technology—creates a new social effervescence. Here, the body is the message of the new electronic media. Communion of emotions generates communication, which generates 'communicracies', forms of liquid power. The law of the state gives way to the law of the group.

It is at this point that the rhetorical and symbolic foundations on which the social construction models of the body traditionally rest are turned upside down. No longer built top down, as with the Christological models, they are being redefined as bottom up. In other words, they start from consensus mechanisms that are wholly similar to those of ancient democracies but are now obtained through virtual 'communicracies', nets of associative action and communication that are construed as a community body. There, aesthetic dimensions are still inflecting power relations, as was the case with Barack Obama in the 2008 US presidential campaign. Television stars belong not only to show business but also to the world of politics (Rein, Kotler, and Stoller 1990), and so politicians make their way into show business. The outcome is an ongoing semanticity that produces deification and mythologization. But in 2008, the model was 'diffused stardom' (Kermol and Tessarolo 1998), and so Obama's body (social body) was created by his supporters: during the campaign, a million volunteers, logged in on Obama's Web site, organized more than 75,000 events in the virtual community. Although it is an extraordinary rhetorical medium of global amplification, the Internet still needs to resort to the logic of communities, as did the ancient Christian ecclesia. Once again, it is demonstrated that, beyond the eternal mechanisms of mass removal and sublimation, the social body still needs the physical body in order to exist.

At the same time, taking part in a similarly new yet ancient rhetoric of power, we have made the beauty of the body (forever estranged from universal aesthetic canons) a myth, a normative overarching category that has become a life goal, an essential ingredient of mass pleasantness. The beauty of the body in the mass imaginary ceases being a subjective fact to become social and cultural, but also liquid. The heartless hedonism that Max Weber feared is now at the extreme of rationalization mechanisms. The assignment to this new body paradigm, which could not be further from the idea of the archetype, illusory and deceptive both in the public and private sphere, does not yet accomplish the task of giving sense to the unrepeatable existence of each subject. Such a task goes beyond the capabilities of the virtual physical body, endlessly reproducible like a mechanical doll but unable to give vigor to a new body model. Its political role, above all, too often brings to mind the always seductive Chinese shadows. No better fate has befallen the crucifix, the religious symbol on which I intentionally dwelled so long. Even the body of Christ must paradoxically become equally devoid of sense in order to assume a completely new meaning, this time inscribed in its very invisibility, as the poetic images of Paola Signorelli (figs. 1–3) suggest.

At the same time, more often than not it is the imaginary body that creates the real body, the daily micro-history that affects macro-history, or, to paraphrase Benjamin (1936), "the digital reproducibility of the political that urges the political development of the public" (Susca and De Kerckhove 2008: xii), thus overturning the power relations between the physical and social bodies and questioning the formation mechanisms of the rhetoric of power. In a certain sense, the five body models presented above (Verdi 1996) are not completely outdated, even in a media communications society in which the role of the state loses its centrality, taking second place to virtual communities. The growth of virtual models has resulted in new 'angel-like' bodies, disembodied but not at all 'exceptional', no longer other-directed but not yet self-directed. It also confuses everyday life with a second, virtual life, again 'deforming' the looks of the human body, which has become an icon in a virtuality that mimics reality, going beyond it but not yet resolving it.

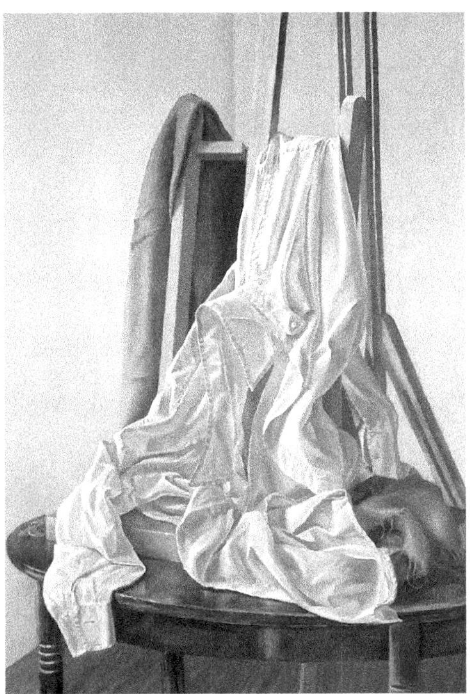

FIGURE 6.1 *Piccola Deposizione* (Small Descent from the Cross). 2007. Oil on canvas. 100 x 70 cm. © Paola Signorelli

"The silence of ordinary, everyday objects suggests a mysterious life of their own outside time ... [they] are bearers of an intelligently formulated and pessimistic message, the leitmotiv of which is the spiritual alienation of modern man."

— *Nicolaas Teeuwisse*

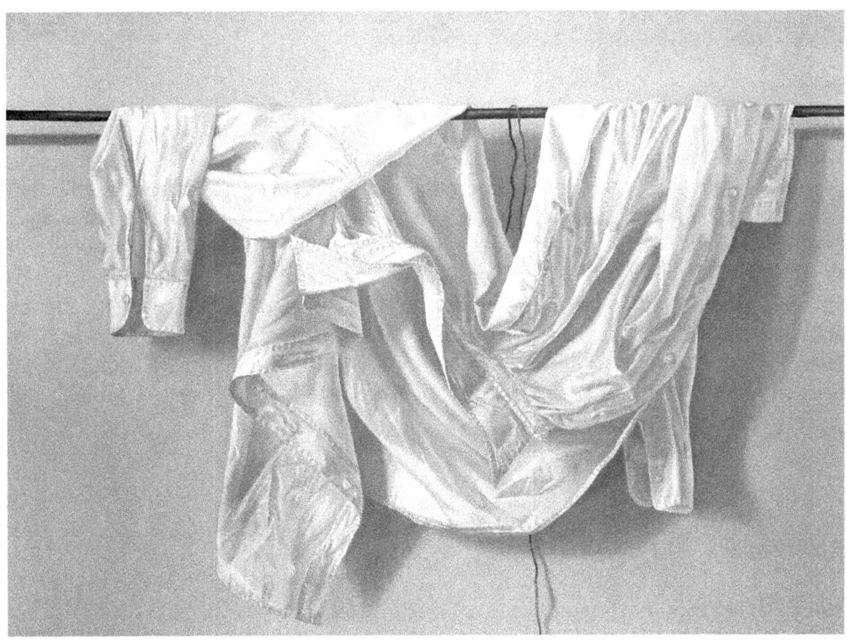

FIGURE 6.2 *Grande Crocifissione II* (Great Crucifixion II). 2006. Oil on canvas. 80 x 120 cm. © Paola Signorelli. "The sensuous beauty of the soft, creased cloth and the clear, vibrant light give the picture a silent, almost metaphysical power and poetry."

— *Nicolaas Teeuwisse*

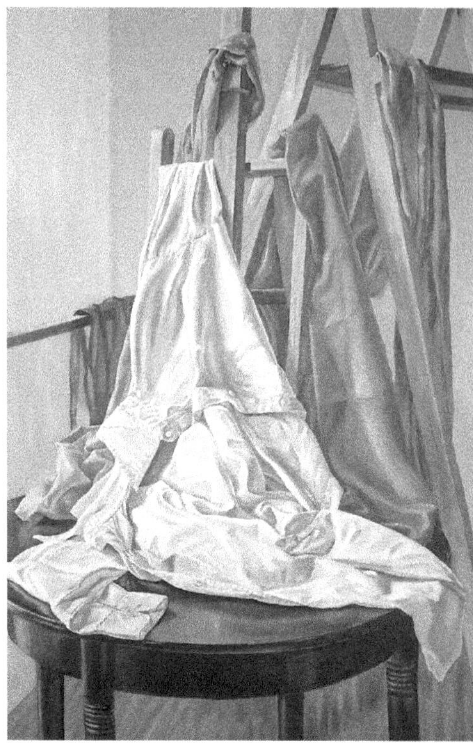

FIGURE 6.3 *Grande Deposizione* (Great Descent from the Cross). 2007. Oil on canvas. 120 x 80 cm. © Paola Signorelli

"This painting offers a world of silence to counter the ubiquitous assaults on our senses by the media ... It is remarkable for its austere monumentalism. It is no coincidence that the composition should be reminiscent of famous prototypes in fifteenth- and sixteenth-century European painting, yet it is also astonishingly unconventional."

— *Nicolaas Teeuwisse*

Laura Verdi is Associate Professor at the Department of Sociology, University of Padua, Italy. Her research topics address especially the sociology of cultural processes (knowledge, music, cinema, popular traditions, social anthropology, etc.) and epistemological questions. She participated in Italy's 2008 National Research Project (PRIN), "Artistic Resources and Cultural Planning," and in the 2007 conference of the Research Network for the Sociology of the Arts at Lüneburg University, "Sustainability: A New Frontier for the Arts and Cultures." A member of several academic associations and societies, her most recent publications include "The Arts and the Future City" (2008), "New Arts for a New Citizenship" (2008), "Tra sociologia ed estetica" (2008), "Arte e società: Il pubblico dell'arte contemporanea" (2009), and "Storia della magrezza" (2009).

References

Alberoni, Francesco. 1968. *Statu Nascenti*. Bologna: Il Mulino.
Ariès, Philippe. 1975. *Essai sur l'histoire de la mort en Occident, du Moyen Age à nos jours*. Paris: Seuil.
______. 1977. *L'Homme devant la mort*. Paris: Seuil.
Bauman, Zygmunt. 2000. *Liquid Modernity*. Cambridge: Polity Press.
Bell, Rudolph M. 1985. *Holy Anorexia*. Chicago, IL: University of Chicago Press.

Benedict, Ruth. [1934] 1946. *Patterns of Culture*. New York: Penguin Books.

Benjamin, Walter. 1936. *Das Kunstwerk im Zeitalter seiner technischen Reproduzierbarkeit*. Paris: Zeitschrift für Sozialforschung.

Braudel, Fernand. 1963. *Le monde actuel: Histoire et civilisation*. Paris: Belin.

Delumeau, Jean. 1987. *Il peccato e la paura: L'idea di colpa in Occidente dal XIII al XVIII secolo*. Bologna: Il Mulino. (Orig. pub. 1983. *Le péché et la peur: La culpabilisation en Occident, XIIIe–XVIIIe siècles*. Paris: Fayard.)

Dorfles, Gillo. 2000. "La sottile differenza tra il folle e l'artista." *Corriere della Sera*, 2 April, 33, 42. http://archiviostorico.corriere.it/2000/aprile/02/sottile_differenza_tra_folle_artista_co_0_0004022877.shtml.

Durkheim, Emile. 1893. *De la division du travail social*. Paris: Alcan.

Furet, François. 1997. "Società borghese, quanto sei fragile!" *Reset: Un mese di idee*, no. 40 (September): 55–63.

Galimberti, Umberto. 1983. *Il corpo*. Milan: Feltrinelli.

Gay, Peter. 1984. *The Education of the Senses*. Oxford: Oxford University Press.

Geertz, Clifford. 1973. *The Interpretation of Cultures*. New York: Basic Books.

Greenhalgh, Michael. 1985. "Iconografia antica e sue trasformazioni durante il Medioevo." Pp. 155–197 in *Memoria dell'antico nell'arte italiana*, vol. 2, ed. Salvatore Settis. Torino: Einaudi.

Guizzardi, Gustavo, ed. 2004. *Star bene: Benessere, salute, salvezza tra scienza, esperienza e rappresentazioni pubbliche*. Bologna: Il Mulino.

Husserl, Edmund. [1931] 1950. *Cartesianische Meditationen und Pariser Vorträge*. Ed. Stephan Strasser. The Hague: Martinus Nijhoff.

Kant, Immanuel. 1970. *Critica del giudizio* [Critique of Judgement]. Roma-Bari: Laterza. (Orig. pub. 1790.)

Kantorowicz, Ernst H. 1957. *The King's Two Bodies: A Study in Medieval Political Theology*. Princeton, NJ: Princeton University Press.

Kermol, Enzo, and Mariselda Tessarolo. 1998. *Divismo vecchio e nuovo: La trasformazione dei modelli di divismo*. Padua: Cleup.

Lavater, Jean G. 1803. *Essai sur la physiognomonie*. Le Haye: n.p.

Mauss, Marcel. 1923–1924. "Essai sur le don: Forme et raison de l'échange dans les sociétés archaïques." *Année sociologique* N.S. 1: 30–186.

Melchiorre, Virgilio. 1989. "Bios, anthropos, ethos." *Studium* 85, no. 1: 19–33.

Mosse, George L. 1996. *The Image of Man: The Creation of Modern Masculinity*. Oxford: Oxford University Press.

Ornaghi, Lorenzo, ed. 1996. *Politica*. Part 1: *Vocabolario*. Milan: Jaca Book.

Parsons, Talcott. 1987. *La struttura dell'azione sociale*. Bologna: Il Mulino. (Orig. pub. 1937. *The Structure of Social Action*. New York: McGraw Hill.)

Pozzi, Enrico. 1994. "Per una sociologia del corpo." *Il corpo*, 1–2 March, 106–144. http://www.enricopozzi.eu/pubblicazioni/ilcorpo/Perunasociologiadelcorpo.pdf.

Rein, Irving, Philip Kotler, and Martin Stoller. 1987. *High Visibility: The Making and Marketing of Professionals into Celebrities*. New York: Dodd, Mead.

Simmel, Georg. 1985. *Il volto e il ritratto: Saggi sull'arte* [The Face and the Portrait: Essays on Art]. Bologna: Il Mulino. (Orig. pub. 1902.)

Susca, Vincenzo, and Derrick De Kerckhove. 2008. *Transpolitica: Nuovi rapporti di potere e di sapere*. Milan: Apogeo.

Verdi, Laura. 1980. *Il regno incantato: Il contesto sociale e culturale della fiaba in Europa*. Padua: Cleup.

_____. 1991. *Il Piacere: Tra storia e società*. Milan: Franco Angeli.

_____. 1996. *Habeas corpus: Figure sociali del corpo*. Milan: Franco Angeli.

_____. 2006. "Corpo sano e corpo salvo: Figure sociali e paradossi dell'arte." *Salute e Società* 1: 88–108; published as a special issue, *Le contraddizioni del corpo: Presenza e simbologia sociale*, ed. Raffaele Rauty. Milan: Franco Angeli.

The Limits of Metaphor

Ideology and Representation in the Zen Garden

ALLEN S. WEISS

The Teramachi shopping mall in Kyoto is the epitome of a certain contemporary vision of Japan: a supercharged, unbridled consumerism couched in an empire of signs. With the exception of its Shinto shrine, the two intersecting streets that constitute this mall consist of storefronts with few decorative touches, other than the mostly inexpensive merchandise on display. However, in this aesthetically bleak environment, one shopkeeper could not resist the centuries-old impulse, typical of Kyoto, to have a small garden at the front of the shop. Such *tsuboniwa*, inspired by the Zen tradition, are small gardens enclosed within an architectural structure (see Katsuhiko 1992, 2002). Nearly every restaurant has such a garden at its entrance. Whether in a courtyard, a storefront, or an alley, just a few square meters suffice. So the shopkeeper in Teramachi designed a sort of *arte povera* garden: a small stone placed alongside a clear bowl of water with plants floating in it, all set on a chair surrounded by six potted plants on the floor, the largest of which has 11 light pebbles set in the soil, and sundry pebbles and large glass beads strewn on a ledge behind (fig. 7.1).[1] This is an ephemeral garden, as it was necessarily dismantled every evening before the shop closed. Moving in its simplicity and frugality, this landscape *bricolage* reveals the minimal conditions of a garden: stone, water, plant. I would

Notes for this chapter are located on page 129.

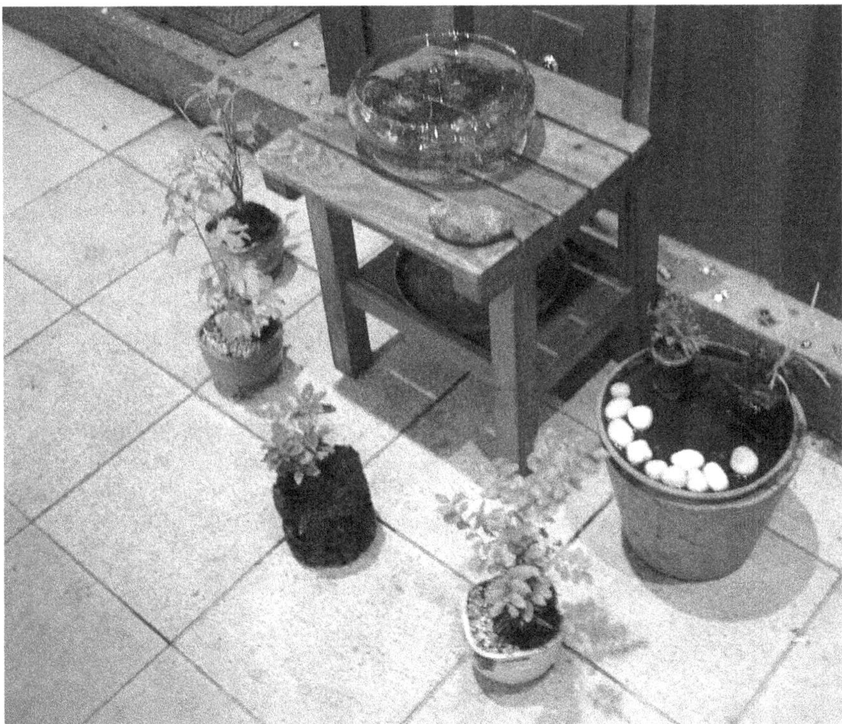

FIGURE 7.1 A shopkeeper's garden in Kyoto

later see, in Zuihō-in, an iconographic source for such a garden: a *bonsai* set between a pottery water basin and a small stand of decorative grass (fig. 7.2). Is this a garden? A metaphor of a garden? A prototype of a garden? Or simply disparate objects related by garden-inspired circumstance?

Material and site, as with form and content, are always already ideologically overdetermined. A narrow storefront (as is the standard in Kyoto), the love of stone and water (as is typical of Zen aesthetics), zoning and safety restrictions (as is the case in every industrialized city), climatic and topographical specifics, and the banal but essential issue of cost: these preconditions always underlie aesthetic choices and iconographic results. What we call 'the state' is the sum total of legal mechanisms that regulate all of these relations. Although Zen is ultimately a form of mysticism, its manifestations are nevertheless fully grounded (in the literal sense of the term) before they become transcendent. The transcendent is situational, and this is perhaps nowhere more evident than in landscape architecture.

One must beware of three major interpretive errors concerning the dry Zen garden (*karesansui*): an anachronistic reading inspired by modernist minimalist aesthetics, a psychologically oriented structural interpretation based on a gestalt figure/ground model, and a confusion of sacred inspiration and material effect. While a garden, painting, poem, or tea bowl may be inspired by Zen, this does not necessarily imply that its use-value is ritualistic or its symbolism theological. In the garden at the Ryōan-ji temple,[2] thresholds serve not as definitive limits or pure barriers, but rather as sites of subtle and often sublime interaction and communication: not concrete figures on grounds, but rather the interpenetration without obstruction that is typical of the Zen experience (see fig. 7.2). In a remark that stresses the essential aspects of representation, miniaturization, and abstraction in the Zen garden, Hannyabo Tessen, an early chief priest of Ryōan-ji, claimed: "Thirty thousand leagues should be compressed into a single foot." The shopkeeper's chair garden in Teramachi might not be extraordinary, but it nevertheless reveals the striking power of the reductive imagination. Perhaps the limit of such abstraction exists in the Myōshin-ji temple complex,[3] where the entrance to one of the buildings is flanked by two absolutely minimal 'gardens'. On the left, a flat square white stone is set into an L-shaped bed of small white pebbles (fig. 7.3), and on the right, a flat black irregular stone is set into a rectangular I-shaped bed of small white pebbles (fig. 7.4). This arrangement offers a complex set of oppositions: L/I, double rectangle/single rectangle, white/black, white-on-white/black-on-white, regular/irregular, thin/thick, smooth/scored. Is this hyperminimal play of binary oppositions mere decoration? Or rather the zero-degree garden? Or perhaps a three-dimensional conceptualization, an ideal prototype, of the dry garden?

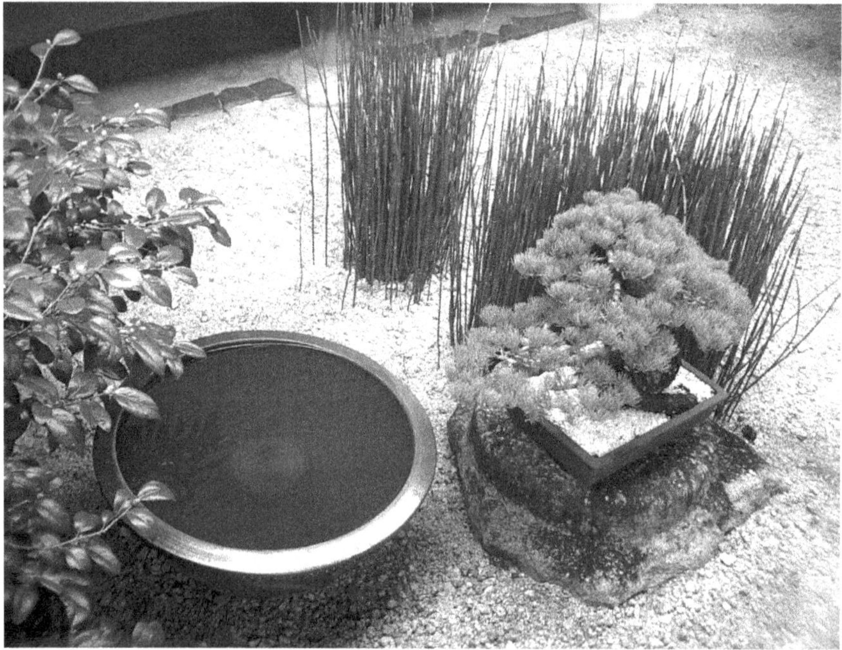

FIGURE 7.2 A miniature garden in Zuihō-in

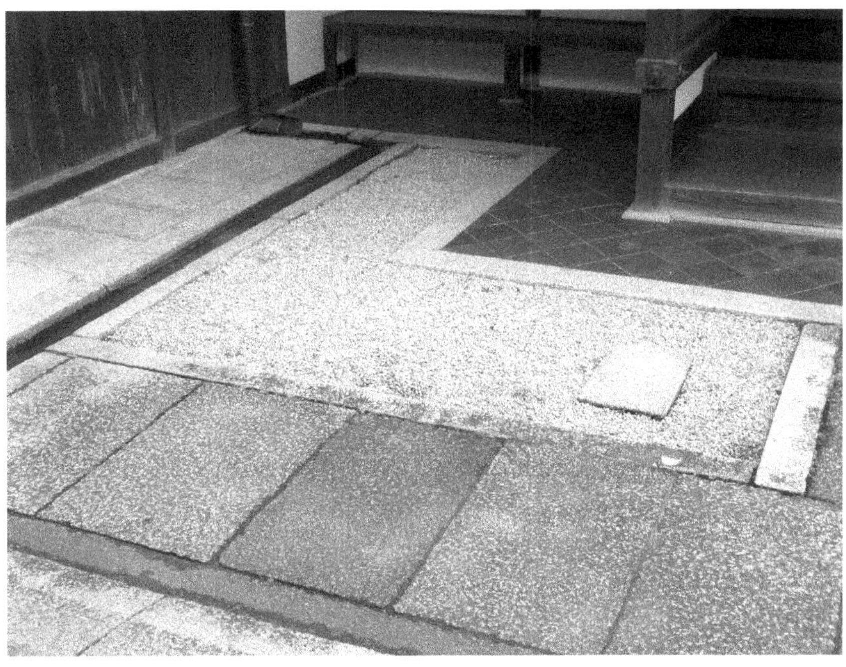

FIGURES 7.3 and 7.4 Gardens at entrance of building in Myōshin-ji temple complex

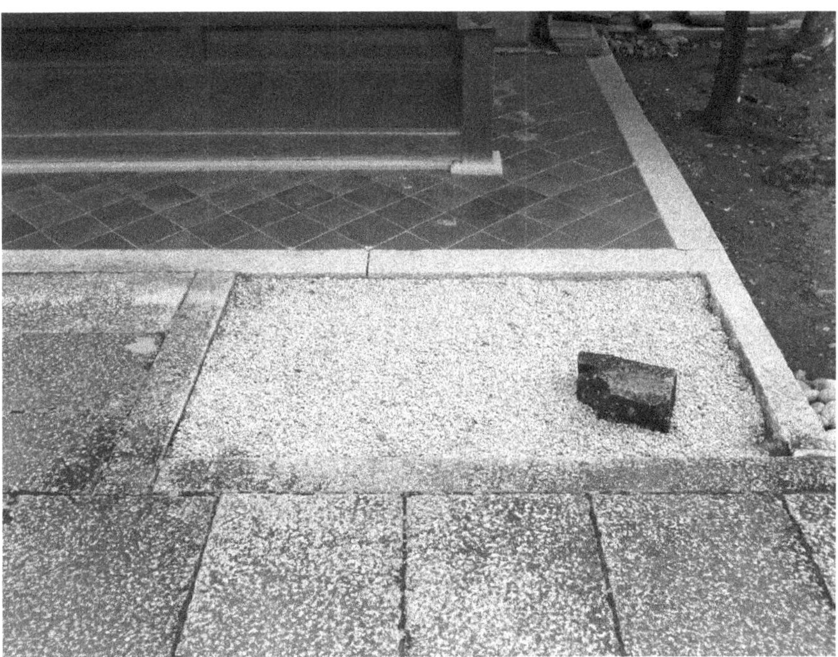

Furthermore, the courtyard reveals the diverse practical and symbolic uses of stone: as border, marker, path, parterre, cairn, sculpture. There is even an altar before which is set a small piles of stones, as if in offering to the gods (fig. 7.5). It is as if the system of binary oppositions visible from the entrance were deconstructed by all that exists within the confines of the courtyard. The apparent minimalism of these dry, stony parterres belies the actual complexity of such gardens, which must always be approached according to their play of scale,

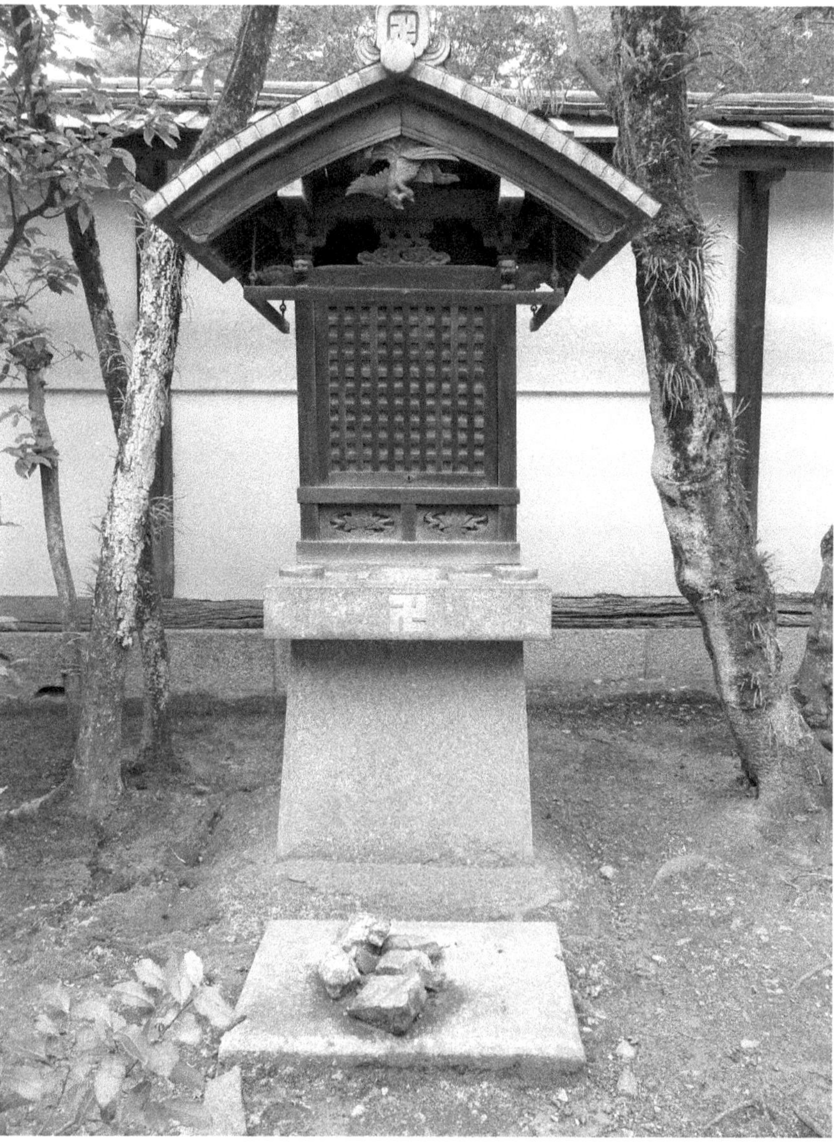

FIGURE 7.5 An altar at Myōshin-ji with an offering of stones

surroundings, climate, motion, temporality, etc. Otherwise, we experience an abstracted picture, not a living landscape. This setting thus simultaneously reveals the minimal conditions of a dry garden and the maximal conditions of visibility, instantiating the claim that 'the richest site is the one most closely observed'. In the Zen garden, this richness is both formal and iconographic, and the resultant equivocation is precisely a source of interpretative latitude and existential possibility.

Much landscape theory suffers from a narrowly construed sense of representation, where rhetorical tropes figure gardens as pictures to be seen rather than fields to be entered, and analytic forms promote a static ontological model based on perspectival projections rather than a dynamic one founded on kinesthetic transformations.[4] These heuristic issues are complicated by the dry Zen garden, most of which cannot be entered, and many of which indeed undergo the most minimal change with the seasons. Furthermore, in the relatively rare instances when motion is considered, it is usually forgotten that the body moves not only laterally and in depth, but also vertically. Both walking and sitting are essential to the Zen sensibility, and both are fully integrated into garden design. Indeed, every Japanese schoolchild who has visited Ryōan-ji—and they are legion—knows that the disposition of the 15 stones in the garden is famed for the fact that from any given viewpoint only 14 stones are visible. Mobility is thus inscribed in the myth of Ryōan-ji, manifested by these incessant comings-and-goings that are certainly inimical to the other use-value of the garden, meditation.

The temple corridors, which are simultaneously walkways and seats, have a double role in defining the spatiality of these gardens, much as the floor, used for both walking and sitting, does in Japanese architecture and design. These gardens are so small that the visual difference between viewpoints is enormous: the angles of vision, relationship between elements, implied horizon lines, effects of closure, degree of framing, play of thresholds, narrative allusions, and symbolic implications are all transformed according to whether one is sitting, standing, or walking. The point of view changes radically as one moves about: it may alternately (and often simultaneously and equivocally) be frontal, oblique, and even aerial. Since the corridors are approximately only 3 feet from ground level, the difference between sitting and standing often entails a prodigious change in viewpoint, from a frontal to an oblique perspective—if such terms still have any meaning in such a context, which is doubtful. Some of these gardens are no wider than the height of an average person, so that one's shadow may well cover an entire landscape. A few steps, even a tilt of the head, may effect transformations of cosmic dimensions. Furthermore, such perspectives share a sense of proportion unique to Japanese aesthetics, one that is determined less by the geometry of perspectival projection than by an innate sense of modularity, formed by the *tatami*—the ubiquitous bamboo floor mat whose proportions establish both conscious and unconscious grids according to which every room, scene, and garden is experienced, not unlike the 'golden section' in Western art (Nitschke 1991). Vision is fulfilled by motion, and perfection is supplemented by reversibility. Certain sites are so subtle that they may not be immediately recognized as gardens and literally passed over as one crosses a walkway or enters a building. A garden, or not a garden: that is the question.

The Zen garden is a perpetual play of thresholds and passages, statics and dynamics, representational views and abstract spaces. Privileged viewpoints constitute a major design feature of all gardens, but they do not necessarily imply a single, fixed, definitive position. Indeed, a perpetual play of dissimulation and revelation (*mie-gakure*) is essential to the experience of Zen gardens. Just as the angle of vision between sitting and standing radically changes perspectives in small spaces, so too does the distance from the garden, so that the view from the edge of the walkway is quite other than that from within the temple just a few feet back. There exist controlled views, partial views, multiple views, counterviews, hidden views, and borrowed views (*shakkei*).

The unequivocal focus of the Zen garden is stones. We find stones with stones, stones on stones, stones representing mountains, stones crushed to gravel, and often just single exceptional stones that all by themselves constitute a landscape. In ancient Chinese and Japanese cosmology, stones are not mere inanimate objects but rather concentrations of cosmic and telluric energy (*ch'i*) flowing in different patterns throughout the universe. Rocks are thus valued for both form and force. Indeed, Zen master Dōgen (1200–1253) insisted that pebbles are sentient beings that participate in Buddha's nature. According to Shinto tradition, certain sites have concentrations of *kami*, supernatural spirits that inhabit the rocks, and particular rock arrangements are used to attract specific *kami*. Rocks are of such great aesthetic importance that one classic Chinese book of painting teaches: "In order to learn to paint, one must invariably learn how to paint rocks. Of all the techniques of using the brush, none are more difficult than those required for rocks, and no subject calls for a greater range of techniques," which is comparable to European Renaissance depictions of clothing, with their intricate folds and extravagant decorations, as a prime sign of painterly virtuosity (Itoh 1973: 48). The Chinese love of rocks may even be surpassed by that of the Japanese, who have designated certain famous stones as National Treasures. Specific rocks may symbolize mountains, both mythological and real, most often Mount Fuji, and they may also represent other natural objects, such as waterfall rocks (*taki-ishi*), so named because their vertical surface patterns suggest cascading water, such as the waterfall rock at Obai-in (fig. 7.6). The priest Zōen, in one of the classics of Japanese landscape art, *Illustrations for Designing Mountain, Water, and Hillside Field Landscapes*,[5] enumerates 57 categories of rocks, reduced from the 361 of Chinese tradition and from the thousands in certain Indian manuscripts. These types include, for example, wave repelling rocks, water cutting rocks, stepping stones, shadow facing stones, ducks' abode rocks, hovering mist rocks, human form rocks, mirror rocks, reverence rocks, demon rocks, vengeful spirit rocks, taboo rocks, triadic Buddhist waterfall rocks. Certain unique stones, such as the Twofold World Rock, Rock of the Spirit Kings, Dragon's Abode Rock, are also identified.

Writers have often insisted that the 15 stones in Ryōan-ji are beyond iconographic determination. Typical of this interpretation, which has practically become the standard Western reading of Ryōan-ji, is that of Thomas Hoover,

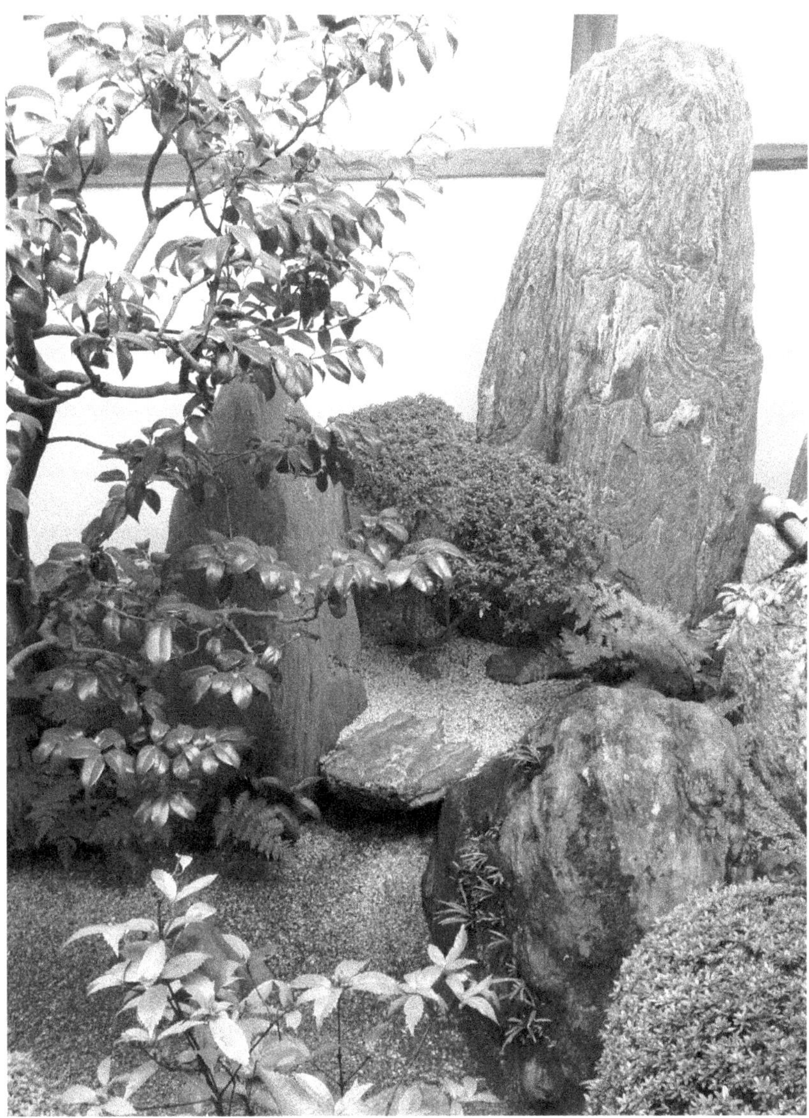

FIGURE 7.6 The waterfall rock at Obai-in, a subtemple of Daitoku-ji

who writes in *Zen Culture* (1977: 105): "Unlike Daisen-in, the garden at Ryōan-ji is not a symbolic mountain scene. It is instead a work of abstract art on a canvas of sand which goes beyond a symbolic representation of a landscape scene to provide a distillation of the very universe. It is internationally regarded as the very essence of Zen, and it is almost impossible to describe, in either words or pictures." Hoover continues, "The first is a symbolic landscape of parched waterfalls and simulated streams drawn in monochromatic granite; the second, a totally non-representative abstraction of stone arrangements in the sand-covered 'flat garden' style" (ibid: 110). Perhaps more telling, because written by a landscape theorist, is François Berthier's claim (2000: 41) concerning Ryōan-ji's abstraction: "It is precisely because the significance of this garden remains vague that it is so rich in meaning: it is because it is shrouded in mystery that it offers everyone a large margin of fantasy." While there is indeed a Zen principle of mystery, obscurity, unknowability (*yūgen*), this in no way obviates consideration of its mythical, representational, and iconographic foundations. The "vague" significance should suggest a broad scope of metaphoricity rather than its lack. Abstraction and figuration are not, in Zen aesthetics, the terms of an antinomy; instead, they are the poles of a profound, complex, and often paradoxical intuition.

Consider the celebrated Fujisan tea bowl (one of eight *chawan* designated as National Treasures), created by the legendary potter Kōetsu Hon'ami (1558–1637), where a subtle effect of slip and ash vaguely resembles Mount Fuji. The resultant equivocation between abstraction and figuration constitutes an ineluctable aspect of Japanese aesthetics and explains the perennial Japanese fascination with images in fog and mist. This equivocation is reinforced by a devotion to chance effects. The accidental and imperfect are essential for Zen, a perfection of the imperfect inherent in so many effects particular to the art of pottery: crackles, cracks, fissures, stains, drips, burns. Manifestations of materiality, chance, and symbolism are often linked, as when a spontaneous, unintentional crack reveals the interior of the clay, or suggests an ideogram or a landscape. Indeed, the crack or imperfection appears to be the zero-degree aesthetic effect in Zen, articulating the contingency of chance effects and the intentionality behind the primal level of representation. This is stressed by the fact that repairs on Japanese pottery are often not made with the invisible mends required by Western restorers, but rather with a filling of urushi lacquer mixed with 23 karat gold dust, so as to highlight the crack. Such is the case, for example, of the famous Seppo (Snowy Peak) tea bowl, also created by Kōetsu, which exhibits not only a spectacular fissure but also where the gold-lacquered repair itself has cracked over time.

One wonders at the aesthetic profundity of this crack upon a crack. Sometimes a crack evokes a landscape, and sometimes it is just a crack. But certain cracks are more perfect than others. Indeed, the profundity of such serendipitous signs is inscribed in the very structure of Japanese calligraphy. The poet Gary Snyder (1990: 18) states it most succinctly in writing of "the gleaming calligraphy of the ancient riverbeds," a metaphor that he makes explicit (ibid.: 108–109): "Mountains and Waters are a dyad that together make wholeness possible ... landforms are a play of stream-cutting and ridge-resistance and ... waters and hills interpenetrate in endlessly branching rhythms ... 'Mountains and waters' is a way to refer to the totality of the process of nature." In suppressing such metaphors, as do certain Western interpreters, a typically Zen equivocation, for instance, the sense of wet dryness and dry wetness, disappears. Essential iconographic features are thus lost, and Zen gardens are reduced to purely formal enterprises.

There is the accidental of the instant and the accidental for the ages. For example, rarely are the walls surrounding the dry garden of Ryōan-ji, themselves National Treasures, discussed. These *aburabei*-style walls, made of clay steeped in oil, are astonishing: centuries-long weathering has caused the oil to seep out in irregular mottled patterns. They are veritable lessons in Japanese aesthetics, instantiating the subtle relations between figuration and abstraction, determinacy and indeterminacy, willfulness and serendipity, denotation and connotation, revelation and suggestion. The walls, a palimpsest of centuries, not only establish the cloistered space, but also emblematize the slow, ever-changing, and cyclical effects of the weather, in stark contrast to the melancholy effects of instantaneous and ephemeral events. These walls are the imperfect, irregular elevation or background against which appear the perfect forms of the garden in its projection, the chaotic ground of the sublime intuition (fig. 7.7). Yet the walls do not function as pure enclosures, like the frames of Western paintings or the alleys of formal gardens, since the borrowed view, however limited, is essential to the constitution of the dry garden. Otherwise, the wall would be of a height to completely obscure the exterior. Here the walls are both poetic sculptural objects in themselves and a middle ground that articulates the foreground of the garden and the background of the environs. But there is also a more curious, more recent, infinitely less noticed and commented upon aleatory effect at Ryōan-ji. Of all the rectangular stones that delimit this ocean of gravel, one is cracked through and through. Even the strongest rock, the greatest mountain, will wear and crack over time: such is the pathos of rock. Given the extraordinary daily care afforded Ryōan-ji, the universal interest that it inspires, and the particularities of Zen aesthetics, it is impossible to imagine that this cracked stone was left there by negligence. Of what might it be an allegory? What does it tell us about Ryōan-ji? About ourselves? About temporality? What is the ephemeral in the face of centuries, of eternity?

Some Zen gardens are representations of the natural landscape, especially the rocky shores of the Inland Sea and the environs of the five mountains surrounding Kyoto. Others are inspired by idealized representations in landscape paintings, notably the iconography of Chinese Sung dynasty landscapes, as well as tales of mythological paradises. That Ryōan-ji has been referred to as a 'garden of emptiness' (*mutei*) is not necessarily proof of its abstraction, since the cosmos is filled with emptiness, as both Zen masters and Western theologians have long taught us. A prime goal of theology is to reconcile humankind to this void, whether through anguish or joy. The void may be metaphoric; the void may be real. The degree of metaphoricity of the dry Zen garden is vast, and the void is but a relatively small aspect of the symbolic realm of the Zen garden. The supposed emptiness of such gardens does not mean that it is beyond iconographic determination, as writers have so often insisted. In *Illustrations,* Zōen goes so far as to suggest that sand alone may suffice to create a landscape scene: "Another type of shoreline scenery is the ebb-tide beach, which has no striking features but simply creates the impression of the tide constantly ebbing and flowing. Here … just by spreading fine and coarse grades of sand and without setting any rocks you can visually re-create

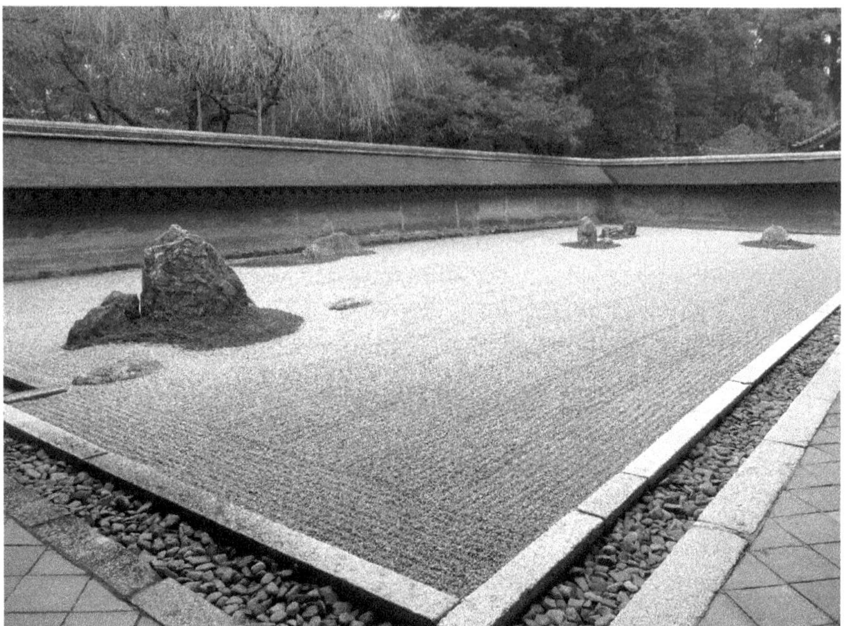

FIGURE 7.7 Ryōan-ji's famous rock garden

a single scenic ambience" (cited in Slawson 1987: 73). This zero-degree effect of dry gardens—originating in the empty sand or gravel fields of sacred Shinto shrines—is described by art historian Yoshinobu Yoshinaga: "The [*karesansui*] garden is an attempt to represent the innermost essence of water, without actually using water, and to represent it at that even more profoundly than would be possible with real water" (ibid.: 74). What is at stake here is the representational quality of symbols and signs. Such is the space of dry water, still waves, proximate distance—the space of the impossible, the space of paradox, the space of Zen enlightenment.

Of all art forms, gardens are the most susceptible to the ravages of time, especially as their temporality is so finely—and often brutally—attuned to that of season and climate, history and catastrophe. All gardens must be considered according to their sundry, and often contradictory, transformations, such that the reality of any garden is one of complex, overlapping, and often anachronistic temporalities. Anachronism is at the core of chronology and iconography, of symbolism and narrative. That a garden element perdures while everything surrounding it changes hardly makes of it an isolated, stable object. What appears as unequivocal presence is always a palimpsest of accidents and forms, causes and effects, reality and myth—a dense web of significations well beyond conscious comprehension and expectation. One need only establish the chronology of each major detail of a garden as proof of the garden's complex and anachronistic structure.

The history of Ryōan-ji is a case in point. First of all, the iconography of the temple of Ryōan-ji is highly syncretic, incorporating Buddhist, Confucian, Taoist, and Shinto elements, the last being noteworthy with regard to the empty space that signifies sacred sites. This complexity is compounded by the fact that the dry garden of Ryōan-ji has often been transformed, although it would be practically impossible to determine how many times and in what manners. Most crucially, in 1606 the iconography changed radically, coinciding with the political and social watershed that followed Oda Nobunaga's unification of Japan, which marked the origin of the unified Japanese state. The sedate monochromatic ink paintings of landscape, bird, and flower motifs in the rooms facing the dry garden were replaced by sliding wall panel paintings (*fusuma*), painted by the circle of Kanō Eitoku (1543–1590), representing extravagant, brightly colored, gold-leaf backed mythological and utopian scenes, including *Tiger and Bamboo*, *The Four Elegant Accomplishments,* and *The Chinese Immortals* (see Onishi and Oba 1993).[6] The lithic outcroppings depicted in these paintings are not mere flights of artistic imagination; rather, they are part of the fully developed iconographic systems of Chinese, Korean, and Japanese painting, as well as of the specifically Chinese genre of scholars' rocks (Mowry 1997). While the abbot's quarters still housed the old monochromatic style paintings, suggesting a theological continuity with more ancient forms, the new temple paintings in the public rooms facing the dry garden were festive displays of courtly ostentation, reflecting the loosening of class barriers that allowed samurai, priests, and artists to intermingle. The complex new relations between classes were articulated by aesthetic means, as they would be, for centuries, by the Zen-inspired tea ceremony. The relation of these utopian iconographies to the dry garden that preceded them is beyond the scope of this chapter, but it is immediately apparent that the jagged, irregular rock formations and the empty gold ground are aesthetically congruent with the iconography of the dry garden at Ryōan-ji. It would be imprudent to assume that the meaning and use-value of the garden remained unchanged when faced with such radical iconographic, cultural, and political shifts. The impulse to see the dry garden of Ryōan-ji as purely abstract is thus anachronistically modernist.

One interpretation of the death of the great tea master Sen no Rikyū (1522–1591) claims that the *shogun* Hideyoshi forced him to commit suicide because of their difference over the question as to whether the appropriate color of the tea ceremony bowl should be red or black (implying, respectively, either extravagance or austerity). This claim is obviously more allegorical than historical, but it points to the profound and complex implications of iconography as it reflects shifts in state power. That a Japanese rock fresh from the Kamo River could represent an ancient Chinese utopia is a sign not of ideological misrepresentation but of the profound richness of symbols and the labyrinth of history. To neglect the image is to misrepresent ideology and to falsify history. In the Zen garden, the rigors of monastic practice, the acute daily attention to detail, the ritualized gestures that make of quotidian tasks a meditative experience, and the devotion to the highest attainments of craftsmanship, all suggest the appropriate manner of approaching these gardens. Our aesthetic vision must be no less exacting. Yet it should not be assumed that such hyperbolic attention to detail suggests a fall into sheer empiricism or that there is a single appropriate manner of viewing such gardens. For Zen implies multiple levels of interpretation, all valid in different manners. There exist what Gregory P. A. Levine (2005: 254) calls a religious, mystical, devotional eye, with its "temple effect," and a secular, scholarly, historical, pleasure-seeking eye, with its "museum effect." Both of these, in their own way, are motivated by "eye-opening" rites, that is, viewing protocols that configure specific ways of approaching such scenes and objects (ibid.: 5). Each person arrives with different beliefs, different expectations, different protocols of viewing. Where one finds the living presence of nature, another seeks a revelation of the transcendental void, while a third discovers sublime beauty. One need not become a Buddhist monk seeking *satori* to appreciate the Zen garden, yet, as with all art, the form and depth of appreciation depend on what one brings to the scene. These temples and gardens are thus simultaneously sites of meditation, magic, devotion, knowledge, curiosity—even commerce, play, and profanation.

There is an oft-told story about Rikyū. One autumn day, he watched as his son Shōan swept and watered the garden path. "Not clean enough," insisted the master, time and again. After an hour, his son replied, "Father, there is nothing more to be done. The steps have been washed for the third time, the stone lanterns and the trees are well sprinkled with water; moss and lichens are shining with a fresh verdure; not a twig, not a leaf have I left on the ground." Rikyū exclaimed, "Young fool, this is not the way a garden path should be swept," upon which he shook a maple tree, randomly scattering its crimson leaves (Okakura 1964: 36). Rikyū's famed pupil, Oribe, one of the greatest tea masters, went so far in Zen mannerism as to sweep his garden clean of leaves and then sprinkle pine needles under deciduous trees. These tales have never been forgotten.

My first visit to Ryōgen-in took place early one morning in December 2007. The garden, brilliant in the morning sunlight, revealed a curious detail: a single crimson maple leaf lay just alongside the left-most rock group. It is almost inconceivable that this could have been an omission during the morning cleaning, as the autumnal maple leaf is revered in Japan, the subject of the greatest attention and admiration. Furthermore, nature itself could not have brought this gift, since the entire morning was of the utmost calm. One could only deduce that the novice or monk entrusted with cleaning and raking the garden that day—conscious or not of the famed tale of Rikyū—had placed this leaf on the otherwise immaculate gravel surface, perhaps in imitation of the aleatory effects of nature, perhaps as a minimal and mannerist aesthetic gesture. This single leaf, not unlike the jar on a hill in Tennessee celebrated in Wallace Stevens's poem "Anecdote of the Jar," refocused the entire garden. According to Zen aesthetics, this suggested a drastic—even if ephemeral and fortuitous— reconstitution of this garden's already sublime aesthetics. In the Zen garden, the fall of a leaf, a ray of sunlight, a sudden rain may offer aesthetic, religious, or utopian possibilities hitherto unimaginable.

Allen S. Weiss teaches in the Departments of Performance Studies and Cinema Studies at New York University. A writer, editor, translator, curator, and playwright, he is the author and editor of 40 books in the fields of performance theory, landscape architecture, gastronomy, sound art, and experimental theater. His publications include *Mirrors of Infinity: The French Formal Garden and 17th-Century Metaphysics* (1995), *Unnatural Horizons: Paradox and Contradiction in Landscape Architecture* (1998), and *The Wind and the Source: In the Shadow of Mont Ventoux* (2005). He recently published his first novel, *Le livre bouffon* (2009), and is now working on the second volume of his gastronomic autobiography, *Métaphysique de la miette*.

Notes

1. All photographs were taken in 2007–2008 by the author.
2. Located in northwest Kyoto, Ryōan-ji is a Zen temple that, with its garden, is one of the Historic Monuments of Ancient Kyoto, a UNESCO World Heritage Site. The Ryōan-ji garden is one of the most acclaimed in the world.
3. This head temple of the Myōshin-ji school of Rinzai Zen is located in Kyoto.
4. For an account of this problematic, see Weiss (1995: 33–46).
5. Referring to the source of this document, Slawson (1987: 51) states that although *Illustrations* is dated 1466, it "contains instructions from earlier periods" and that Zōen, who is "credited as its original compiler," lived prior to the eleventh century.
6. The recent discovery that these screens, donated to the Metropolitan Museum of Art in New York, belonged to Ryōan-ji has significant implications for the iconographic study of this garden.

References

Berthier, François. 2000. *Reading Zen in the Rocks*. Trans. Graham Parkes. Chicago, IL: University of Chicago Press.

Hoover, Thomas. 1977. *Zen Culture.* New York: Random House.

Itoh, Teiji. 1973. *Space and Illusion in the Japanese Garden.* New York: Weatherhill; Toyko, Kyoto: Tankosha.

Katsuhiko, Mizuno. 1992. *Masterpieces of Japanese Garden Art*. Kyoto: Shoin.

______. 2002. *Landscapes for Small Places: Japanese Courtyard Gardens.* New York: Kodansha.

Levine, Gregory P. A. 2005. *Daitokuji: The Visual Cultures of a Zen Monastery.* Seattle: University of Washington Press.

Mowry, Robert D., ed. 1997. *Worlds Within Worlds: The Richard Rosenblum Collection of Chinese Scholars' Rocks.* Cambridge, MA: Harvard University Art Museums.

Nitschke, Guenther. 1991. *The Architecture of the Japanese Garden: Right Angle and Natural Form.* Cologne: Taschen.

Okakura, Kakuzo. 1964. *The Book of Tea.* New York: Dover.

Onishi, Hiroshi, and Takemitsu Oba. 1993. *Immortals and Sages: Paintings from Ryoanji Temple.* New York: Metropolitan Museum of Art.

Slawson, David A. 1987. *Secret Teachings in the Art of Japanese Gardens: Design Principles, Aesthetic Values.* Tokyo: Kodansha.

Snyder, Gary. 1990. *The Practice of the Wild: Essays.* San Francisco, CA: North Point Press.

Weiss, Allen S. 1995. *Mirrors of Infinity: The French Formal Garden and 17th-Century Metaphysics.* New York: Princeton Architectural Press.

Chapter 8

Images of Transgression

Teyyam *in Malabar*

DINESAN VADAKKINIYIL

In the context of religious and communal practice in the Indian state of Kerala, *teyyam* rituals are manifested by and identified with particular deities. One such, in the ritual complex of North Malabar, is the *teyyam* or deity of Muttappan. In contrast to the Brahmanic and hegemonic discourse of state ideology, Muttappan highlights the importance of *teyyam* as both deity and ritual in symbolic representations of community. Muttappan is in itself an image of power that unsettles all other images of state power and caste hierarchy.

My purpose here is to analyze the deity Muttappan in relation to the changing structures of the Indian state. This particular *teyyam* has the potency to deterritorialize and reterritorialize, continually reinforcing itself, asserting its autonomy and transgressing boundaries. Its potential to do this—and the way that it does so—will be examined in this chapter. My analysis of Muttappan will proceed by discussing the relationship between power and ritual worship, the politics of the devaluation of the latter as 'art', and the assertion of autonomy within caste structures.

Notes for this chapter begin on page 148.

I begin by presenting an instance of how *teyyam* emerged in the situation of a nascent colonial state coming up against an existing kingdom, with the latter trying to reassert its power while being eroded in the presence of the former. I will explore some of the ways in which colonial and post-colonial Kerala discursively constructed *teyyam* as 'devil worship', a process wrought within the rationality of Western modernity and missionary zeal to help the 'natives' 'progress' and become 'civilized'. In the post-colonial period, this approach has been maintained, although with differences. The state no longer rejects *teyyam* outright by construing it as devil worship; rather, *teyyam* is incorporated by devaluing its capacity to effect change and regeneration and by turning it into an art form. Hence, from 1960, discussion has centered on *teyyam* as an art (folk, popular, village, or classical). But a reading of the mythologies of *teyyam* will show that it is concerned with the great inequalities of the past. Reducing *teyyam* solely to art is making it empty and part of the structure of the state. Once adopted by the state, *teyyam* could be seen as an artifact that represents national identity and hence could be incorporated into Onam, the largest festival in Kerala, where it is displayed as part of the state's cultural heritage. As a result, when India observes Republic Day on 26 January, *teyyam* appears at the nation's capital during the celebrations. In this re-presentation, we can see the paradox of *teyyam*: it has the potential to resist powers of the state, yet at the same time it has been co-opted within the state's structure.

In contemporary ritual worship, *teyyam* continually reinforces caste divisions and at the same time recenters them in relation to the community. Muttappan, being an exemplar of modernity, has the potential to cross borders and to resist caste or any other kind of domination. Thus, the image of opposition to state practice is situated in Muttappan's marginality and outsider status.

Teyyam: Rite and Contests

Exclusive to North Malabar, *teyyam* is a form of ritual worship of ancestor spirits and local deities wherein the bodies of *teyyam* specialists become vehicles (in dance, possession, speech, etc.) for the manifestation of specific deities or spirits.[1] Most people in Malabar who might be broadly classified as Hindus, regardless of their caste or class, participate in the worship of *teyyam*. The sacred spaces of *teyyam* worship are mainly the courtyards of the *taravad* (matrilineal joint family) or lineage shrines. However, changes are occurring. Muttappan, for example, is a new *teyyam* whose sacred locale might be a taxi stand, a housing estate, a shopping complex, or the household of a newly settled small family not living as a joint family (Vadakkiniyil 2009). The word *teyyam* is considered to be derived from the Sanskrit word *daivam*, meaning god.

The right to perform *teyyam* belongs exclusively to those once considered to be members of lower castes or 'out groups'. The rite starts with the performer invoking the deity that he is going to manifest and reciting the deity's mythical story. Once invoked, the performer's body and face are painted in the manner appropriate to the deity that he is becoming. The manifestation of the *teyyam* in its most complete and ordered form is achieved when the *teyyam* performer is masked and dressed in the regalia of the deity. The performer-as-*teyyam* then goes before the shrine of the deity, and the ritual moves toward the events of its finale. These may involve possession, sacrifice, the giving of gifts, and the blessing of worshippers. *Teyyam* as a whole is a complex aesthetic ensemble involving music, song, dance, and occasional dramatic events, among many other happenings.

Those who enact *teyyam* (the person who manifests the *teyyam*, the musicians, and the assistants) do so as a paid ritual service to specific *teyyam* shrines and their relevant communities.[2] Usually, they are not from the community at whose *teyyam* shrine the ritual is performed. The permanent officiants come from the group or community that owns the shrine. These officiants include priests who conduct regular ritual practices concerned with the maintenance of the shrines and who engage in ritual acts involving dance and possession. These actions express the power of *teyyam* but do not involve either the dress or the ritualistic events that are normally associated with *teyyam* as a ritual form.

The history of the East India Company as the colonial power since 1795 and the opposition of contemporary ritual practice to the dominant state power can be construed as a struggle between colonial pragmatism, on the one hand, and the encompassing power of the potency of *teyyam*, on the other. It is in this context that the designation of ritual came to be seen, over time, as (mere) art, stripped of its religious significance.

Between the years 1792–1795, the Kolattiri, the king of North Malabar, lost his sovereign political authority, and the entire region came under the rule of the English East India Company. Kolattiri attempted to regain his lost power by proposing to conduct a coronation ceremony for his successor. In effect, this action would resacralize the kingship, the authority of which was being threatened by the British presence. The coronation or resacrilization would address the goddess of the ruling royal lineage, Thiruvarkatt Bagavati, a female divinity in the *teyyam* complex. In the pre-colonial conception of state power in Malabar, it was believed that the kingdom was under the protection of Bagavati and that she authorized the rulership of the king and the order of state power. Kolattiri conveyed his decision to conduct the ceremony to the administrative heads of the East India Company stationed in his (former) territory. But the Company turned down his request, stating that he was defying the authority of the "government of the ceded province" with a view "to attaining his former state of independence" (Swai 1978). The king was attempting to gain acknowledgment from the British that their power was conditional on the goddess, on the sacred. A further motivation behind such a request, I suggest, was that the king wished to augment his own power, for if the company agreed, it was tantamount to the British accepting the authority of the king and his royal lineage, founded as it was in their connection to and worship of Bagavati. The Company responded to Kolattiri by asserting that he was acting like one who did not understand "his relative situation with the Company at present" (ibid.), that is, Kolattiri did not seem to grasp that his power depended on the authority of the British rather than a goddess.

In the second quarter of the twentieth century, when the anti-colonial movement was at its peak, *teyyam* emerged with another potency. Nationalists countered the colonial characterization of India as a superstitious and barbaric land by projecting *kathakali* as a superior form of dance drama and *kalari* as the pre-colonial system of training warriors of the state in martial techniques (Zarilli 2000). However, nationalist fervors often sidelined *teyyam*, viewing it as mythical and irrational and as an impediment to development. One social reformer criticized the practice of *teyyam*, arguing that it was instrumental in reproducing the caste system and the exploitation of the depressed classes. Meanwhile, leftist revolutionaries, especially Communists, explored the possibility of using *teyyam* as a means of resistance against colonial and feudal forms of domination. The death and deification myths of *teyyam* deities were interpreted as resistance to elite power, especially the power of landlords and the colonial state. Thus, leftist intellectuals interpreted the myths of *teyyam* as living evidence of class exploitation. One result of these interventions was the realization among the exploited that their hitherto taken-for-granted social position as members of lower castes was not naturally given. Attempts to redefine their position emerged from within, placing *teyyam* at the center of the tension.

The rhizomic dimension of *teyyam* and its potential to resist exploitation and bureaucratic order made it difficult for the political parties of the Left and the independent Kerala state to reject *teyyam* in the way that colonialism did, that is, by characterizing it as superstitious, irrational, and uncivilized. On the other hand, to incorporate *teyyam* into the fold of the state structure as a religious practice was difficult for a secular state and for a political theory that perceives religion to be an ideology that creates false consciousness. It is in this predicament that the discursive construction of *teyyam* as an art form emerged. Taking insights from Wayne Ashley (1993), Phillip Zarrilli (2000: 201) argues that in post-colonial Kerala both the state and the Communist Party accepted *teyyam* and other such traditional arts, "but only if they were historically decontextualized, shorn of the vestiges of the regressive feudalistic, superstitious belief systems of the past, and made accessible to 'the people' with new content."

In this situation, *teyyam* was invoked both inside and outside Malabar. It appeared beyond its conventional sacred spaces, crossing over into the realm of stages, public processions, and overseas city centers. In such modern spaces, *teyyam* emerged as an instrument for disseminating political positions, as a decorative piece that makes a public event spectacular, as a dying art seeking protection and support from philanthropists. Within Malabar, seminars and discussions were held that dissected the status of *teyyam* as an art form. *Teyyam* began to be referred to in literature and in common speech as 'traditional art', 'art form', 'folk art, 'religious art', 'ritual art', 'popular art', or 'classical art', and the ritual practitioners were described as 'artists'. State institutions, so-called progressive thinkers, and the organs of print culture debated the nature of *teyyam* and whether it could be considered an art (Kerala Sangeetha Nataka Academy [1977] 1987; Kurup [1985] 2000). All of them discursively constructed *teyyam* as an art and effectively tried to position it within the fold of the state or state-like institutions. In such discourses, *teyyam* emerged as an arboreal, bereft of its capacity to transcend boundaries (Deleuze and Guattari [1988] 2002). This, I would argue, is an aspect of the centralizing of a rhizomic potency—the encompassing of the unencompassed. *Teyyam* has thus primarily become an art, an art of Kerala, a sign of its unique culture, and a symbol of religious unity in the academic, political, and popular discourses of the second half of the twentieth century. Such an argument may be advantageous for the elites who have constructed a unified 'secular state'—one that provides room to incorporate the dynamic potential of *teyyam* within the state system and dominant political orders.

My focus now turns to the myth and ritual practice of Muttappan-*teyyam* in order to explore the dimensions and potency of this male divinity as a 'line of flight' (in Deleuze's sense) in contemporary Malabar and beyond. Here we will see him emerging more in the secular spaces that modernity has created, rather than in the traditional ritual spaces of *teyyam* worship. Muttappan has achieved great significance in urban centers and even among migrants abroad. Although he has long been worshipped, his popularity is expanding. What is particularly interesting in my view is that the ideas and practices that elaborate about this deity extend a logic that is already integral to him and that is of a rhizomic kind. Muttappan is not a deity who is connected to the *taravad*; he operates outside the domains of bounded land and kinship and previously established communities. Rather, as I will explore, he is a *teyyam* who appears to be relevant to situations of deep uncertainty and who is also a vital factor in the creation of new relationships, often where these have not existed before. The consideration of Muttappan that I present here demonstrates further the way that potentialities within *teyyam* can continually develop and open out to meet the circumstances and contingencies of the diverse and differentiating processes of everyday life.

I now provide a brief overview of Muttappan's major characteristics and mode of appearance, leading into a consideration of the principal myths concerning his origins and rites, which condense aspects of his key potencies. From this I will examine how the capacities that he embodies are expressed and thus made apparent in certain contexts and situations of contingency. I examine how these may relate to his growing popularity, itself a factor in realizing and expanding upon potentialities already immanent within this deity.

Muttappan and His Embodied Potencies

As a *teyyam*, Muttappan is not tied to a particular caste, matri-clan, or lineage. Features that he embodies, extending well back into pre-colonial times, indicate a being who is non-hierarchical and non-territorial, unlike other divinities in the *teyyam* complex. Muttappan-*teyyam* seems to have been worshipped by numerous communities and in different forms. This is also true for many female divinities, but their particular forms are connected with political and social differentiations of lineage and caste. Muttappan has fewer forms, and, since they are not associated with specific communities, he can settle anywhere. He has little in the way of a stable abode and travels easily. A highly pragmatic god, he can engage in matters of daily exigency. In contrast to many other more settled divinities, he does not necessarily demand enduring devotion.

Muttappan might be conceived of as a figure on the way to becoming an ancestor, through whom relations will come into existence. Furthermore, since he is not attached to settled groups of kin or to the houses of kin, he is a being of the outside and of the margins, even beyond human habitation. Associated with open terrains and non-territorialized spaces that are unrestricted by boundaries of order and rule, Muttappan is sometimes conceived of as a forest dweller, a wanderer, or a solitary figure living in a cave. Outside of all place, he can be located in any place.

Until the beginning of the twentieth century, Muttappan was worshipped primarily in rural areas. He protected fields and crops, especially those in the open and unbounded areas used for swidden agriculture. A guide and helper to the hunter, Muttappan, typically represented as bearing a bow and an arrow, also guarded cattle as transient wealth. He defended against sorcery and acted in judgment on those who engaged in theft or otherwise attacked the vulnerable.

The *teyyam* of Muttappan usually appears as a simple, infirm old man (see fig. 8.1). He has a white moustache and beard and wears a red loin cloth. His body is painted with purifying turmeric, he has a pot belly, his back is hunched

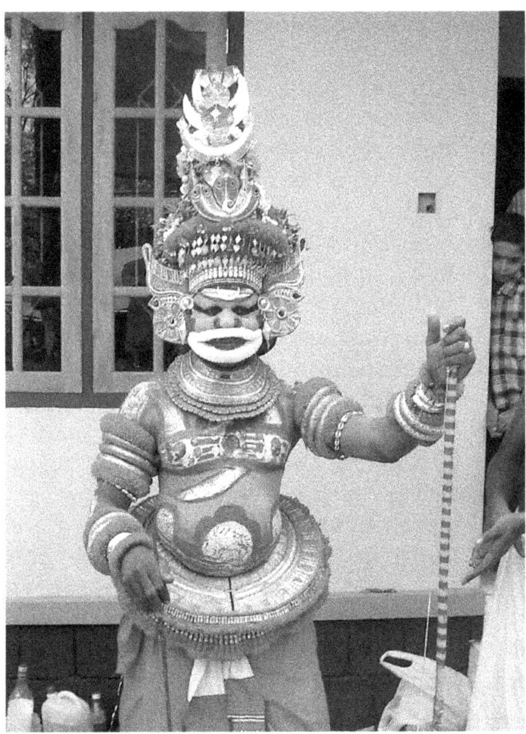

FIGURE 8.1 Muttappan. Photograph provided by author.

by age, and his lips tremble in the palsied manner of those of very advanced years. His conical headdress (*kodumudi*) is made from a variety of medicinal flowers and plants, predominant among which is *thulasi* (L. *ocimum sanctum*, holy basil).[3] This plant, which is used in *ayurveda* (the traditional Hindu medicinal system), is understood to cure humoral imbalances and associated illnesses and diseases, including those of anxiety and stress. The main head-piece, which represents matted hair and/or a coiled python, also has cobras set into it. Muttappan's healing and magical powers as a sorcerer are indicated by this headdress. He is commonly associated with the god Siva and more recently with Ayyappan.[4]

Unlike the *teyyam* of *taravads*, Muttappan can be invoked and worshipped at any time or in any place. There is no restriction on when or where Muttappan's *teyyam* may be performed. He can be manifested as a *teyyam* at inauspicious times as well as auspicious, and his appearance is not limited by any societal status rules regarding purity and pollution: "I can come in the darkest days of the monsoon and in the bright hot days of summer. I may come whether the king is being crowned or whether he is being cremated." Muttappan does not demand a permanent shrine, and he will appear in any unconsecrated place. A shrine is frequently made for him following his *teyyam* performance in a specific site. In other words, Muttappan is a being who is continually originating, radically differentiating anew, but according to the demands of the situation. Shrines and new stories (myths) of origin, thoroughly grounded in the turmoil of the present, follow in his wake. There is speed in his motion, as reflected in the rapidity of his rites, unlike the slow building of momentum and conserving of energy that are characteristic of the deities in the temples and shrines of long-settled communities. Muttappan requires nothing elaborate for storing his weapons and is content with the simplest of settings (a wooden plank as an offering table, an oil lamp, a stool) and the barest of essentials in the way of ritual objects. His manifestation is easily facilitated. The terms that are used to refer to the places in which Muttappan appears—a cave or cooking shelter (Nair 1981: 180) or a small dusty space—indicate that he is prepared to appear in the lowliest and filthiest locations. Even in the most polluting sites, his presence and potency have a counteracting force.

In the past and today, Muttappan has been worshipped at places of danger and transition, at the borders between different political and social territories, at the thresholds of entry and egress. Conceived as a wandering sage, a healer, and a magician, he mediates between social and political difference, extending relations where there are none and turning back the dangers that may be present. Unlike other *teyyam*, Muttappan does not operate through a medieval imaginary of an order built around caste, power, rank, or status. He does not demand any prescribed services denoting hierarchy: no blacksmith is required to sharpen his weapons (his sword is blunt); a launderer is not needed to supply clean clothes; a village astrologer does not have to set an auspicious time for the performance of his rite; a carpenter is not required to make a sacred stool. In my view, it is the non-hierarchical dimension of Muttappan and his thoroughly conjunctional and mediational character that underpin his increasing popularity.

Muttappan's foundation myths are very much a part of popular consciousness. Here I want to outline a major Muttappan rite that is performed in rural and urban areas. Additionally, I will give particular attention to Muttappan's dual capacity to deterritorialize and to reterritorialize.

Myths of Muttappan as a Line of Flight

The most well-known myth of Muttappan is as follows:

> There was an old Brahmin couple named Ayyankara Vazhunnavar and Padikkutty living in a remote village of North Malabar. They were childless, despite many years of praying and undertaking numerous vows. One day, when Padikkutty went to bathe as usual in a nearby stream, she had a general sense of something unusual, as if of a strange presence. While immersing herself in the stream, she heard drumming and the sound of brass anklets. Emerging from the water, she saw a basket set on a small rock by the bank. Padikkutty rushed to the spot to see a smiling baby boy lying in the basket. She took the boy into her house and described her experience to her husband. He understood the boy to be a god's gift. The couple named him Muttappan and brought him up as their son.
>
> But the hopes and expectations of the Brahmin couple did not last long. Going against Brahmin custom, the boy mingled freely with people from lower castes. He wandered with them to hunt and fish, eating whatever they caught and drinking intoxicating liquor. On occasion, Muttappan brought meat and fish into his house, offending Brahmanic rules of purity and pollution. This outraged the village as a whole. Ayyankara Vazhunnavar and Padikkutty scolded Muttappan and demanded that he give away his unruly behavior. Muttappan decided to leave his adopted home and took up a life as a hunter and wandering mendicant. Before departing, he revealed that he was not an ordinary human being but rather a divine incarnation born to protect the world.
>
> After leaving the house, he went to Kunnathurpadi to lead an ascetic life inside a cave. Whenever he felt thirsty, he would climb a nearby palm tree to drink the toddy made by Muthoran Chandan, a member of an out-caste community. Chandan was aware of what was happening when he saw an old man climbing his tree. He prepared to shoot him down with his bow and arrow, but as he was about to do so, Muttappan changed Chandan into stone.
>
> Chandan's wife, Chakki, was alarmed at his failure to return, and with tears in her eyes went in search of Chandan. She came to the palm tree where she found a strange stone and an old man sitting on the treetop, drinking toddy. Suspecting that something dreadful had happened and that the old man was no ordinary mortal, she prayed to Muttappan, saying that if he returned her husband, she would worship Muttappan as a *teyyam* and offer him ritual food. Satisfied and impressed with Chakki's honesty and innocent sorrow, Muttappan brought Chandan back to life. The couple then started to worship Muttappan and routinely offered him toddy, meat, fish, coconut, and boiled beans at his cave.

A major theme in this myth and others is that Muttappan is a transgressive figure. He is sometimes portrayed as the result of impossible or unlikely unions: one has him born of a union of Siva and Vishnu in their male forms (Namputhiri 1990), another has him as a child of incest (Vayaleri 1996, 2007). In two stories that I have collected, he is born into one caste and brought up in another, either going from high to low or from low to high (Elayavoor 2006: 234–235; Kannan 2007). In the central myth, he refuses the rules governing inter-caste relations and challenges conventions regarding property. In most of the myths, he breaks customs and rules and dies a violent death, to be reborn as a *teyyam*, sometimes as a result of resisting the cruelty or exploitation of dominant castes (Nair 1981). In one myth, he dies trying to return to a community that had expelled him because of his incestuous birth (Vayaleri 2007). Muttappan is in constant movement or transition; he is a nomad, and as he moves he deterritorializes and also reterritorializes.

In the most popular myth, Muttappan enters Chandan's domain and breaks down his defenses, turning him into stone, making Chandan into his own boundary. But he is recognized and accepted by Chandan's distressed wife Chakki, who declares that she will give a food offering to Muttappan. This offering, in itself, disregards pollution rules and embeds no hierarchy. Muttappan restores Chakki's well-being by bringing Chandan back to life. In effect, Muttappan reterritorializes in a way that is inclusive of Chandan and recodifies (through the substantialization of food) an order that is not founded on the hierarchization of difference. Muttappan's reterritorialization is not on the basis of kinship or caste but instead insists on the formation of relationships through the gift, within which inheres no principle of rank, status, or power and, therefore, no boundaries, separations, or rejections. In a sense, the gift to Muttappan is outside a discourse of purity and pollution; it is even destructive of such a discourse, due to the pollution wrought by its offering.

As such, via the mediation of Muttappan, relations can be established in social contexts of heterogeneity, mixture, flux, and strangeness, all of which Muttappan embodies. Furthermore, the advantage of Muttappan is that he can overcome the rejection of difference and the dangers and uncertainties that lie hidden in the new (which may sustain previously experienced forms of hierarchy), or else express new forms of which, for example, the imagination of a medieval past can be a metaphor. Muttappan overcomes them by countering them with potencies that are the most negative of all. He is the positive of the negative, representing the potency of the healer, the magician, and the sorcerer. Muttappan is both the dangerous potentiality of places and spaces of migration, of new settlement, and of transience and, at the same time, the antidote to the injuries, risks, and suffering that are immanent or actualized in them. This is powerfully expressed in his *teyyam* form and especially in his headdress, which combines the destructive, the protective, and the reconstitutive. The understanding that this mountain of medicinal herbs is also matted hair has significance in the argument that I present. It is a sign not only of the wandering sage, of Siva, of the renouncer who is outside society, but also of the mystic or the soothsayer, who expresses the hidden and may bring it under control.[5]

The Rite: Muttappan's Hunt for a Place in the World

Muttappan's major rite is performed in urban areas, often in places of new settlement. The ritual centers on a process of re-creation and on the formation of relations through the distribution of a gift that recognizes no hierarchy. Muttappan's gift and the relations he constitutes through it can be seen as overcoming 'the poison in the gift' (Raheja [1988] 1997), that is, the dangers that may flow through the gift, such as envy and the desire for that which another possesses. This, I note, is also embodied in an aspect of Muttappan's theft of Chandan's toddy. Muttappan is involved in the forming (or re-forming) of relations in circumstances where there is often a lack of relationships or where relations do not yet exist. He emerges in contexts where people are individuated or in some way socially isolated and may consequently have an intensified fear of the other. Muttappan overcomes all this by mediating the formation of relations and simultaneously distributing (administering) the antidote to counteract the dangers, desires, and fears that may be present in alienated, competitive, and individualized environments.

Muttappan's rite is performed to celebrate a diversity of occasions, for example, getting marriage, securing employment, building a new house, or returning home from work in the Gulf states (the major source of income in Malabar). These events reflect wealth and success—and they also attract envy. To counter this, Muttappan performs at storefronts to protect the owners and the merchandise (see fig. 8.2). He will also appear in the event of theft in order to punish the

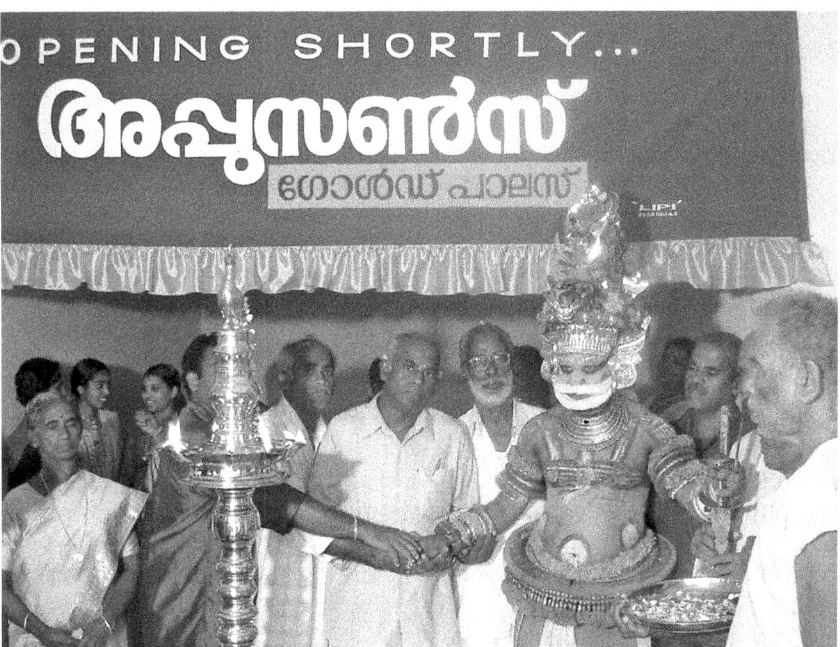

FIGURE 8.2 Muttappan inside a shopping complex. Photograph provided by author.

culprits and to assist in their capture. He will be worshipped following the successful outcome of a court case. His rite is performed during the advent or resolution of a great variety of misfortunes.

The rite itself is over quickly. It takes little more than an hour to perform, although Muttappan will usually stay at his place of performance for a couple of hours (sometimes for as many as six), distributing his blessings and gifts. In return, he receives offerings, generally in the form of a small amount of money, that acknowledge and recognize his protection. The rite is performed by a male belonging to a *teyyam*-performing lower caste. The performance is ordinarily held in the courtyard of a house or else in an open space within a neighborhood, but it may also be performed at crossroads, at bus and railway stations, at taxi stands, in marketplaces, and occasionally at shopping complexes. At all of these places, Muttappan will put up his simple, temporary shrine. Recently, there has been a tendency to erect more permanent shrines, an indication of the further growth of his popularity as Muttappan becomes more and more an important god.[6]

His rite starts with a short song of invocation that calls him from his mountain abode in the eastern hills of Malabar. The performer initially appears dressed in a red loin cloth and wearing a diadem, but without body or facial painting. Muttappan is his own priest, for upon completing his invocation he will have his body and face painted, put on his headdress and costume, and then manifest as himself. The god stands by a stool that he has placed beside the offering table and, for about 15 minutes, sings his mythical song of origin and exploits. The ritual song (*tottam*) as a whole tells of a royal hunt in the forest, in itself a deterritorializing/reterritorializing event. I present a summary of the key episode, the killing of the wild boar:

> King Hariyapuran with his hunting dogs [the dog is Muttappan's vehicle], armorer, and other servants climbed the mountain to hunt. Nets and barricades were placed to trap the prey. A huge wild boar, as big as the world itself, startled by the shouting and clamor of the hunters, ran from its forest hideout. It escaped the trap, but when it reached the river bank, a hunter—a Vedan, an out-caste forest dweller—shot an arrow and wounded the boar. It tore through the village, uprooting its crops of plantain, mango, yam, taro, and arrowroot, finally to fall by a rock. Tracking the trail of blood, the hunters found the boar. Hariyapuran gave everyone their share, including the dogs. Only the Vedan was left out. However, all of those gathered were aware of the Vedan's plight and that it was he who had brought down the boar, and so they gave a portion of their own share to him.[7]

This event is part of a well-known mythic tradition of the incarnation of Vishnu as a wild boar who creates the world by lifting it on his tusks from the ocean depths. The story that Muttappan sings is of a regenerative sacrifice in which the boar, while destroying the crops of the village, plows the earth for a new emergence. It is thematic of the myth as a whole, the wild boar being symbolic of death and continuous re-creation. The act of redistribution—the point of the song—overcomes the hierarchical, exclusionary act of the king by recognizing the crucial involvement of the humble Vedan (the outsider) in securing the success of the hunt.

Finishing the recitation of his ritual song, Muttappan first receives an acknowledgment and blessing from the person who has asked for the performance. Then, in a state of possession and carrying an arrow, he dance-mimes the hunt. First, Muttappan bathes in self-purification, cleans his weapons, and feeds his hunting dogs. In a following hunting dance (*pallivetta*, or royal hunt), he gestures the searching out of game, aiming his arrows but missing until he finally hits the target—a coconut symbolic of the sacrificial wild boar. The events end with an act of (re)distribution. Muttappan presents betel leaves, toddy, flowers, and herbs plucked from his headdress to all of the onlookers.

In the rite, Muttappan might be seen as a combination of the critical elements of both his popular myth of origin and his ritual song. He is at once king and Vedan, high caste and low, simultaneously embodying their disparity and conjunction. Within a reality that he both destroys and re-creates, Muttappan draws in those who were hitherto excluded. He mediates the formation of new relations in contexts of individualization and heals the grounds of envy. Muttappan might be conceived of as a kind of fixer, a figure for 'reassembling the social' in situations of its disassemblage and fracture. He is himself an assemblage, a being of internal tensions brought together, a plateau of intensity (Bateson 1972; Deleuze and Guattari [1988] 2002).

Muttappan: A God of Assemblage and Transience

Muttappan's popularity has grown chiefly in urban centers and among migrants who have left the domains of *taravad* and interconnected relations of kin, as well as among those whose sets of relations are constantly in flux or who are dependent on movement, such as itinerant workers, migrants, and traders. He is popular among the poor and the vulnerable, who are often cut off from the support of kin and are exposed to anxieties because of the pressures and difficulties of providing for their families. Muttappan is a common icon for worship, and his image appears alongside those of well-known Hindu deities in the worshipping room of many houses. Some houses even have stickers over their doorways declaring that "Muttappan is the savior of the house." But this should not obscure the fact that he is also increasingly important among the more wealthy, especially merchants and traders.

The history and stories surrounding Muttappan's emergence in Kannur (a major city in the northern region of Kerala state) support my understanding of this deity as a god of assemblage and transience. The accounts I relate may also be regarded as new myths of origin that extend beyond the myths founded in the rural traditions mentioned earlier, even though these myths have continuing importance in urban centers. In this connection, I briefly discuss three stories in popular circulation, all of which claim that Muttappan first began to be worshipped in the area after being introduced by manual workers employed on the construction of the railway near Kannur early in the twentieth century. Later a shrine to Muttappan was built at Kannur railway station, and it has since grown in importance. Currently, Muttappan performs every Friday at the shrine, and free food is distributed.[8] Since the establishment of the Kannur railway shrine more than 20 Muttappan railway shrines have been built along the line of rail through North Malabar reaching to Mangalore in southern Karnataka state.

The first story says that Muttappan was brought by manual laborers from the outskirts of Thalasseri, the main seat of the British colonial government in Malabar. The story recounts that the railway workers felt isolated, now far from their rural homes, which were in an area where Muttappan was an important god. It is said that they began to worship Muttappan, calling on him to protect them from the dangers of their work in an unfamiliar social environment. From this beginning, the important shrine to Muttappan developed.

The second story/myth associates the development of Muttappan's shrine at Kannur railway station with the mislaying of a liquor consignment for the British colonial army. The railway employees and the parcel officer immediately involved understood that they would be blamed for its disappearance and in all likelihood punished by dismissal. The fearful employees prayed to Muttappan to help them, vowing that they would give him his preferred offering (namely, *paimkutty*)[9] should they find the lost consignment. The night before it was due to be handed over, the parcel officer had a dream showing him where the consignment was concealed. He rushed to the spot that he had dreamed of and retrieved the lost liquor. As a result, the relieved employees began to offer Muttappan *paimkutty* in the parcel office itself. Thus began the tradition of the Friday Muttappan-*teyyam* at the station.

The third story/myth concerns a British engineer in charge of constructing the railway who became a worshipper of Muttappan. He had to build a number of bridges, the largest of was intended to span the Valapattanam River approximately three miles to the north of Kannur railway station. Despite repeated attempts to build the bridge, he was unsuccessful. One suspicion was that obstacles were set in the way of the project by forces associated with the kingdom of Kolattiri, whose *taravad* house and shrine were situated close by. Work came to a standstill until an old man from the village suggested that if the engineer worshipped Muttappan, who lived near the river bank, his problem might be solved. Reluctantly, the engineer offered *paimkutty*. To his surprise, all hindrances were removed, and the bridge construction was completed. In gratitude, the engineer permitted his workers to build a shrine to Muttappan near the railway station.

These stories, themselves myths of one of the first major urban shrines to Muttappan, clearly extend his earlier rural-based associations into the contexts and situations of modernity. He occupies a major line of flight, the railways, and is tied to contexts of migration and situations of vulnerability at work and an unfamiliar environment. He is a point of assemblage, joining persons in relations who are in a common situation of vulnerability. He overcomes barriers to movement (the bridge), and, in the last story, there is a sense that he negates the obstacles of old borders and their forces of protection, such as those of the pre-colonial kingdom of Kolattiri. Muttappan's pragmatism is underlined when he provides assistance to the British engineer.

I conclude this section with an incident that involves the spread of Muttappan's potency beyond Kerala into the neighboring state of Tamil Nadu and its capital, Chennai. The event concerns an October 2005 performance by Muttappan that was arranged by three brothers in the driveway of their restaurant on the outskirts of Chennai. The organizers were second-generation migrants from Malabar who had lost contact with their parental village and *taravad*. The performance of Muttappan-*teyyam* was in recognition of his protection of the brothers, whose ownership of the land on which their restaurant now sits was contested by a former state minister of Tamil Nadu. Their father, at one time an influential civil servant in Tamil Nadu but now deceased, had bought the land but had not put it to use during his lifetime. A close family friend of the father, the ex-minister, claimed that the land belonged to him and should be returned, despite the fact that the brothers' father had been dead for 15 years. The brothers ignored the claim, for they had possession of documents proving ownership. The ex-minister sent thugs (*goondas*) to threaten the brothers, and eventually the case was taken to court.

At the height of this crisis, the brothers made appeals to Muttappan for help and asked him to ensure that the court case would be settled in their favor. Soon after, the eldest brother, who already had some association with the Tamil Nadu film industry, encountered a well-known film actress who was able to introduce him to Tamil Nadu's chief minister and influenced the latter to intervene. The chief minister told the ex-minister to stop his threats of physical violence and to await the court's decision. The atmosphere of extreme tension immediately dissolved, and the court accepted the brothers' claim. They were able to go forward with their plans for a modern drive-in restaurant, employing more than 60 staff members.

Their celebration of Muttappan was an elaborate affair, arranged inside the restaurant and attracting over 100 guests, including members of the film industry and other businesses, as well ordinary workers from Kerala and Tamil Nadu. Many of those who had never seen Muttappan before immediately accepted his divinity. Indeed, a Tamil film actor who attended asked Muttappan to name his newly born granddaughter. Not only was Muttappan introduced to the world of Chennai, but he was also seen to be capable of overcoming established power, denying its border and property claims (as in Muttappan's main myth). I note his potency as a being of assemblage, capable of forging ties where they did not exist, and his role as a catalyst who brings together persons of heterogeneous backgrounds and ties.

Muttappan on Cyberspace

Here I will briefly analyze *teyyam* in cyberspace as an image of power/opposition in relation to outsider status, new identity, and traveling. This should, I think, highlight the importance of *teyyam* as both deity and ritual in the symbolic representations of community, in contrast to the Brahmanic and hegemonic discourses and panoply of state ideology. Thus, the image of opposition to state practice is situated in Muttappan's central role in relation to marginality, outsider status, and so on. Here I will also investigate how *teyyam* is faring in cyberspace, a medium where members of the Kerala diaspora meet.

Muttappan continues to display his assemblage potency in which social hierarchies and kinship have no relevance. Moreover, while all divinities in *teyyam* complexes assume significance as beings of identity and their representation, Muttappan remains less inclusive than the other *teyyam*. However, an understanding of this feature, as well as the way that the *teyyam* may realize their potentiality (and also limitations), requires an explanation of the particular complexities of the Internet and the kinds of domains in which aspects of the *teyyam* are expressed. To do so, I will refer to three types of Internet space: general Web sites, blog sites, and Orkut, a social networking service akin to Facebook. I will show that in a relatively short period of time, upon the development of blogs and Orkut, *teyyam* shifted from being a mere object of representation to becoming an important cyber-medium for the articulation of social relations.

Further, I will consider how the constraints of the Internet have led to an interactive discourse on *teyyam* that followed a more explicit realization of the potentialities of *teyyam*, certain aspects of which are more embedded in the actual lived practice of *teyyam* rites. I suggest that the very fact that the Internet places limits on the development of sociality (a 'thin' sociality as distinct from a deeper sociality of face-to-face relations) forces a kind of discourse or discussion, an elaboration of content, that replaces what may be described as the communicative lack of the Internet. As a result, the discourse, operating as a kind of compensation for this lack, leads to a revelation about aspects of *teyyam* that are embedded in and/or, in their realization, make explicit and expand upon, or perhaps change, dimensions of the *teyyam* concerned.

General Web sites are informational on a range of matters relating to Kerala in which more specific cultural information can be included. On these sites, *teyyam* is by and large presented as an art of Kerala, a sign of the state's unique culture and a symbol of the religious symbiosis of Kerala society. In other words, *teyyam* here appears as mere representation. Some effort has recently been made to open up the general Web sites for interactive discussion, but they are extremely limited as a basis for building interpersonal networks and a discourse in which people can exchange feelings and opinion.

Tourism provided the initial impetus for these general Web sites, where *teyyam* is usually presented as a relatively undifferentiated tradition and, in modernist secular terms, as an art form whose local specificity and relevance to daily life have been reduced. There are a few Web sites that are more or less exclusively about *teyyam*. They express deeper understandings of *teyyam*, but still within the paradigm of representation of exotic Malabar. More recently, general Web sites concerning *teyyam* have begun to express local knowledge, as well as a sense of the experience of *teyyam*; however, as with other similar Web sites, there is little capacity to enter into dialogue and discussion. Although a more locally based understanding is beginning to emerge, the very technical limitations of such a Web site (regardless of the fact that it is principally directed at foreign tourists) place restraints on the poietic capacity of Internet-mediated interaction to effect a further poiesis of the import of *teyyam*. Lacking the means for a more potent dimension of discursive interaction, general Web sites are restricted in their ability to bring forth some of the deeper dimensions of *teyyam* or to realize some of its potentialities.

Blogs are designed to overcome some of the restrictions of general Web sites and are oriented to the development of cyber communities. They have a technical capacity to realize some aspects similar to *teyyam* in its local and situated contexts. A blog is a personal publishing Internet platform with an interactive format that provides space to post comments, express opinions, and list links to other blogs and discussions. By 2001, migrants from Malabar—mainly to the Middle East but also including India—had entered into active blogging (blog writing). Initially, all of them wrote in English, but soon blogs written in Malayalam began to appear, and blog discourse now occurs in both languages. However, while the blogs in English remain largely monologic, those that appear in Malayalam all tend to be interactive and to form active cyber network communities.

The use of Malayalam to write about *teyyam* is a conscious attempt not only to re-establish connections with one's native land but also to form an exclusive community of native language speakers. Blogs express personal experience and rarely engage abstract scholarly opinion or present state-mediated mainstream views. They are an open space often expressing alternative understandings to the hitherto dominant Brahmanic and Sanskritized interpretations. Moreover, they are a space in which new cyber-social relations can be created. These features are exemplified by the Malayalam blogs. A site named *perumkaliyattam*, created by a person who had migrated away from his home locality in Kerala (as is mainly the case with those who contribute to the site, forming what is known as a collaborative blog) shows aspects of the new direction. The person who started the blog was anguished by the fact that he could not attend important rites in Kerala, and his creation of the blog illustrates a desire to use this medium in a thoroughly emotional and social way. It assumes an intensity, or a wish for such an intensity, that the actual rituals offer to those who participate in person.

The blog *perumkaliyattam* is not concerned with any specific *teyyam*. All kinds of *teyyam* are discussed, and there is an urgency among the contributors to imagine themselves into the world of *teyyam* and assert their common identity as people from Malabar. At the center of the emergent and imagined community of the site is a blogger known as 'Kannuran', who identifies himself as being from the Malabar region of Kannur. On his own personal blog,[10] he recounts an event exposing his former ignorance concerning *teyyam*. On a short visit home, he was asked by some of his brother's friends about *teyyam*, as a performance was then taking place at his local shrine. Embarrassed by his lack of knowledge, he decided then and there to pursue information. Kannuran is a writer of fiction, and he began to use *teyyam* as a trope in his stories. As a result, he has become a crucial source of knowledge in the dissemination of information relating to the myths of *teyyam* and the details of *teyyam* rites.

Through intensive discussions and interactions, the *perumkaliyattam* blog site community has become an agency for a reimagining of *teyyam* in which *teyyam* achieves a new vitality and simultaneously becomes integral to the formation of relationships that are reinforced through the building of a shared knowledge. Further, the cyber community does not gloss over difference, as in state-mediated discourse. Rather, through the articulation of the diversity of *teyyam*, the site is able to weave together migrants from differing localities into a communing Internet group. Heterogeneity is not erased in the establishment of identity, as in state discourse. Moreover, the migrants, distant from home, are enabled, at least in an imagined sense, to reconnect with their *taravads* and localities of birth. The participants in the blog site are able to establish relations that overcome the divisions and separations that social dissimilarities of various kinds might otherwise promote.

The capacity of the blogosphere is expanded in a social networking service known as Orkut, the most popular such service in India. Orkut is a Google-based social networking site that is "designed to make your social life more active and stimulating."[11] It enables users to create their own 'communities' using the 'forum' (or 'message board') Web application, a successor of the 'bulletin board' systems and 'news groups' of the 1980s and 1990s, respectively. A cursory review discloses that there are Orkut communities for almost all of the cultural/ritual forms in Kerala, but they vary in number and popularity. For example, the results of my search (carried out on 9 March 2009) reveal that the number of Orkut communities available for *teyyam* (including general and individual *teyyam*) is 120, which is nearly three times more than its nearest rival, *kathakali* (which has only 44 communities). The most common *teyyam* who has Orkut communities is Muttappan, a trans-local *teyyam* (with 39 communities). It is conceivable that the anti-elite and trans-class dimension of Muttappan, on the one hand, and the *taravad* and community, on the other, contribute to the relatively greater number of Orkut communities formed with respect to them.

Earlier I explored the potency of Muttappan as a deterritorializing, rhizomic being, who is becoming increasingly popular in towns and in sites of migration. On the Internet, his growing popularity is reflected in the fact that he accounts for most of the *teyyam*-focused cyber communities.[12] These Web-based communities extend the deterritorializing dimension of Muttappan, a capacity, I suggest, that is at the heart of his popularity. What is stressed in the Orkut communities for Muttappan are his anti-caste, 'secular', and class dimensions: he has the ability to unite people as a class or, at least, to give expression to a sense of class belonging, which the context of migrant life in the Middle East (where many of the site participants reside) might be expected to accentuate.

The Orkut communities dedicated to Muttappan are fueled by a sense of alienation and nostalgia and by a concern to make a difference back in Kerala. The social intensity of the participation, via Muttappan Orkut sites, in the offline realities and actual circumstances of lived existence in Kerala finds many expressions on the Internet. And here, I think, there is real connection. The image of Muttappan, as he pragmatically works in everyday life in a diverse range of situations in Kerala, is extended to become the way that he is imagined and brought into being on the Internet. There is a degree of consonance between the Internet Muttappan and off-line existential realities in Kerala, as well as elsewhere. I have documented Muttappan-*teyyam* performances in the Middle East that demonstrate a certain unity among people from Kerala as both Keralites and migrant workers in a common circumstance of existence.

The zeal expressed by many participants in the Muttappan Orkut communities has a revolutionary feel, which contributes to the sites being experienced as social communities, rather than merely cyber communities. However, as in any deterritorializing dynamic, there is always a tension toward reterritorialization that may erect new barriers and obstacles. As we have seen, there are some indications that Muttappan is becoming associated with new class-dominant interests and not the poor and vulnerable, such as the Kannur railway workers described earlier. Other new divisions of modernity are possible, such as the formation of relations based on ethnicity rather than on the prior basis of sociality or caste structures.

Conclusion

Teyyam ritual worship is thoroughly engaged with the everyday realities of human existence. It is through the internal dynamics of ritual—and the ritual virtuality (Kapferer 1997, 2005, 2006) that it generates—that personal realities and other aspects of lived existence in their great diversity are confronted, dealt with, and renegotiated.

Muttappan-*teyyam* is a ritual practice within which relations between art and the state are set at odds. The co-optation of ritual practice in the service of the state (e.g., to promote tourism or to encourage a sense of national identity) renders that practice vulnerable to conflicting expectations of a religious form that can be reduced in its potency to an art form. The aesthetics of power adopted by the Indian state in the service of ruling groups is manifested in taking recourse to a free use of diverse symbolic practices that are manufactured for public consumption as artistic display. Such practices gloss over differences of caste and class in a performance of nationalist solidarity. Conversely, the suppression and devaluation of oppositional groups and communities in the past and present continue to be materialized within local social and cultural contexts as structures of devotion and belief. At the same time, Muttappan provides, through ritual and deity, an escape from everyday political and social exigencies and a space wherein such exigencies can be re-formed by a community of interacting others, either in person or through blogs and Orkut networks.

Muttappan is not a being of emergence or transcendence. His dynamic is one that can be described as the clearing of space, the breaking down of barriers, divisions, and separations. He is a being that forces things together that might otherwise be apart. He is a being of the moment, of the event, of the situation, of the ongoing and multi-linear flux of existence, overcoming any bounding, hierarchizing, striating force or potency that might rise up in his path. Muttappan's modernity is one of decentering, destabilizing fluidity. His power is growing, particularly in towns and among new urban settlers and migrants, and his appeal is increasing among all social classes.

After closely observing Internet sites that facilitate the formation of networks and networking (especially blogs and Orkut), I have argued that their potency lies not in the technological tools they provide but rather in how people appropriate these tools for a successful human enterprise (Rheingold [1993] 2006: 54). While the Internet is a continuously developing technology that facilitates (as it also constrains) the formation of cyber communities, its potentials are already conditioned within social-cultural dynamics. In the same way, Muttappan is, in his person, both a symbol and an actuality of social relations engaged in the ongoing construction of cultural and political ties that do not owe their formation to agencies removed from the actions and situations of their everyday existence.

Acknowledgments

This chapter benefited from intense discussions and debates with Bruce Kapferer and Judith Kapferer, and I wish to express my deeply felt gratitude to both of them. I thank the members of the Department of Social Anthropology at the University of Bergen for their encouragement and support. I am also indebted to the *teyyam* performers whom I met during my research, especially Podikkalam Parambil Kunhirama Peruvannan (Sreestha), Kavinissery Rama Peruvannan (Kadannappalli), Prakasan Peruvannan (Chovva), Kundora Santhosh Peruvannan, and Rajesh Peruvannan.

———————————

Dinesan Vadakkiniyil is Assistant Professor in the Department of History, Government College (under the University of Calicut), Perambra, Kerala, India. Previously, he was the Academic Coordinator of the Kerala Council for Historical Research, Thiruvananthapuram, Kerala. He received his PhD from the Department of Social Anthropology at the University of Bergen, Norway. Currently engaged in fieldwork leading to a major work on the Bagavathi (goddess) cult in Kerala, he has recently contributed articles in leading journals on ritual facial paintings and color symbolism. His areas of interest include ritual studies, the modern history of Kerala, and social theories.

Notes

1. The fieldwork upon which this ethnography is based was conducted in the region of Payyanur in the Kannur district in the northern part of the Indian state of Kerala.
2. A close observation of the actual ritual practices reveals that the contemporary monetary payment is an aspect of the modernity of the rite. In previous times, payment was not typically made in money. Instead, betel leaves served the purpose, which explains the latter's continuing importance in *teyyam* ritual. The present practice of inserting money

inside a bundle of betel leaves is a way of canceling the monetary dimension and reasserting the continuation of caste services and the importance of the obligatory relation.
3. If *thulasi* is not available in abundance, leaves of *thumba* (*Leuca Indica*) are preferred. One of my informants said that tradition also permits them to use the leaf of the *koovalam* (*Aegle marmelos*) to make the *kodumudi*. All are highly valued medicinal plants.
4. There are different interpretations of the divinity of Ayyappan. He is believed to be a Dravidian god of hunting or a village god. The myth that is now widely prevalent in Kerala treats him as a god in the Brahmanic religious pantheon who was born out of the union of Siva and Vishnu. For more details on Ayyappan as a Dravidian deity, see Dumont (1970) and Whitehead ([1921] 1983). For an integrated discussion, see Osella and Osella (2003) and Younger (2002).
5. Obeyesekere (1981) conceives of the long knotted hair that is typical of sages and mediums as a boon from the gods or as a sign that the sages are possessed by gods, such as Siva or Suniyam, a sorcerer.
6. Many of these features of Muttappan parallel the emergence in Sri Lanka of Suniyam, who evolved from being a magician, sorcerer, and demon/god of the village boundaries to his contemporary significance as a powerful god of protection and punishment with his own shrines. Suniyam, like Muttappan, is a god appealed to by the weak and the poor, as well as by merchants and those who fear the envy of others. See Kapferer (1997) and Gombrich and Obeyesekere (1989).
7. The *kodumudi* (mountain peak) headpiece of Muttappan achieves some interpretative possibilities in the context of this *tottam*. Thus, the headpiece metaphorically indicates Muttappan as a god (the boar) who rises through the earth and generates it anew.
8. See http://www.videowired.com/watch/?id = 1394654773.
9. *Paimkutty* is a food offering package that consists mainly of pulses, smoke-dried fish, coconut, and toddy.
10. See http://www.kannuran.blogspot.com.
11. See http://www.orkut.com/about.
12. In September 2007 there were only 19 communities for Muttappan, but this had increased to 23 by April 2008 and to 39 by the middle of February 2009.

References

Ashley, Wayne. 1993. "Recodings: Ritual, Theatre and Political Display in Kerala State, South India." PhD diss., New York University.

Bateson, Gregory. 1972. *Steps to an Ecology of Mind: Collected Essays in Anthropology, Psychiatry, Evolution, and Epistemology*. London: Jason Aronson.

Deleuze, Gilles, and Felix Guattari. [1988] 2002. *A Thousand Plateaus: Capitalism and Schizophrenia*. Trans. Brian Massumi. London: Continuum.

Dumont, Louis. 1970. *Religion/Politics and History in India: Collected Papers in Indian sociology*. The Hague: Mouton.

Elayavoor, Vanidas. 2006. *Vatakkan Ithihyamala*. Kottayam: Current Books.

Gombrich, Richard, and Gananath Obeyesekere 1989. *Buddhism Transformed: Religious Change in Sri Lanka*. Princeton, NJ: Princeton University Press.

Kannan, V. V. 2007. *Muthappan Puravritham*. Kottayam: DC Books.

Kapferer, Bruce. 1997. *The Feast of the Sorcerer: Practice of Consciousness and Power*. Chicago, IL: University of Chicago Press.

______. 2005. "Ritual Dynamics and Virtual Practice: Beyond Representation and Meaning." Pp. 35–54 in *Ritual in Its Own Right,* ed. Don Handelman and Galina Linquist. New York: Berghahn Books.

______. 2006. "Virtuality." Pp. 671–684 in *Theorizing Rituals: Issues, Topics, Approaches, Concepts,* ed. Jens Kreinath, Jan Snoek, and Michael Stausberg. Leiden: Brill.

Kerala Sangeetha Nataka Academy, ed. [1977] 1987. *Teyyam*. Thrissur: Kerala Sangeetha Nataka Academy.

Kurup, K. K. N. [1985] 2000. *Teyyam: A Ritual Dance of Kerala*. Thiruvananthapuram: Department of Public Relation, Government of Kerala.

Nair, Chirakkal T. Balakrishnan. 1981. *Thiranjedutha Prabhanthangal*. Thrissur: Kerala Sahithya Academy.

Namputhiri, M. V. 1990. *Thottampattukl Oru Patanam*. Kottayam: National Book Stall.

Obeyesekere, Gananath. 1981. *Medusa's Hair: An Essay on Personal Symbols and Religious Experience*. Chicago, IL: University of Chicago Press.

Osella, Filippo, and Caroline Osella. 2003. "'Ayyappan Saranam': Masculinity and the Sabarimala Pilgrimage in Kerala." *Journal of the Royal Anthropological Institute* 9, no. 4: 729–754.

Raheja, Gloria Goodwin. [1988] 1997. *The Poison in the Gift: Ritual, Prestation, and the Dominant Caste in a North Indian Village*. Chicago, IL: University of Chicago Press.

Rheingold, Howard. [1993] 2006. *The Virtual Community: Homesteading on the Electronic Frontier*. New Haven, CT: MIT Press.

Swai, Bonaventure. 1978. "Notes on the Colonial State with Reference to Malabar in the 18th and 19th Centuries." *Social Scientist* 6, no. 12: 44–65.

Vadakkiniyil, Dinesan. 2009. "*Teyyam*: The Poiesis of Rite and God in Malabar, South India." PhD diss., University of Bergen.

Vayaleri, Kumaran. 1996. *Kurichiarude Jeevithavum Samskaravum*. Kottayam: Current Books.

______. 2007. *Adhivasi Puravrutham*. Kottayam: DC Books.

Whitehead, Henry. [1921] 1983. *The Village Gods of South India*. New Delhi: Cosmos Publications.

Younger, Paul. 2002. *Playing Host to Deity: Festival Religion in the South Indian Tradition*. Oxford: Oxford University Press.

Zarilli, Phillip B. 2000. *Kathakali Dance-Drama: Where Gods and Demons Come to Play*. London: Routledge.

www.ingramcontent.com/pod-product-compliance
Ingram Content Group UK Ltd.
Pitfield, Milton Keynes, MK11 3LW, UK
UKHW021911060726
6981IPUK00004B/77